THE SECRET POWER of
MASONIC
SYMBOLS

THE SECRET POWER of
MASONIC
SYMBOLS

THE INFLUENCE OF ANCIENT SYMBOLS ON THE PIVOTAL MOMENTS IN HISTORY AND AN ENCYCLOPEDIA OF ALL THE KEY MASONIC SYMBOLS

ROBERT LOMAS

FAIR WINDS

© 2011 Fair Winds Press
Text © 2011 Robert Lomas

First published in the USA in 2011 by
Fair Winds Press, a member of
Quayside Publishing Group
100 Cummings Center
Suite 406-L
Beverly, MA 01915-6101
www.fairwindspress.com

15   14   13   12   11   1   2   3   4   5

ISBN-13: 978-1-59233-450-6
ISBN-10: 1-59233-450-4

Library of Congress Cataloging-in-Publication Data available

Cover design by Peter Long
Book production by Mighty Media, www.mightymedia.com
Black-and-white illustrations by Mike Wanke, except on pages 184, 202, 203, 204,
205, 206, 214, 225, which are courtesy of www.tracingboards.com

Additional photo credits
Istockphotos.com: p. 21, 33, 36, 67, 69, 70, 107, 108, 109, 110, 164, 166, 168
Gettyimages.com: p. 128
Photononstop/Superstock: p. 172, 180, 186,
The Irish Image Collection/Superstock: p. 226

Printed and bound in China

Dedicated to my daughter in a very important year.

CONTENTS

THE HIDDEN INFLUENCE
OF ANCIENT SYMBOLS

⸺•⸺

ANCIENT MASONIC SYMBOLS HAVE SHAPED WHO WE ARE TODAY, and they can still powerfully affect our lives. This book will lead you into that secret symbolic world.

Until recently, only a select group of people were aware of the importance of symbols within the fabric of modern Western society. This group had received extensive training in the use and power of symbols and been taught how to recognize the influence that could flow from the display of certain secret symbols of power in public places. The group knew that the ability to understand symbols is an ancient skill possessed by all humans but that the influence of particular symbols on human actions is universal.

Recent popular literature has latched onto this idea, and it has become a subject for extremely successful fictional thrillers. In particular, Dan Brown's *The Lost Symbol* has taken as its main theme the search for a great symbol of power. But is that symbol real? And do symbols actually have the power that novelists attribute to them?

One group in particular thinks they do, and for them, the study of symbols has become an important part of their lives. It may be coincidental, but many members of this group have been prominent figures in the history of humanity. They have helped formulate modern science and forged the republics that brought freedom to the masses. They have been influential writers, musicians, industrialists, scientists, astronauts, and politicians. But above all, they have belonged to a secret order that has spent the last 600 years studying the way symbols interact with human beings to bring about progress or disaster. These people are the Freemasons.

Beginning in the late fifteenth century, Freemasonry described itself as "a peculiar system of morality, veiled in allegory and illustrated by symbols." The purpose of this book is to provide an authoritative guide to the secret symbology of Freemasonry. We will start with a biography of the symbols that have shaped

Western civilization and then reveal little-known facts about the influence of these powerful symbols on society.

Symbols speak to us at a far deeper level than writing. The fundamental ideas of Masonic teaching are deeply rooted in the use of symbols. Some of the symbols that Freemasons use date back to humans' first attempts to carve symbols into stone. Some 200,000 years ago, humans developed speech, and then about 70,000 years ago, they discovered the visual language of symbols. Some 4,000 years ago, those early symbols were developed into alphabetic writing as a way to encode speech. It is through symbols that humans have expressed their most abstract ideas. As we will see, modern scientific studies reveal that all humans have innate emotional reactions to symbols in general, but it is Masonic symbols in particular that evoke the most positive emotional responses.

Symbolic thinking is deeply rooted. It began over 70,000 years ago with the first known use of symbols by human beings. Those symbols are still in use today and transcend any differences in human language. The archaeological record has huge gaps, but the first ritual use of symbols can be seen in the shamanistic symbols in the cave paintings of northern Europe, which were created about 30,000 years ago.

For well over 2,000 years, since the time of Plato, many people have believed that a realm of perfect symbols exists. With careful training, an individual can be shown how to communicate with this realm and discover the true nature of these symbols. Plato developed this idea into a theory, which is deeply embedded in Masonic symbology. It is this Masonic tradition that has preserved and developed the ancient emotive symbols and led to the discovery of mathematical symbols.

During the seventeenth century, symbolism branched out in two ways. One was the use of loosely defined symbols to create images, emotions, and feelings within a ritual context, and the other was to help the human mind to reason. This later route is *mathematics,* and it has led to a deep understanding of the world.

There are three main types of symbols:

1. *Emotive symbols* encode feelings and aspirations. These are the oldest of all symbols. They have been widely used to communicate emotion to illiterate people.

2. *Speech symbols* encode the sounds of language and enable humans to communicate through time and space. At one time, these symbols were tightly restricted to an elite group and often linked to religion.

3. *Mathematical symbols* encode a means of understanding and predicting reality. Freemasons helped develop algebra and calculus, which in turn produced these counting symbols.

Using symbology, Freemasonry has been able to communicate its ideas by means of a unique and universal language. Once an idea has been formulated using symbols, it can be transmitted without corruption. This guarantees a continuity of tradition. A modern Mason carries out his symbol work in exactly the same way a Mason did 500 years ago. The Mason of today faces the same fundamental problems in his quest for Truth that a Mason living in the fifteenth century had to face, and the symbols provide the same answers.

Approximately sixty basic symbols are taught to aspiring Master Masons as they progress through the various degrees of Freemasonry. These symbols are introduced as a candidate masters each of the successive degrees of the Craft, the Mark, and the Royal Arch. Eventually, the symbols are combined into pictorial narratives called *tracing boards*. There are six tracing boards, all conveying different philosophical messages.

In the United States, many Grand Lodges have allowed the study of traditional Masonic tracing boards to fall out of common use, which has resulted in a shortage of Masonic instruction about the ancient symbolism. As Bro. Thomas W. Jackson—a thirty-three-degree Mason and Ruler of the Northern Masonic Jurisdiction of Scottish Rite Freemasonry in the United States—stated in the Masonic journal the *Northern Light:*

> Tracing Boards are now rarely used in North American Grand Lodges, ... and I caution you, that it will take concentration on your part [to understand the symbolic ritual of Freemasonry] as a result of our lack of teaching the esoteric qualities of Freemasonry and our failure to make use of the meanings of the Tracing Boards.[1]

Tracing boards, which are displayed in British and other European lodges, are used as visual aids to help with instruction and also for meditation and reflection. When the United States was founded, tracing boards and their symbols were regularly used by Freemasons.

Masonic symbols evoke emotions that cannot be conveyed by language alone. They also have an allegorical role and surface on everyday items from bank notes to jewelry, and in the facades of state buildings. But Freemasonry has an even larger influence: The symbols of mathematics are used to manipulate conceptual abstractions. Two of the most influential mathematical thinkers, John Wallis (who invented algebra) and Isaac Newton (who invented calculus and physics), received Masonic instruction in the use of symbols.

Freemasonry's secret method of symbolic teaching, which its ritual describes as "illumination by symbols," has exerted a powerful influence on key individuals in history. Why, for example, do U.S. presidents make a Masonic sign when being inaugurated? It is because the first president of the United States was a Freemason, and he deliberately introduced key items of Masonic symbolism into his inauguration. But the symbolic teaching of Freemasonry has been felt throughout history:

- Oliver Cromwell, the first Lord Protector of the Republican Commonwealth of Great Britain, chose to be portrayed standing between the two porchway pillars of Freemasonry.

- The Masonically inspired French Revolution adopted the great tripartite motto of "Liberty, Equality, Fraternity." This motto is one of the sets of symbolic names given to three working pillars of the Masonic lodge, portrayed symbolically as Doric, Ionic, and Corinthian.

- The great statement of intent, "No taxation without representation," was generated by the brethren of St. Andrew's Lodge in Boston and became the spark that kindled the greatest Masonic document of all times: the U.S. Constitution. The idea for a written constitution came from the actions of Bro. Benjamin Franklin.

For over 500 years, the symbology of Freemasonry has fostered a secret stream of radical ideas running just beneath the surface of popular culture. These ideas, illuminated by public symbols hidden in full view, have influenced and shaped the society we live in.

The earliest statement of Masonic aims and objectives was created as a crude set of symbols in the late fifteenth century. These symbols, which had been drawn and redrawn since humans first discovered how to make marks on rocks, were painted on sailcloth and laid on the floor of the first Freemasons' lodges to teach the brethren. Since then, Freemasons have displayed and taught the hidden meanings of these symbols. Freemasons have long known that continual exposure to symbols changes how people think.

The symbols have been used by three major republics whose leaders were all inspired by the symbolic importance of brotherhood, relief, and truth. The emotive power of these symbols reminds people of basic truths about the human condition. The two pillars that frame the image of Oliver Cromwell in the famous etching of him as protector of the Commonwealth also frame George Washington as the first president of the United States. Citizens of the United States are reminded of these pillars whenever they pick up a dollar bill.

Despite these significant facts, no illustrated guidebook to the basic ideas of Masonic symbology has been published, and the story of the symbols has remained mysterious. Until now.

PART ONE

THE SECRET
INFLUENCE
OF SYMBOLS

FOR TWO THOUSAND YEARS, SINCE THE TIME OF the philosopher Plato, people have understood that there is a source of pure symbols existing in a spiritual realm of perfection. Plato taught that with careful training an individual could be shown how to communicate with this realm and discover the true nature of these symbols. He developed a way to investigate the truth carried by shapes that it is deeply embedded in Masonic symbology.

The first Freemasons were stoneworkers, employed to carve symbols of religious power into public places of worship. They recognized the power of symbols and realized that symbols were able to influence people's thoughts and actions. They studied the ancient symbols and learned how they had influenced the development of human thought.

The Masonic tradition preserved and developed the ancient emotive symbols and from its practice of symbolic reasoning created an environment which influenced the advancement of society. This book shares secret knowledge that has taken five hundred years to learn.

CHAPTER I

WHY SYMBOLS ARE MORE POWERFUL THAN WORDS

SYMBOLS MADE US HUMAN

A *symbol* is a pictorial device that evokes a concept in its entirety. It bypasses the intellect and talks straight to the heart. Our intellect analyzes, but our heart synthesizes. So a symbol evokes understanding without needing to convey verbal information.

Around 120,000 years ago, a new species of primate appeared in Africa. Its scientific name is *Homo sapiens*, but we know this creature as the modern human. When this species appeared on the earth, there were already other similar but more widespread species of humanoid apes, such as the Neanderthals. Yet the *Homo sapiens* were different. They were different because they could tap into the mystic power of understanding that is inherent in symbols. Symbols have helped humans develop a unique form of consciousness that no other animal has.

All the races of humans are much more closely related than most of us realize. You might be even more surprised to know how closely we are related our primate cousins, the African apes. Our genes are about 98 percent identical to those of an ape, and we share large chunks of our DNA sequence with all other life forms on the earth, even bacteria.[1]

All humans are descended from a single female that lived in Africa less than 200,000 years ago. She is popularly called "Mitochondrial Eve."[2] As geneticist Bryan Sykes puts it: "'Mitochondrial Eve' ... lies at the root of all the maternal ancestries of every one of the six billion people in the world. We are all her direct maternal descendants."[3] Our common maternal ancestor lived only a few thousand generations ago. And her earliest descendants drew the first symbols and tapped into their power.

In the following chapters, you will learn about the power of these symbols, the history of their interaction with humans, and how humans' differential advantage came about because they evolved a type of brain that benefits from a direct relationship with the symbols. This symbiotic relationship began during our early evolutionary history and continues to influence our development in ways most of us are often unaware of.

There is, however, a secret group of specialists who have spent the last 500 years working with these symbols. They learned how symbols can advance the human condition by enabling us to share understanding. This group is the Freemasons, and their declared purpose is to study and understand symbols.

Ask any Freemason the question What is Freemasonry? and you will get this answer: a peculiar system of morality, veiled in allegory and illustrated by symbols. For 500 years, Freemasons have used a system of allegorical ritual and exposure to the mystic power of symbols to sensitize their members to the life-changing power these symbols have. Freemasons continue to experience the deep understanding that symbols can inspire and their power to change the way humans develop.

When humans were first exposed to symbols' mystic power, they changed from brute animals into human beings in a way we still struggle to understand. James Shreeve, a well-known anthropologist, sums up the puzzle presented by this abrupt change:

> Human beings—modern humans, *Homo sapiens*—are behaviorally far, far away from being "just another animal." The mystery is where, how, and why this change took place. ... An "all-important transition" did occur, but it happened so close to the present moment that we are still reeling from it. ... Something happened that turned a passably precocious animal into a human being.[4]

Anthropology records how and when this change happened but offers no explanation. It is my contention that humanity came into contact with a powerful force outside itself that has interacted with our collective mind ever since. This force is carried and communicated by symbols. In later chapters, we will discover that symbols are part of a great cosmic language that transmits deep understanding about the secrets of the universe.

In 2001, when Shreeve wrote the statement just quoted, it was thought that humanity's relationship with symbols began only 30,000 years ago in the deep, dark caves of northern Europe. Then, much earlier evidence of the power of symbols came to light in a cave in southern Africa. The *Times* of London reported it:

> A pair of decorated ornaments unearthed in a South African cave
> have been dated at more than 70,000 years old, proving that human
> beings could think abstractly and appreciate beauty much earlier than
> is generally accepted.

THIS MASONIC TEMPLE DISPLAYS THE ANCIENT LOZENGE PATTERN CARVED INTO THE ARCH ABOVE THE MASTER'S CHAIR. Copyright and reproduced by permission of the Library and Museum of Freemasonry, London and Painton Cowen

The engraved pieces of ochre, a type of iron ore, are by far the oldest examples of symbolic art—a standard benchmark for recognizably modern thought and behavior. The earliest similar objects, from Europe, were made less than 35,000 years ago, and subtle intelligence is usually held to have begun at this time.

The find at Blombos Cave, 180 miles from Cape Town in the Western Cape, will therefore completely revise one of the first chapters of human history.

It indicates that not only did the first human beings evolve in Africa and spread throughout the world, but that they became mentally sophisticated by the time they did so.

This helps to explain the ease with which *Homo sapiens* supplanted other human relatives, such as the Neanderthals in Europe, and thus the development of the modern human race.

All the anatomical features of *Homo sapiens* are known to have evolved in Africa between 150,000 and 130,000 years ago, but the question of when the species began to behave in modern fashion has remained more elusive.

The Blombos Cave, discovered by Professor Chris Henshilwood of the Iziko South African Museum in Cape Town, resolves the debate decisively.[5]

I am a Freemason, and I have been trained in the Masonic system of symbol sensitization. When I saw the image these long dead humans had carved, I recognized it immediately.

I know them as the Masonic lozenge. It is an image I see every time I look at the floor of my Masonic lodge or at a Masonic tracing board.

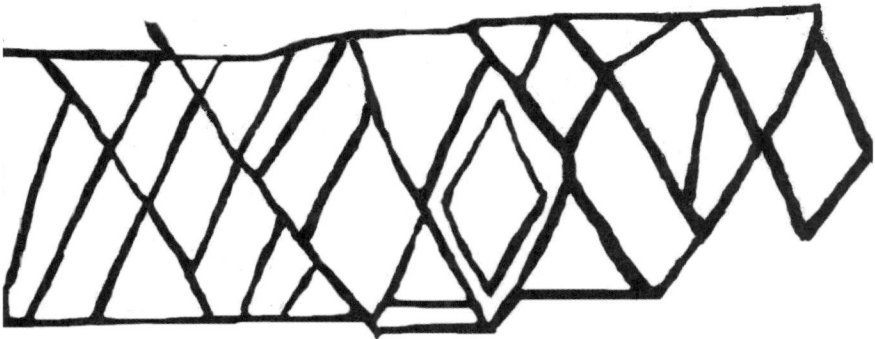

SYMBOLS BEGAN IN DARK CAVES

That ancient primeval lozenge symbol is alive and well today. If you look around, you will see it built into the facades of buildings and in the logos embroidered on sports clothing and mounted on the hoods of cars. Why has it been drawn and redrawn for 70,000 years? Because simply looking at it creates emotions and insights, deep in our unconscious minds, that we enjoy. We respond to its power and feel good about it.

After this first symbol, there is a large gap in the archeological evidence of the interaction of symbols with humans. The next evidence occurred some 40,000 years later, when our ancestors starting drawing pictures on the walls of the caves of Europe. These early humans kept their relationship with symbols a secret. They did not display the symbols on their buildings, clothing, and possessions, but they crawled miles underground into distant, dark caves to experience the deep pleasure of seeing the symbols by the flickering flames of simple torches. It was not until 1879 that evidence of the symbols our ancient ancestors painted was found on rock walls. The first to be recognized were images of bison on the walls of a cave at Altamira in Spain. Then further symbols were found in caves at La Mouthe and Tuc d'Audoubert in France.

These symbols were hidden deep underground, far along narrow tunnels thousands of meters long. The symbols' purpose could never have been public display. They were difficult to reach, and seeing them required unreliable rush lights and burning brands (the remains of which were found in the caves). The humans who drew them needed great courage to venture into those dark depths with only a flickering, feeble light to guide them. Yet they struggled through these tunnels to draw a wide range of symbols. Prehistoric art historian David Lewis-Williams describes the symbols:

> [There are] animals, such as bison, horses, aurochs, woolly
> mammoths, deer and felines. ... There are also occasional anthropo-
> morphic figures that may or may not represent human beings. Some
> of these are therianthropes (part-human, part-animal figures). ... Then
> there is an image type that is exceptional in the ways that it is made —
> handprints. Finally, there is a multiplicity of signs, geometric forms
> such as grids, dots, and chevrons.[6]

A 30,000-YEAR-OLD IMAGE OF AN IBEX WITH MAGNIFICENT HORNS FOUND IN ORANGE SANDSTONE IN A CAVE IN BUCKSKIN GULCH IN UTAH (UNITED STATES).

It is not the drawings of beasts or people that have the most influence on humans. Rather, the symbols that really affect us are the geometric forms. They drive our emotional responses and evoke an understanding of concepts that we struggle to put into words.

It is symbols of the type that first appeared at Blombos that show the continuing interaction between the evolving human mind and the evocative shapes of the symbols.

Analytical psychologist Carl Gustav Jung confirms that symbols speak to us of "things beyond the range of human understanding." They tap into a source of knowledge that is not normally accessible to our conscious minds. Jung defines such symbols as

> a term, a name or an image that may be familiar in daily life, yet it possesses specific connotations in addition to its conventional meanings. It implies something vague, unknown or hidden from us. ... Thus a word or an image is symbolic when it implies something more than its obvious and immediate meaning. It has a wider "unconscious" aspect that is never precisely defined or fully explained. Nor can one hope to define or explain it. As the mind explores the symbol it is led to ideas

that lie beyond the grasp of reason. ... Because there are innumerable things beyond the range of human understanding, we constantly use symbolic terms to represent concepts that we cannot define or fully comprehend.[7]

Jung goes on to expand this idea:

> There are unconscious aspects of our perception of reality. ... Even when our senses react to real phenomena, sights, and sounds, they are somehow translated from the realm of reality into that of the mind. Within the mind they become psychic events, whose ultimate nature is unknowable (for the psyche cannot know its own psychical substance). Thus every experience contains an indefinite number of unknown factors, not to speak of the fact that every concrete object is always unknown in certain respects, because we cannot know the ultimate nature of matter itself.[8]

But what is this knowledge, and where does it come from? These questions have haunted the human race for at least 2,500 years. Greek philosopher Plato (427–347 BCE) thought that symbols came from a transcendental world of perfect and beautiful forms that can be reached only by the human soul. He believed that the most important human knowledge is recalled by the soul from the time before it was born. He said that if we consider our knowledge of equality, then we have no difficulty deciding whether two people are equal in height. But they are never exactly the same height. It is always possible to discover some difference—however minute—with a more careful, precise measurement.

All the examples of equality we recognize in ordinary life approach but never quite attain perfect equality. However, since we realize truth from our experience, we must somehow know for sure what true equality is, even though we can never see it.[9] This kind of thinking led to the discovery of the symbols of geometry and mathematics, which opened up humans' understanding of reality.

THE HEAVEN OF PERFECT SYMBOLS

All the symbols we see around us are imperfect instances, but we have an inner knowledge of abstract things, such as truth, goodness, beauty, and equality. These are the *Platonic forms*: abstract entities that exist independently from the physical world. Plato said that ordinary objects are imperfect and changeable, but they faintly echo the perfect and immutable forms of their symbols. Later, you will see how many of the key symbols that have influenced human development are found among these Platonic forms. Although we can never draw a perfect square, a perfect equilateral triangle, or a perfect lozenge, we know what they are because our soul knows their symbolic, perfect forms.

Plato argued that we cannot possibly have knowledge of these perfect forms through any bodily experience, so our knowledge must be a memory that our souls carry from the transcendental place where the symbols exist in perfect form. Plato, whose ideas inspired part of the Masonic teachings, believed that the world is essentially intelligible but that our intellect, not our senses, has the ultimate vision of true being. We understand the world through the deep knowledge that is conveyed into our hearts by symbols.

Both Plato and Jung tell of a reality that lies beyond normal human consciousness and can only be reached through symbols. This symbolic knowledge has a spiritual or transcendental dimension, which has been the subject of Masonic study and teaching over the centuries. Aniela Jaffe, a student of Jung's, confirms that the early cave symbols have a spiritual power:

> Animal pictures go back to the last Ice Age (between 60,000 and
> 10,000 BCE). They were discovered on the walls of caves in France
> and Spain at the end of the last century, but it was not until early
> in the present century that archaeologists began to realize their
> extreme importance and to inquire into their meaning. These inquir-
> ies revealed an infinitely remote prehistoric culture whose existence
> had never even been suspected. Even today, a strange music seems
> to haunt the caves that contain the rock engravings and paintings.
> According to the German art historian Herbert Kuhn, inhabitants of
> the areas in Africa, Spain, France, and Scandinavia where such paint-
> ings are found could not be induced to go near the caves. A kind of

religious awe, or perhaps a fear of spirits hovering among the rocks and the paintings, held them back. Passing nomads still lay their votive offerings before the old rock paintings in North Africa. In the 15th century, Pope Calixtus II prohibited religious ceremonies in the "cave with the horse pictures." ... This goes to prove that the caves and rocks with the animal paintings have always been instinctively felt to be what they originally were—religious places. The spiritual power of the place has outlived the centuries.[10]

Jaffe confirms that these symbols were intended to be viewed in secret to create a sense of awe and to inspire action on the part of the observers. As she explains,

In a number of caves the modern visitor must travel through low, dark, and damp passages till he reaches the point where the great painted "chambers" suddenly open out. This arduous approach may express the desire of the primitive men to safeguard from common sight all that was contained and went on in the caves, and to protect their mystery. The sudden and unexpected sight of the paintings in the chambers, coming after the difficult and awe-inspiring approach, must have made an overwhelming impression on primitive man.[11]

SYMBOLS LIKE THESE WERE INTENDED TO BE VIEWED IN SECRET TO CREATE A SENSE OF AWE FOR THE OBSERVER. Connection Blue/Alamy

Symbols appeared first as secret devices drawn in the hidden confines of caves, to be viewed only by those brave enough to venture into their depths. But over the next 25,000 years, symbols would come out of the darkness and into the light.

HOW HUMANS LEARNED TO LIVE WITH SYMBOLS

By the early Neolithic age, or about 12,000 years ago, symbols were being carved into all sorts of portable artifacts. The late Professor Marija Gimbutas of UCLA made these early portable symbols her lifelong study. She said the most frequently occurring symbols developed independent lives of their own. Everywhere humans moved, they engraved certain types of symbols around them—on rocks and on artifacts such as pots and sticks. These symbols were rooted within the consciousness of the people who drew them and, as I show, remain there to this day. According to Gimbutas, "The old European sacred images and symbols ... are too deeply implanted in the psyche to be uprooted."[12]

These symbols track humanity's evolution from simple hunter-gatherers to sophisticated farmers, and Gimbutas believed it was possible to decipher their importance and meanings. As she said:

> Symbols are seldom abstract in any genuine sense; their ties with nature persist, to be discovered through the study of context and association. In this way we can hope to decipher the mythical thought which is the *raison d'etre* of this art and basis of its form. My primary presupposition is that they can best be understood on their own planes of reference, grouped according to their inner coherence. They constitute a complex system in which every unit is interlocked with every other in what appear to be specific categories. No symbol can be treated in isolation; understanding the parts leads to understanding the whole, which in turn leads to identifying more of the parts.[13]

Gimbutas was right. It is possible to decipher the meanings and importance of these enduring symbols. They have a hidden power that they exert on humanity. I discovered this by testing whether the deep power of the ancient symbols still affects modern human minds.

THE ANCIENT SYMBOLS STILL WORK

To test how deeply these ancient symbols are implanted in the psyche of modern humans, I conducted a series of tests on volunteer students to see how they responded to them. I used a technique called *galvanic skin response (GSR)*, which measures the degree of emotional arousal a symbol causes. This technique is founded on the idea that you have no control over what makes you sweat. Using GSR made it possible for me to monitor what was happening in parts of students' brains they were not consciously aware of. When they felt strong emotions, their brains forced them to sweat. Sweat is a good conductor of electricity, so the more the students sweat, the easier it became to pass an electric current across the surface of their skin. They were not consciously aware that it was happening, but I was able to measure it.

GSR is one of the key tests that has been used as a lie detector for many years. But recently, a group of scientists at the Wellcome Department of Cognitive Neurology, of University College London, used functional magnetic resonance imaging to scan subjects' brains to see exactly which parts caused these GSR-measurable sweats. The areas involved are the left medial prefrontal cortex, bilateral extrastriate visual cortices, and cerebellum. These are parts of the brain that create emotions. So symbols are not evoking understanding in our heart but in our left medial prefrontal cortex. The heart is a more romantic metaphor, however.

The sweat response happens when our attention activates these emotional parts of our brain. It is an evolutionary response that makes sure that even if we are concentrating on something else, our attention can be drawn to important events outside our bodies. It works by causing us to feel an inexplicable (i.e., not something we can consciously control) emotional response to some stimuli that we may not consciously be aware of. The key areas contributing to this response are in the limbic system of the brain—an area below our normal level of consciousness. But our consciousness certainly feels the emotions it produces. This is how symbols evoke understanding in our hearts.

The fact that our brain has this built-in indicator of the emotional impact of symbols has allowed me to study how people from different backgrounds respond to symbols. I work at an international business school, and for my research, I had access to volunteers from around the world. I was able to test people who had been brought up in British, African, Asian, American, European, and Chinese cultures and had been taught to read in different writing systems, using different methods of recording words, and speaking different native languages. I tested equal numbers of females and males in each culture/alphabet group. I repeated this test over a number of years, and my results have been consistent.

I took a set of twelve shapes: six from modern contemporary jewelry and six ancient symbols. One of the symbols was from Blombos, and the rest were of the type associated with the spread of farming societies. I chose modern jewelry because its decorative motifs are designed to appeal to people.

I set up a GSR meter between the thumb and forefinger of the right hand of each volunteer. Once the volunteer's baseline reading stabilized, I showed him or her a card with an image on it. I allowed the volunteer to look at the image for at least a minute, until his or her GSR settled again. Then I noted the reading before showing the volunteer another image.

When I analyzed the results, I found that all the ancient symbols caused a consistent change in galvanic skin response. The implication of this test is that the ancient symbols caused an emotional response in my test subjects. The responses to the modern jewelry shapes were less consistent. But I could not tell from these data if the response to the ancient symbols was positive or negative. Did the subjects like these symbols, or did they find them disturbing? Because the subjects' responses were subconscious, I soon found that there was little point in asking them how they felt about the images. They struggled to articulate their feelings.

The only sure way to uncover the subjects' feelings was to conduct a follow-up survey using the same subjects but asking different questions about the symbols that caused their emotional responses. In this survey, I asked the subjects to rank the same set of images in terms of attractiveness.

I placed the twelve images I had used for the GSR test on a table in front of each subject and asked him or her to examine them. (The actual images used are shown at right.) Next, I asked the subject to hand me the image he or she found most attractive. I recorded the subject's choice and placed the card out of sight. I then asked the subject to pick

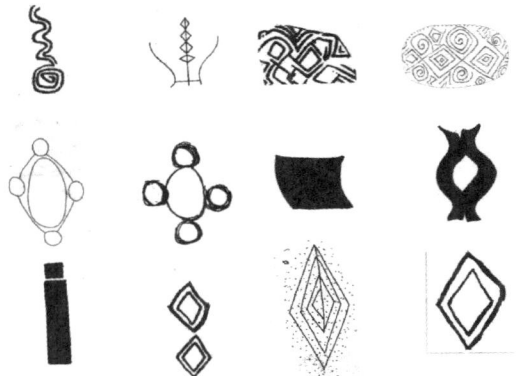

the most attractive of the remaining images. This process continued until only one image was left.

In this way, I created a ranking system for the images. Each image had a possible ranked value of 12 to 1. When I had completed the full sample, I calculated an average attractiveness score for each image. All the top-scoring images were images that caused a significant GSR response. The sweating I had measured was the glow of pleasure, not a cold sweat of fear.

The top five symbols, scored according their attractiveness, appear below.

Note that a Blombos symbol was found to be significantly attractive, even after 70,000 years.

The most significantly popular symbol is one that Gimbutas recorded in many similar forms between Anatolia and Orkney. It is an elaboration of the 70,000-year-old Blombos lozenge, and it has been paired with a spiral. Gimbutas noted that the spiral became particularly popular as a pottery symbol in southeast Europe around 6300 BCE and spread west.

There were no statistically significant differences between volunteers from different ethnic groups. But no matter what nationality they were or what native language they had learned to speak, read, and write, there were significant differences between males' and females' responses. Specifically, females found the spirals more attractive, whereas males were drawn to variations of the lozenge and V-shape. Both males and females found the ancient symbols of the lozenge and the spiral consistently more attractive than the shapes taken from modern contemporary jewelry.

These symbols would not have persisted for so long simply because they were pretty. Human views of beauty change. Rather, it seems some transcendental evolutionary force burned the symbols into our brains. Based on my research, I could conclude that human brains are hardwired to like particular symbols, so there must be an evolutionary payoff. But I still had to uncover it.

PICTURES CAN TRANSFER THOUGHTS

Betty Edwards, a professor of art at California State University, noticed how certain persistent symbols interact with humans. She found that her students could see consistent meaning in some drawings:

> Students ... suddenly see that drawings (and other works of art) have meaning. I am not, of course, referring only to drawings of things — portraits, landscapes, still-life subjects. That kind of meaning ... can be summed up in a few words. But meaning is also expressed in the parallel visual language of a drawing, whether it represents recognizable objects or is completely non-objective. This different kind of meaning requires a different kind of comprehension. A drawing, to be comprehended for meaning, must be read by means of the language used by the artist, and that meaning, once comprehended, may be beyond the power of words to express. Yet in its parts and as a whole, it can be read.[14]

When we look at abstract shapes, parts of our brain relate to the emotions and thoughts that were in the mind of the person who drew the shapes.[15] This emotional response is the same one I found in my volunteers.

Sensitivity to the emotive message of symbols is innate but can be trained and enhanced. Edwards describes this process in terms of drawing:

> In its simplicity, drawing is the silent twin to reading. Both reading and drawing can be done at any age from early childhood to the final day of a lifetime, if the eyes last that long. Both can be done in almost any environment, at any time of the day or night, by any person of any age who has minimal physical and mental health. ... Prehistoric human drawings predate written language by about ten thousand years. It seems possible that a language of drawing may derive from innate brain structures, just as verbal language apparently derives from innate structure. The fact that you know (part of) the parallel visual language already — though you perhaps don't know that you know it, indicates at least a possible innate brain structure for visual language. How, then, to tap into your natural ability to use — and

understand the expressive power of this visual language? Clearly, by drawing—and by learning how to draw—just as we tap into the power of verbal language by learning how to read and write.[16]

Drawing images allows people to express ideas or feelings that are too complicated or imprecise to fit into the straitjacket of written language. According to Edwards, "Drawings can show relationships that are grasped immediately as a single image, where words are necessarily locked into a sequential order."[17] Words have to be processed by marching into your mind in single file, whereas ideas encoded in pictorial symbols flow into your heart in parallel waves.

When humans discovered how to make long-lasting marks, the first thing they developed was a visual language of symbols that did not encode words but rather conveyed emotion. This secret language of symbols is still open to us. Freemasonry teaches that different symbols work on our minds in different ways and that some symbols are more powerful than others.

Edwards developed a technique she called *analog drawing*. It involves exercises for which the goal is to "dredge up that inner life of the mind by using an alternative, visual language [analog drawings] to give it tangible form—in short, to make inner thought visible."[18] The images Edwards's students drew to represent the concept of "femininity" immediately attracted my attention, as they were similar to the early emotive geometric shapes my volunteers liked.[19]

In particular, one of Edwards's analog drawings of femininity showed what looked like an image of the ancient Blombos lozenge.[20] Yet Edwards could not have been aware of the Blombos symbol, as it was not found until twenty years after she recorded this image. It appears to be a universal symbol of femininity—a subject that always interests young males. Was this why my male students rated it so highly?

Edwards said that teaching her students to become sensitive to symbols made them better thinkers. This is a lesson Freemasonry has been teaching for hundreds of years.

I asked a number of artist friends to use Edwards's analog method to draw their own symbols of femininity, without explaining why I was interested or giving any indication of what I expected. The images, shown on the next page, have similar features to Edwards's findings.

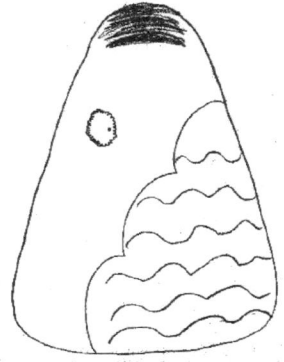

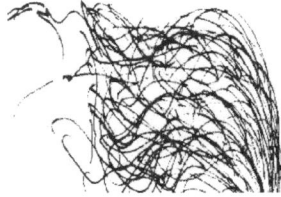

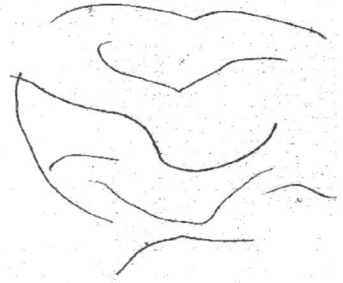

SYMBOLS TAUGHT US HOW TO THINK

Symbols and language evolved together and are a key part of what defines us as human. The cave paintings in Lascaux, Chauvet, and Altamira show that symbols were used to influence reality 30,000 years ago—specifically, to increase success in hunting and to increase fertility among the people. Professor of prehistory Steven Mithen describes the sudden surge in modern behavior that symbol exposure caused: "There was a cultural explosion ... 60,000 —30,000 years ago. ... *H. sapiens sapiens* ... adopted certain forms of behavior never previously seen, ... notably the origins of Art."[21] The "Art" Mithen is talking about are the symbols of animals, people, and platonic forms that were drawn deep inside the underground cave systems.

The oldest symbols drawn by modern humans date back to 70,000 BCE and were geometric. By 35,000 BCE, a mixture of pictorial and geometric symbols had been drawn across Eurasia and North Africa.

In the following chapters, we will see how three major types of symbols drove the development of human civilization:

1. *Emotive symbols* encode feelings and aspirations. These are the oldest of all symbols and date back over 70,000 years. They have been widely used to communicate emotion to illiterate people.

2. *Speech symbols* encode the sounds of language and enable humans to communicate across time and space. At one time, these symbols were tightly restricted to an elite group and often linked with religion and a ruling class.

3. *Counting symbols* encode techniques of measuring, recording, and keeping track of how many possessions you have and eventually gave birth to the cosmic language of mathematical symbols.

As each new group of symbols appeared, it interacted differently with humanity but always brought about changes in the organization of society. Symbols make humans different from other animals. It was Freemasonry's study of these ancient, transcendental symbols that led to the greatest breakthroughs in human achievement.

CHAPTER 2

HOW SYMBOLS TURNED HUNTERS INTO FARMERS

SYMBOLS LET US COMMUNICATE WITH THE DEAD

The first symbols, discovered over 70,000 years ago, still have the power to influence us today. Symbols made us human, and as we developed them, they taught us new skills. The appearance of one particular type of symbol changed human society by teaching people how to cooperate in the hunt.

A CAVE PAINTING FROM NEWSPAPER ROCK IN UTAH (UNITED STATES) SHOWING A HUNTER AND HORNED SHAMAN SUCCESSFULLY COOPERATING TO KILL FOR FOOD.

Carl Jung said that symbols arise in "our unconscious psyche." This is the inarticulate part of our mind that keeps a vigilant watch on our surroundings. If we did not have such a built-in survival feature, we would have died out long ago. Our ancestors would have been surprised and eaten by lions while they admired the smoothness of a pebble, unaware of what was going on around them. But if we were not able to ignore our surroundings and concentrate on detail, we would never have learned how to hunt in tribes, to farm our food, or to build cities.

Jung believed that our unconscious psyche, which interacts with symbols, plays an important role in the development of the human mind. He did not put forward any theory of how symbols work, but he showed that archetypal symbols have an enormous impact on an individual, shaping his or her emotions, ethical and mental outlook, and relationships with others and affecting his or her whole destiny. Von Franz, one of Jung's students, sums up this idea:

> The archetypes, or archetypal symbols, act as creative or destructive forces in our mind: creative when they inspire new ideas, destructive when these same ideas stiffen into conscious prejudices that inhibit further discoveries. To Jung, his concepts were ... heuristic hypotheses that might help us to explore the vast new area of reality opened up by the discovery. ... If all men have common inherited patterns of emotional and mental behavior [which Jung called the archetypes or archetypal symbols], it is only to be expected that we shall find their products [the results of acting under the influence of these shared archetypal symbols] in practically every field of human activity.[1]

Professor Gerald Edelman, director of the Neuroscience Research Institute and winner of the Nobel Prize in Physiology in 1972, has studied how ancient emotive symbols interact with the human mind. I had the good fortune to meet Dr. Edelman and to discuss his views on the evolution of human consciousness when he visited my own university to deliver a keynote speech at our Darwin Centenary Conference in September 2009. Edelman identified two important evolutionary drivers that developed the human mind. These are distinct modes of thought referred to as *logic* and *selectionism*. Edelman states, "There are two main modes of thought—logic and selectionism (or pattern recognition). Both are powerful, but it is pattern recognition that can lead to creation, for example, in the choice of axioms in mathematics. If selectionism is the mistress of our thoughts, logic is their housekeeper."[2]

Symbols live much longer than any human. We can look at the symbols drawn by our ancient ancestors 70,000 years ago and feel the same emotional response as they did. My GSR tests prove this. Symbols enable human thoughts and aspirations to transcend the limits of our short life span.

Evolutionary theory says that change is driven by the interaction of competing forces. The appearance of emotive symbols was only the beginning, not the end, of the story of their interaction with humans. A symbol's ability to transmit emotional and creative ideas across time and space confers enormous advantage on any human who becomes sensitive to the symbol's power.

Emotive symbols are of two types: geometric and realistic. The *geometric* emotive symbols were the first to appear but did not initially have a great impact on human progress. The symbols that gave humanity that first push were the *realistic* symbols associated with hunting and gathering. The realistic symbols were eventually surpassed by the more powerful geometric emotional symbols. Even so, the realistic symbols still play a role in the Masonic symbolic repertoire.

SYMBOLS HELPED HUNTERS

The creative explosion of human thought in western Europe 30,000 years ago was driven by realistic emotive symbols. Professor David Lewis-Williams, an academic expert in prehistoric art, describes what happened:

> To seek a driving mechanism for the West European Creative
> Explosion, ... we need to consider the divisive functions of image-
> making. In doing so, we distance ourselves from earlier functionalist
> explanations, such as art for art's sake, sympathetic magic, binary
> mythograms, and information exchange, all of which see art as con-
> tributing to social stability. The most striking feature of the west
> European Upper Palaeolithic is a sharp increase in the rate of change,
> ... greater diversity in the kinds of raw materials used for artifact manu-
> facture, the appearance of new tool types, the development of regional
> tool styles, socially and cognitively more sophisticated hunting strate-
> gies, organized settlement patterns, and extensive trade in "special"
> items. Even more striking is the explosion of body decoration, elabo-
> rate burials with grave goods, and, of course, portable and parietal

images [images drawn deep in caves]. It is clear that all these areas of change were interdependent—they interlocked. They were not a scatter of disparate "inventions" made by especially intelligent individuals; rather, they were part of the very fabric of a dynamic society.[3]

Symbols were being woven into the thinking processes of humanity. They were creating and spreading ideas by forcing everyone who viewed them to identify with the emotional state of the person who drew the symbol. In this way, symbols drove the cooperative tribal effort to hunt effectively and feed the growing group.

HUNTING SYMBOLS LIKE THE ONES SHOWN HERE (A HERD OF AUROCH, AN EXTINCT SPECIES OF WILD CATTLE, BEING INFILTRATED BY HUNTERS) HELPED DRIVE THE COOPERATIVE EFFORT OF HUMANS TO HUNT AND FEED.

The impact of hunting symbols on human development provides dramatic support for Edelman's theory. He says that mental imagery, provoked by seeing and recalling symbols, helps humans thrive in the real world. He calls this the evolution of *higher-level consciousness*.

The symbols of hunting made it possible for groups of humans to share their mental representations. And this caused humanity's dramatic progress. Lewis-Williams draws on Edelman's research to help explain this evolutionary mechanism:

> Higher-order consciousness involves the ability to construct a socially based self-hood, to model the world in terms of the past and the future, and to be directly aware. Without a symbolic memory, these abilities cannot develop. ... Long-term storage of symbolic relations, acquired through interactions with other individuals of the same species, is critical to self-concept. ... Edelman explains the evolution of higher-order consciousness in neurobiological terms, but we need not consider all the details here. ... The difference between primary consciousness and higher-order consciousness is that members of the species *Homo sapiens*, the only species that has it, can remember better and use memory to fashion their own individual identities and mental "scenes" of past, present, and future events. This is the key point. ... The pattern of modern human behavior that higher-order consciousness made possible was put together piecemeal and intermittently in Africa. ... It seems likely that fully modern language and higher-order consciousness were, as Edelman argues, linked: It is impossible to have one without the other.[4]

This is the key to understanding the realistic symbols of hunting scenes, animals, and hunters, secretly drawn deep within the dark caves.

Our brains had reached an evolutionary stage where we were ready for wider access to the transcendental eternal Platonic heaven of symbols. This developing relationship with symbols made us different from our Neanderthal cousins. The symbols were shaping the inner structure of our evolving brains. Lewis-Williams explains how these cave symbols were used:

> We saw that a crucial threshold in human evolution was between two kinds of consciousness, not merely between moderate and advanced intelligence. Neanderthals were able to borrow only certain activities from their new *Homo sapiens* neighbors not because they were hopelessly bemired in animality and stupidity but because they lacked a

particular kind of consciousness. They could entertain a mental picture of the present and, by learning processes, sense the presence of
danger or reward. But they were locked into what Gerald Edelman
calls "the remembered present": Without developed memory and the
kind of fully modern language that must attend it, they were unable
to enter into long-term planning [or] initiate complex kinship and
political systems.[5]

This is why the symbols of hunting were hidden deep in caves. They conferred
power on those who could access their representations of hunts and chases, noble
beasts, and brave hunters. Those who were invited to view the symbols saw birds
and bison, deer, and horses—all flowing along the walls with rampant and successful hunters in pursuit. These individuals felt the emotive power of the symbols
and carried that inspiration out with them, enhancing their own hunting skills and
becoming inspired to lead the hunt.

Lewis-Williams says the purpose of the images was to enable the tribal leaders
of the hunting bands to engage with the spirits of the animals they hunted. Doing
so would ensure that the group could find and kill enough prey animals to survive.
Images of these leaders appear in the cave and are often shown as *therianthropes* (i.e.,
part human and part animal symbols), implying that they can think like a hunter and
like a prey animal and so lead the human band to the food it needed.

There is a consensus among neurologists, art historians, psychologists, philosophers, and physicists that humanity's close encounter with realistic emotional
symbols created a new dimension of human possibility. Without the interaction of
symbolic representation, there could be no gods and no godlike aspirations.

Over time, symbols emerged from the depths of the caves into the light and
mutated into powerful symbols of gods and goddesses. These symbols, as well as
the beliefs they transmitted, made the next step possible: the change from hunter-
gathering to farming.

SYMBOLS TAUGHT FARMING

Hunter-gatherers had an easier lifestyle, lived longer, and worked less than the early
farmers. Yet humanity decided to opt for the hard slog of subsistence farming. After
some 3.5 million years of living a successful nomadic lifestyle, humans gave up the

idyll of hunting-gathering and chose the hard work, uncertain harvest, and winter worry of farming. It was the spiritual power of these symbols that caused humans to exchange the thrill of the chase for the muddy squalor of the farmyard.

When *Homo sapiens* first evolved as a species, they lived in small, economically self-sufficient, family-based groups. They found their own food and made their own weapons, tools, and other necessary items. Only after some of these primitive groups settled down, learned how to grow crops, raised livestock, and built houses did villages emerge. From these villages came new social concepts and institutions—such as the division of labor, large building projects, and intricate social organizations— that laid down the foundations of civilization. The true secret of why farming began was hidden in the symbols these early farmers carried with them.

Geneticist Jim Wilson carried out a survey of the native Orcadian population, who live north of Great Britain. He identified the maternal heritage that had the largest effect on this population as coming from the area we now call Turkey. The Orcadians' ancestors came from Anatolia, where a city known as Çatalhöyük had thrived. This city did not prosper by farming, however. Its citizens made their living by making stone knives and trading them for food with passing hunter-gatherers. But it was from Çatalhöyük that the first farming settlements originated and then spread over the whole world. And it was in Çatalhöyük that the new symbols of farming emerged. Wilson's analysis showed that farming was spread by women, and as I show, the symbol of farming began as a symbol of womanhood.

This farming symbol was observed by the late Professor Marija Gimbutas. She has documented a whole range of ancient symbols for the last 30,000 years:

> Symbols ... constitute a complex system in which every unit is inter-
> locked with every other in what appears to be specific categories. ...
> The religion of the early agricultural period of Europe and Anatolia is
> richly documented. Tombs, temples, frescoes, reliefs, sculptures, figu-
> rines, pictorial paintings, and other sources.[6]

This symbol combines lozenge and spiral symbols. It is about 7,000 years old and was discovered by Gimbutas in eastern Yugoslavia. She described it as a "loaf-shaped clay object which was probably a model of sacred bread made as an offering to the Pregnant Goddess."[7] Early farmers made bread with symbols on them, rather like the hot cross buns that modern-day Christians make to celebrate Easter, and they also made miniature clay tokens of their loaves.

The oldest version of the combined symbol that Gimbutas recorded is shown at the bottom-right below.

Gimbutas knew how the symbol stamp was used because it was found alongside the token clay model of an embossed sacred loaf.[8] The clay token of a loaf of bread (shown below), impressed with these sacred symbols, is around 9,500 years old.

By 6500 BCE, these symbols had spread west into Europe.[9] The table below shows the dates of the growth of farms from Anatolia to the west coast of Europe.[10] Recognizable versions of the lozenge and spiral symbols spread with the expansion of the farming villages, as the diagram shows. The oldest symbols are in the East and the most recent in the West.

DATED CIRCA 7,500 BCE: ANATOLIA, TURKEY

DATED CIRCA 7,500 BCE: ANATOLIA, TURKEY

DATED CIRCA 6,000 BCE: SOUTHERN ITALY

DATED CIRCA 5,000 BCE: BOSNIA

DATED CIRCA 4,000 BCE: NORTH-EASTERN ROMANIA

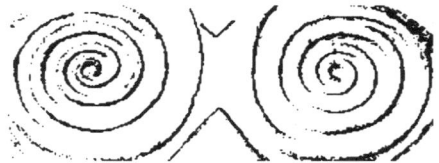

DATED CIRCA 4,000 BCE: MALTA

DATED CIRCA 4,000 BCE: MALTA

DATED CIRCA 3,500 BCE: IRELAND

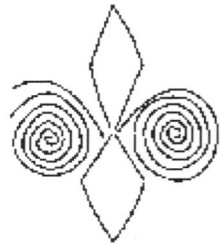

DATED CIRCA 3,000 BCE: NORTHERN SCOTLAND

ANCIENT SYMBOLS FOUND IN A BIRTHING CHAMBER

The dates of the appearance of the lozenge and spiral symbol match the sequence of the changeover from hunting-gathering to farming. The symbols traveled with the farmers, helping and inspiring them in the difficult times of establishing a farm in the trackless wilderness. At first, I was puzzled as to the significance of the symbols, but Gimbutas's collection held an important clue. She had recorded a realistic statue of a woman's torso, overlaid with the emotive geometric lozenge and spiral symbols. It was a Rosetta Stone linking realistic womanhood symbols with emotive geometric farming symbols.

Gimbutas also discovered that the lozenge and spiral symbol was used in rituals of birth and farming at Çatalhöyük. As she explains:

> In the early Neolithic, peoples constructed ... birthing shrines. At Çatalhöyük ... excavations revealed a room where inhabitants apparently performed rituals connected with birthing. They painted the room red, reminding us that red, the color of blood, was the color of life. Stylized figures on the walls illustrate women giving birth, while circular forms and wavy lines painted nearby may symbolize the cervix, umbilical cord and amniotic fluid. A low plaster platform could have been used for actual birthing. The color and symbolism in the room suggest that people regarded this as a religious event and that they accompanied it with ritual.[11]

The circular forms and wavy lines were the lozenge and spiral shape also found on the token model of the symbol-impressed loaf. Gimbutas points out that symbols of a pregnant Earth mother were

> frequently unearthed near bread ovens. She [the pregnant Earth mother] personified the analogy between human and animal pregnancy and the annual cycle of plant germination, growth, and harvest.[12]

Archaeologist James Mellaart excavated altars within birthing shrines at Çatalhöyük and found offerings of grain preserved between layers of red clay on symbolic altars.[13] More recently, similar "votive deposits," including carbonized barley seeds, have been found covered over in post cavities.[14] Gimbutas found that the ritual of adding grain seeds to symbolic clay figures spread along with the practice of farming. As she explains:

> The early Cucuteni (Tripolye) culture, which dated from circa 4800–3500 BC, provides us with the clearest insight into Neolithic rituals honoring the pregnant vegetation goddess. … Figurines showed traces of grain, and some sixty figurines bore evidence of grain impressions on the surface. … When technicians x-rayed these very porous clay figurines, they found three grain types (wheat, barley, and millet) stuffed inside. … Here we have powerful evidence for a ritual associating grain, flour, and baking, performed for the goddess in order to assure abundant bread.[15]

The ritual importance of placing seeds within the layered clay was the clue to understanding the symbolic goddess figures and the symbols carved on the female torso. It reveals a context for the combined realistic and geometric figure, which dates from around 5000 BCE.[16]

Drawing the symbols flattened out, instead of wrapped around the torso, reveals a familiar symbol. Gimbutas found that the egg-shaped buttocks were decorated with energy symbols—whorls and concentric circles—which are naturally occurring patterns created by the shadow of the noon sun.[17] At right is a drawing of the unfolded symbol.

Gimbutas's collection is evidence of the long-term use of the lozenge and spiral symbol, which I show still retains the power to fascinate my students.

Gimbutas placed the symbol in a ritual religious context:

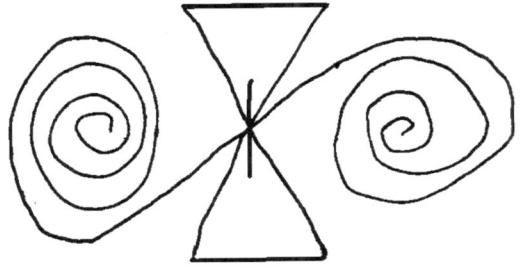

> Innumerable Neolithic figurines preserved in their original settings the intimate richness of Old European spirituality. ... Their makers incised them with symbols, such as two or three lines, spirals or meanders, a chevron or a lozenge. ... Artisans could create schematic figurines easily, and, like the Christian cross, in religious practice these figures communicated the same symbolic concepts as the more representational art. These simplified images ... express a sacred message.[18]

The geometrical emotive symbols were embossed onto semirealistic images of the fertile female form before becoming freestanding symbols. The symbolic importance of the various parts of the female torso relate to the symbols. The downward-pointing triangle is a symbol of the vulva and womb "sprouting life and giving birth."[19] The upward-pointing triangle formed by the spread of the woman's legs, symbolized death and the womb as tomb. This use can be seen in the structures of "horn-mouthed tombs" that were built at this time as symbolic wombs to house the dead.[20] According to Gimbutas,

> The caves, crevices, and caverns of the earth are natural manifestations of the primordial womb of the Mother. Burial in the womb of the earth is analogous to planting a seed, so it is a simple step to expect new life to emerge from the old.[21]

Now the emotive power of the combined symbol becomes easy to explain. The upward-pointing triangle represents death and the act of planting a seed in the womb. The downward-pointing triangle represents the new life that will come in the spring. The points of these triangles meet at the vulva of the goddess and at the intersection of the double symbol of fertility, which is the goddess's exaggerated and fertile buttocks. As shown below, the V-shape, or chevron, when topped off to form a lozenge, or diamond shape, is a pattern that is created by the shadows cast on the land by the rising and setting sun as it moves through the seasons.

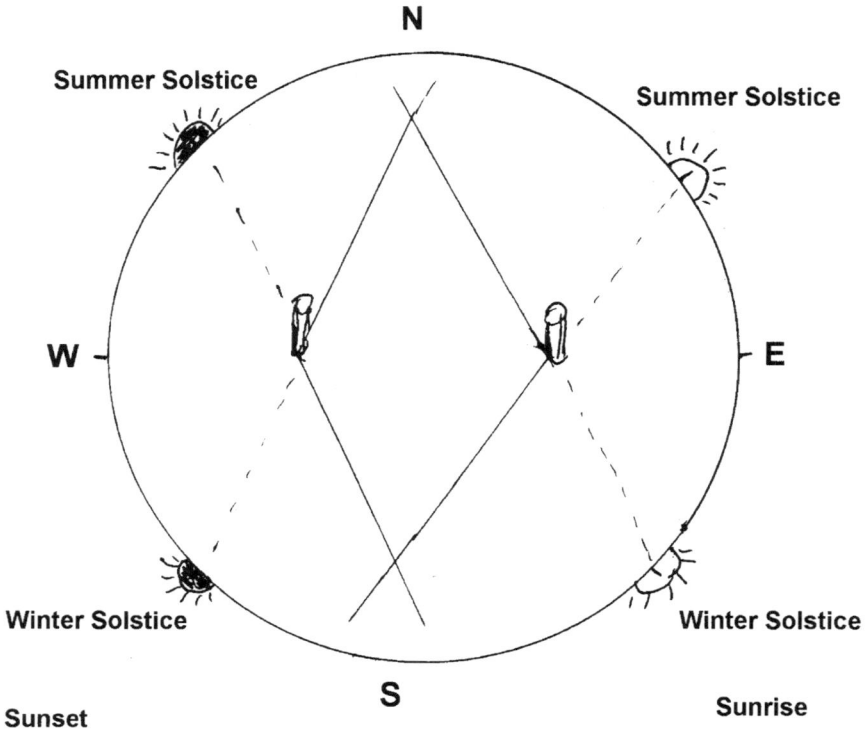

The further north, the taller and thinner the lozenge shape becomes. In latitudes near the equator, the lozenge becomes short and fat.[22] I have used this observation to check the shapes of many lozenges, including the earliest ones ever found (70,000 BCE at Blombos Cave) and found them to be consistent in locating the latitude of the site where they were engraved.[23] Likewise, the shape of the two spirals, which was superimposed on the buttocks of the goddess can be created by marking out the path of the sun's shadow during the seasons, with each spiral taking three months to appear. This observational symbolism is carried out by plotting the fall of the tip of the shadow of the freestanding pole at midday.[24] The symbol traced out by the natural movement of the sun draws out the pattern that appears on the woman's buttocks.

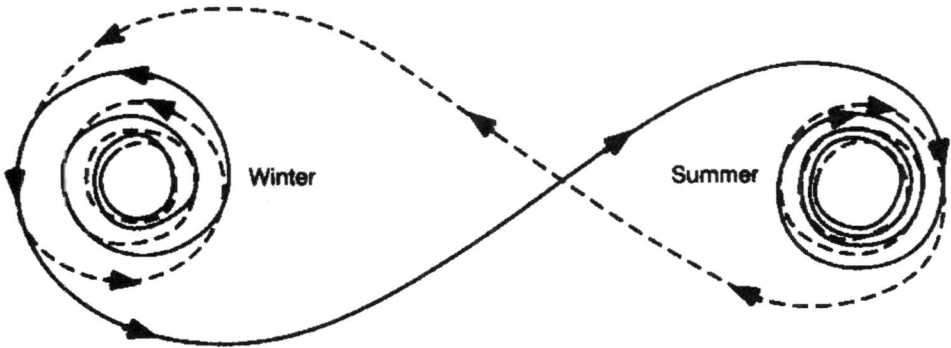

As farmers became more successful and more settled, they began to build not just villages but also large communal structures. The farmers used these structures for religious rituals and carved their religious symbols on the walls to inspire them to continue to labor on their land. Below is the image of the farming symbol displayed on the wall of a massive tunnel mound at Newgrange in Ireland. It dates from about 5,000 years ago.

The two lozenge shapes are taken from the extreme latitudes of the British Isles. They intersect where the downward-pointing triangle meets the upward-pointing triangle. This is the place where the spring spiral of the sun's path meets the spiral of the beginning of summer. This season is known as *spring* or the *vernal equinox*. It is the time to plant seeds for the autumn har-

vest. The mundane meaning of the symbol is "Plant your dead seed in the womb of Mother Earth at the vernal equinox, and by the end of the summer, it will be reborn as abundant grain to give you bread through the winter." Not only is this a powerful geometrical emotive symbol, but it can also be read as a textbook on how and when to farm grain.

Both elements of this symbol can be found in the Masonic teaching about symbols. The spiral and lozenge are key elements in the second-degree tracing board.

As humans became more settled, they created a new form of symbol that transmitted more precise information than these early emotive symbols. Individuals with knowledge of this new symbol would create the first empires. Symbols were about to change the human species again. They would facilitate a concept of wealth and the power that wealth can bring.

CHAPTER 3

HOW SYMBOLS
CREATED KINGDOMS

THE IMPORTANCE OF COUNTING

About 9,000 years ago in Mesopotamia, in a land then called Sumer, a group of symbols appeared that made it possible for humans to count objects and to keep records of what they owned. These symbols emerged in the small farming villages that were starting to appear and made it possible for farmers to keep track of their produce. Using these symbols marked the beginning of wealth and also suggested the potential for power and domination.

Before humans farmed, they had no domesticated pack animals to carry things. Hunter-gatherers had to carry their possessions in their hands or on their backs as they followed meandering herds of prey animals. This limited what they could own, in terms of both size and weight. These people had no wealth and little incentive to count their few bits and pieces. But when they stopped hunting-gathering and began to farm, they accumulated goods.

As farming settlements became more widely established, so did the number, value, and weight of an individual's personal goods. For the first time, people were able to own homes where they could live for the rest of their lives. And with the domestication of animals, ownership extended to flocks and herds of semi-tame beasts. But for the early farmers to survive through the winter without hunting, they had to keep track of their reserves of food and domesticated beasts. This was when a new form of symbol revealed just how useful it could be.

Counting symbols began on farms. The clay token loaves that we saw in the previous chapter were not toys; rather, they provided a way of keeping track of the number of loaves that had been baked. Archaeologist Denise Schmandt-Besserat, professor of Middle Eastern studies at the University of Texas, has studied and classified over 8,000 of these symbolic counting tokens that have been excavated from all over Sumer. She explains the purpose of these tokens:

> A system of tokens, ... small clay objects of many shapes—cones,
> spheres, disks, cylinders, and so on—served as counters in the pre-
> historic Near East and can be traced to the Neolithic period, starting
> about 8000 BC. They evolved to ... [keep] track of the products of
> farming, [and] then ... [as more cities grew] to keep track of goods
> manufactured in workshops. The development of tokens was tied to
> the rise of social structures, emerging with rank leadership and com-
> ing to a climax with state formation.[1]

The tokens began as miniature clay models of the actual goods they symbolized. Grain was stored in conical clay storage vessels, so a measure of grain was
represented by a small cone. Oil was kept in ovoid jars, and so a measure of oil was
symbolized by a small clay ovoid. For two measures of oil, two ovoids were kept.
Tokens were used for various animals and various types of food. For each object that
a record of quantity was needed, a token was made to symbolize the individual item.

Knowing this, the purpose of making clay symbols of embossed loaves makes
sense. Those people who made a number of loaves for use in trade at a forthcoming
festival would need to keep a token for each loaf to know how many they had in stock.

Two new functions of symbols were beginning to emerge. Schmandt-Besserat
explains what was happening in the ongoing interaction between humanity and the
power of symbols:

> The earliest evidence of signs, in the form of notched tallies, date
> from the Middle Paleolithic. ... Symbolism was used both in rituals
> and, at the same time, for the compilation of concrete information.
> From its beginnings in about 30,000 BC, the evolution of symbolic
> information processing in the prehistoric Near East proceeded in
> major phases, dealing with data of increasing specificity. First, during
> the Middle and late Upper Paleolithic, ca. 30,000–12,000 BC, tal-
> lies referred to one unit of an unspecified item. Second, in the early
> Neolithic, ca. 8000 BC, the tokens indicated a precise unit of a par-
> ticular good. ... The name of the sponsor/recipient of the merhandise
> [was] indicated by seals.[2]

A group of individuals soon saw a chance to prosper by seizing a share of everyone else's goods. Today, we call this process taxation. But before you can tax someone, you need to be able to measure what he or she has. The symbols of counting spawned the accountant and the tax collector.

Here are examples of those early symbols. Below are cone tokens, which were used to indicate measures of grain (after Schmandt-Besserat):

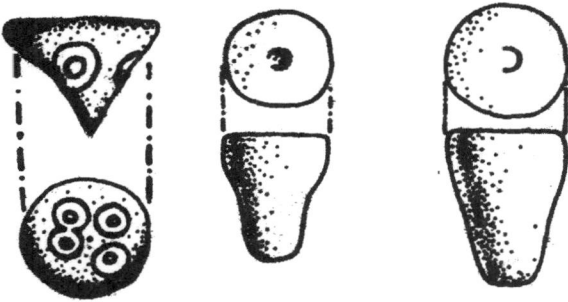

These are ovoid symbols, which were used to indicate measures of oil (after Schmandt-Besserat):

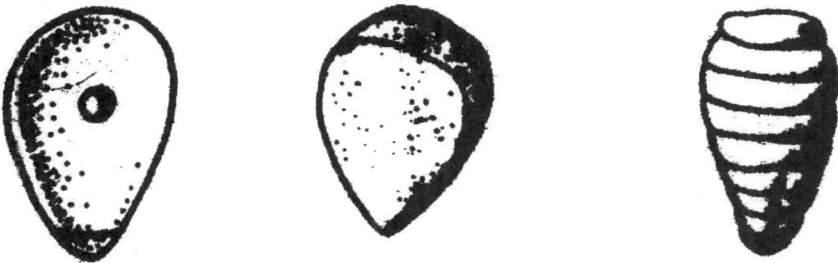

Here are some animal head symbols. They were used to indicate how many of each animal was owned (after Schmandt-Besserat):

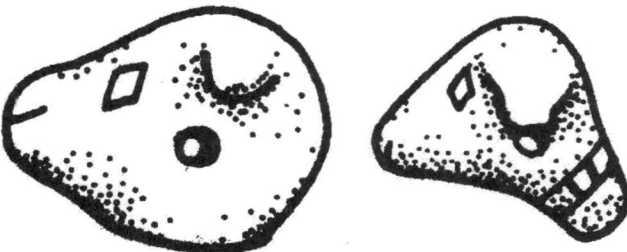

Finally, here are some animal skin symbols (after Schmandt-Besserat):

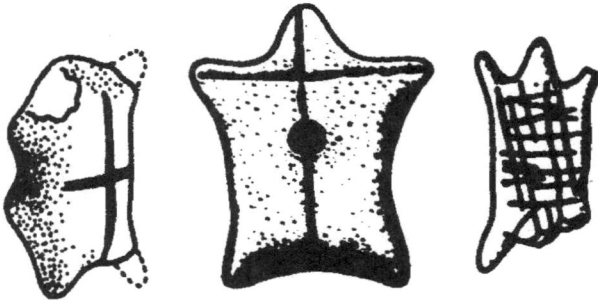

Some of the tokens had holes in them to allow them to be strung on a cord and kept together. Symbols without thread holes were sealed inside clay containers, which served as envelopes when people needed to carry about their symbols.

The hunter-gatherers had not needed long-range communication. They lived in small self-contained bands, and their main concern was successful hunting. They followed the herds and harvested wild food. They traded for tools, such as stone axes and obsidian knives, by swapping food or live captured animals with communities such as Çatalhöyük.[3]

The farmers, however, were different. They also needed stone tools, unless they lived by an outcrop of obsidian or flint, in which case they made implements, like the people of Çatalhöyük. Successful farms could exist only on fertile land, so farmers stayed in one place. They traded tools from passing bands of hunters but had to keep track of what they owned and had available to trade. The farmers needed symbols of counting.

THE FIRST SYMBOLS

Ancient symbolic tokens have been found throughout Israel, Iran, Iraq, Turkey, and Syria. They were fired to harden them and make them last. Schmandt-Besserat realized that they were part of a larger symbolic system when she found small and large cones, thin and thick discs, small and large spheres, and even fractions of spheres, such as half and three-quarter spheres.

The purpose of these symbols became clear when Leo Oppenheim, an archaeologist from the University of Chicago, found a container in Nuzi, northern Iraq, dating from about 2000 BCE. It was sealed and intact. On the outside was writing, and inside was a selection of the symbolic tokens that Schmandt-Besserat had seen proliferating across the farmers' lands. The discovery was the key to decoding the symbols' purpose. The inscription on the container was a list of the forty-nine different animals owned by a shepherd named Ziqarru. Inside the container were groups of seven different symbolic tokens. By linking the twenty-one "ewes-that-lamb," described on the outside, with the twenty-one identical symbol tokens inside, the first steps were taken to link symbols' shapes with objects.[4]

The farmers became wealthy and measured their wealth by assigning a symbol to each object. Then they began to produce more food than they could eat. A hierarchy quickly emerged, which demonstrated that it was possible to live off a food surplus without working to produce it. The new potential overlords joined forces and used sacred emotional symbols to impress on the farmers the need to placate their gods.

Soon, one of the most powerful symbol groups would come into being, and these would be the precursors to writing. Schmandt-Besserat sums it up:

> The consequences of this discovery are significant. Writing resulted not only from new bureaucratic demands but from the invention of abstract counting. ... Counting was not subservient to writing; on the contrary, writing emerged from counting.[5]

The token-symbols established a mode of concrete counting, an idea that appeared long before the discovery of the abstract numbers of mathematics.

These symbols enabled humanity to think and plan for the future, instead of just reacting to everyday needs. As the realistic tokens of the clay ovoids of oil jars became geometric symbols of a measure of oil, so humanity came to rely on them to help it organize itself.

The token-symbols were first used as mundane counters or realistic images and helped humanity keep track of its foodstuffs and other basics of daily life. Symbol users could manage goods and build an economy because they had access to instruments of power. They had emotive—geometric or realistic—symbols that they used to manipulate people's feelings, and they had counting token-symbols that enabled them to manage food production. These two types of symbols created new social patterns and enabled data to be manipulated for the first time.

THE SYMBOL OF NEWGRANGE

Around 3500 BCE, a preliterate elite on Orkney—a group of islands off the north coast of Scotland—was able to persuade, or force, the local population to build three massive stone ring structures, a village with a large meeting hall, and an enormous tunnel mound: the Ring of Brodgar, the Stones of Stenness, the Ring of Bookan, the neolithic village of Barnhouse, and the mound of Maes Howe, respectively. The Ring of Brodgar took over thirty years to complete, at a time when the average lifespan was about twenty-four years. The Barnhouse great hall and village took at least another ten years to build, and the massive mound of Maes Howe took a further fifty years. The reason for building these sites was religious, as the sacred symbol of the double lozenge and interlaced spirals was used at the sites. Here is the symbol as displayed by the Orkney farmers/builders (right).

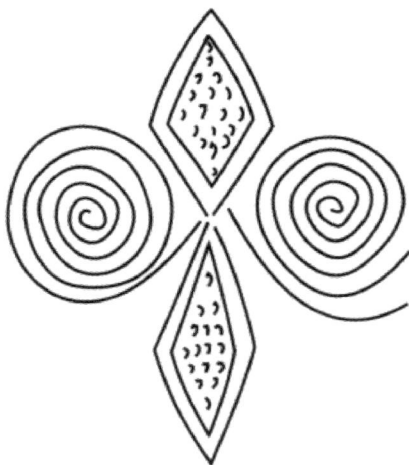

Three even more spectacular temples to preliterate geometric emotive symbols were built in the Boyne Valley of Ireland around 3200 BCE. Three massive tunnel mounds were built and their interiors covered in geometric emotive symbols. The most striking is a large engraving of the sacred farming symbol on the rear footstone of the mound of Newgrange.

The symbols of counting and recordkeeping would soon evolve and change humanity fundamentally. And a new group of alphabetic symbols was about to join forces with the basic sounds of speech and greatly extend the range of language.

THE IMPORTANCE OF WRITING SYMBOLS

Writing is a special form of symbolic magic. It enables me to converse with a friend in a distant country and understand her reply, instantly. It lets my dead mother tell me about the trauma of her childhood, which she would never talk about when she was alive. And it lets the ancient inhabitants of the first cities of Sumer, in Mesopotamia, recite to me the stories of their first king, Gilgamesh.

The symbols of writing do much more than encode the spoken word. They also make it permanent and so give it greater authority. And they allow it to be carried to distant regions without corruption.

It is no coincidence that the symbols of writing appeared at the time of the rapid growth of the cities of Sumer. Dense populations of city dwellers needed more complex social organizations than did isolated farm families or hunting groups. City people had more wealth to steal, so they built defensive walls to increase security. They lived together for social reasons and built meeting places, monumental temples, and palaces. They protected their wealth from roving thieves by using counting symbols to provide effective economic records.

Archaeologist W. John Hackwell studied the emergence of alphabetic symbols of writing and drew attention to the role of the custodians of religious symbols, the priests:

> Since life in Mesopotamia centered around the temples, such economic record keeping was probably the function of the priests. Indeed, some archaeologists have suggested that the invention of writing was the result of a demand for more efficient recording than the clay tokens offered. Perhaps it was the priests who invented the idea.[6]

But priests did not simply decide to invent writing in order to make the Sumarian city-state work more efficiently. Interpreters of sacred geometric symbols had 5,000 years of opportunity to extend their influence by inventing writing, but they never accomplished this. All that happened was that people in small, isolated communities (such as Malta, Orkney, and Ireland, for example) were persuaded to work long, hard hours to build structures to display the sacred symbols—presumably with the payoff of feeling good inside. The overlords realized that they could hold ceremonies and rituals to exploit this human response. They lived in luxury but did not feel the need to take part in the daily toil of farming that fed their community.

The symbols of writing did not come about because of social change. They caused that social change. They were an untapped source of influence on humanity, and their emergence made the growth of city-states and empires inevitable. The cities of Sumer and the later empires of Assyria, Egypt, and Babylon all grew out of the mystic power of writing symbols.

At first, every item to be recorded had to have a special realistic token-symbol made to represent it. Different tokens-symbols were needed to count quantities of grain (cones) and quantities of oil (ovoids). But having concrete symbols for counting particular things was a turning point in information processing. They inherited from their Paleolithic ancestors a way of abstracting data from reality and preserving it in symbols. The new symbols of writing made long-distance communication possible.

The symbols also brought about a higher-order consciousness, as Schmandt-Besserat explains:

> Corresponding to the increase in bureaucracy, methods of stor-
> ing tokens in archives were devised. One of these storage methods
> employed clay envelopes, simple hollow clay balls in which the tokens
> were placed and sealed. A drawback of the envelopes was that they
> hid the enclosed tokens. Accountants eventually resolved the problem
> by imprinting the shapes of the tokens on the surface of the enve-
> lopes prior to enclosing them. The number of units of goods was
> still expressed by a corresponding number of markings. An enve-
> lope containing seven ovoids, for example, bore seven oval markings.
> The substitution of signs for tokens was a first step toward writing.
> Fourth-millennium accountants soon realized that the tokens within
> the envelopes were made unnecessary by the presence of markings
> on the outer surface. As a result, tablets—solid clay balls bearing
> markings—replaced the hollow envelopes filled with tokens. These
> markings became a system of their own which developed to include
> not only impressed markings but more legible signs traced with a
> pointed stylus. Both of these types of symbols, which derived from
> tokens, were picture signs or "pictographs." They were not, however,
> ... pictures of the items they represented but, rather, pictures of the
> tokens used as counters in the previous accounting system.[7]

An example of this can be seen in the shape of one of the first symbols used by the Sumarians in a type of writing called *cuneiform*. It is the symbol for barley, which is simply a drawing of a plant stem with symbolic seed heads branching off it. The seed heads are shown using the traditional downward-pointing V, or chevron, which

Gimbutas explains was a long-established symbol of the mother goddess of farming.

Here is the cuneiform symbol for barley (right). Notice the series of Vs, or chevron symbols, placed on the stem:

The chevron symbols have a separate religious significance. As Gimbutas explains:

> Chevrons, V's, zig-zags, M's, meanders, streams, nets, and tri-lines are frequent and repetitious in Old European symbols. ... We shall begin our journey with the Goddess's hieroglyphs, the V and chevron. ... Graphically, a pubic triangle is most directly rendered as a V. This expression and its recognition are universal and immediate. It is, nevertheless, amazing how early this bit of "shorthand" crystallized to become for countless ages the designating mark of the Goddess.[8]

The use of a series of downward-pointing Vs in the first writing symbol for barley symbolizes the divine origin of farming. As explained earlier, farming started as a series of irrational symbolic religious acts of spring planting by women devotees of a farming goddess. This apparently irrational religious symbolism rapidly conferred evolutionary advantage on its followers and contributed to the success of farming.[9]

The chevron symbol made the leap from inscriptions on realistic figurines of the goddess to freestanding religious symbol around 18,000 BCE. Gimbutas explains:

> [We see] little figurines [of the Goddess,] ... their divine generative function emphasized by a large pubic triangle. Some of them are decorated by a series of panels, each with a somewhat different chevron design—chevrons in columns, opposed, or inverted. These figurines, tentatively dated to circa 18,000–15,000 BC, are of inestimable value for the insight they afford into the antiquity of the V in connection with an anthropomorphic goddess.[10]

As I show in a later chapter, Freemasonry preserves the symbol of the chevron in the shape of the Master's square.

The first writing symbols of cuneiform were more closely linked to their counting-token ancestors than to the sounds of spoken language. They were representations of words for objects, so each word had to have its own symbol. Such a symbol is called a *logogram*, and every word needs to have a distinct symbol. Everyone must learn all of these logograms if he or she is to read and write. Learning the symbols required tremendous effort, and so their use was restricted to a limited number of skilled people.

The system of privilege that drove the expansion of Sumer was linked to the power of the newly discovered writing symbols. According to Schmandt-Besserat:

> During the period from 3500 to 2500 BC, Sumer had a redistribution economy involving three main components: (1) a temple which conferred meaning and pomp on the act of giving; (2) an elite who administered the communal property; and (3) commoners who produced surplus goods and surrendered them to the temple. This redistributive economy relied upon a system of record keeping and, indeed, could not have succeeded without it. This function was fulfilled in the third millennium BC by cuneiform writing and, going further back in time, by tokens.[11]

As cuneiform exploited the writing symbols, they evolved to represent the sounds of syllables of speech instead of words. This meant a smaller set of standardized symbols could be memorized, which simplified the tasks of writing and reading. Here is a later cuneiform symbol for the word *barley* from around 600 BCE (right).

The small triangular shapes were made by pressing a stylus into soft clay.

However, for the purpose of encoding speech, this system was still complex and used over 2,000 symbols, each of which had to be memorized.

Writing symbols mutated into a different set of logograms in Egypt, where they were called *hieroglyphs*. Each hieroglyph is one of four types. It can be an alphabetic sign, which represents a single sound (although the Egyptians took most vowels for granted and did not write them down). It can be a syllabic sign, which represents a combination of consonants. It can be a stylized picture of the object it describes (rather like the barley symbol shown earlier), in which case, it is followed by an upright stroke to indicate that the word is complete with the one sign. Or it can be a determinative, which is a picture of an object to help the reader understand an abstract idea. The Egyptians used only alphabetic hieroglyphs to sound out imported words and so failed to discover the real power inherent in the alphabetic symbols of writing.

I have provided below my first name, Robert, written in alphabetic hieroglyphs.

As you can see, it is not an easy script to write. To become a good writer would require a good deal of practice. Nevertheless, this group of writing symbols helped the ancient Egyptians become wealthy and successful. But the symbols of writing had another trick to play on humanity.

FORTUNE FAVORS THE SYMBOL WRITER

The Canaanites, or Phoenicians, were a mixture of desert dwellers and sea traders. They lived in a series of small city-states along the western seaboard of the land of Canaan. The alphabet they adopted later spread to the struggling kingdom of Israel, and the Jews used its symbols to record the stories of the Bible. The Phoenicians manufactured and traded glass and high-quality purple dye. But most important of all, they were skilled seamen who ranged far and wide to trade. They had little time for the complex and clumsy symbols of cuneiform or hieroglyphics, but they discovered that a small set of symbols could stand for all the possible sounds of a complete spoken language.

Alphabetic symbols empower a small group of geometric images (usually thirty or fewer) to represent every sound that a speaker can utter. These symbols quickly became the dominant type of writing symbol among the Phoenician traders. As Hackwell points out:

> The Sumerian writing system became abstract and linear. Archaeologists and experts in ancient Semitic languages expected to find evidence that the users of cuneiform took the next logical step— that of using signs to represent clusters of sounds, called syllables. But such is not the case. The Canaanites appear to have bypassed that concept when they discovered the alphabet, for they recognized that speech consisted of basic sounds that could be represented with a very few signs.[12]

Between 1200 and 900 BCE, a Canaanite symbolic alphabet appeared that could preserve and transmit any thought that could be put into words in Hebrew, Phoenician, or Aramaic. The symbols of that alphabet appear below.

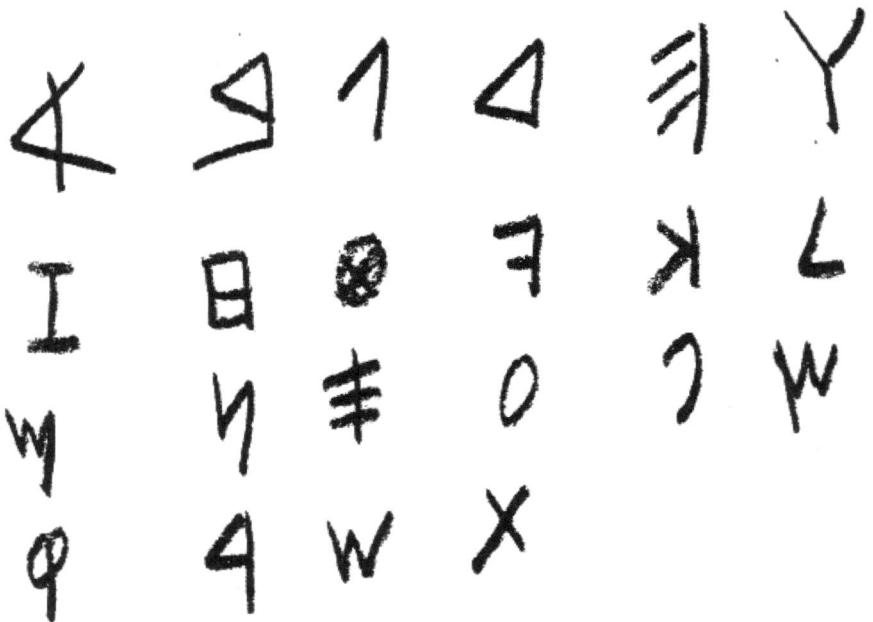

And here is my name written in Phoenician symbols. (Note that I have written it from left to right, not right to left, as the Phoenicians would have.)

At the time David became king of the Jews, the Phoenicians were using an alphabet of just twenty-two geometric symbols, which could store and transmit any word that a Phoenician could say. These were the writing symbols that carried a message from King Solomon to King Hiram of Tyre, seeking help to build the iconic Temple of Jerusalem. The symbol of that famous temple and the role it played in creating a system to understand Masonic symbology will be discussed later in this book.

The symbols of writing quickly spread to Greece. There, they powered the explosion of classical knowledge and preserved the words of Socrates and Plato and the works of Euclid for us to read today. The Greek alphabetic symbols spread to Rome and gave birth to the Latin alphabet.

A NEW ALPHABET APPEARS

So far, we have seen four waves of symbols that have driven the progress of humanity. The first symbols were geometric emotive symbols. As farming became established, the geometric emotive symbols reappeared and became more powerful. At first, they were drawn on top of the realistic images, such as loaves of bread and images of fertile women, but eventually, they became separate, purely geometric images. At first, they were engraved onto portable objects, such as figurines and tokens of sacred bread, but as the cult of farming became more successful, they were used to adorn permanent buildings (such as the Newgrange complex).

As settled communities grew and become more prosperous, humans started to own more objects. And so, a set of symbols emerged to help them count things. The cumbersome way of counting with a token for each animal or jar of oil gave way to a new set of abstract number symbols that could count anything, real or imaginary. These new symbols had no limits. They could count anything, no matter how large.

They could count the stars in the universe or the grains of sand on a beach. This concept was new and far beyond the capability of concrete symbol counting.

Used initially as a means of administering and controlling the actions of people, this new class of symbols proved to have the power of storing and increasing knowledge. (And notably, the Freemasons came to distrust written language, as it can easily become a tool of repression. Freemasons insisted on teaching using emotive symbols and poetic verbal metaphors.)

The power of symbols within writing is limited by their failure to be unambiguous. This was not a problem for emotive symbols, as they create unambiguous empathic feelings. The power of symbols has created a complex society that is very different from the groups of hunter-gatherers who first scratched the simple lozenge symbol on scraps of red ochre. In fact, the early symbols have never gone away, but today, we humans pay more attention to the newer language symbols, because they speak to our minds in words. The older symbols work in different, more subtle, less obvious ways, so we feel them in our hearts but cannot explain why they make us feel as we do.

Over 500 years ago, Freemasonry recognized that some parts of our brains have a strange yet powerful relationship with particular symbols. As a Freemason, I am aware of symbols and their importance.

To understand how and what symbols do to our minds, we need to look inside our heads. There is something in the human brain that gives symbols their sacred power.

CHAPTER 4

THE POWER OF SYMBOLS
ON THE HUMAN BRAIN

HUMANS HAVE TWO MINDS

The human brain has evolved to recognize and respond to symbols, but this is the part of the brain that feels rather than speaks. This evolution makes it almost impossible for us to put into words the effect symbols have on us. Yet the emotions symbols can trigger between humans have changed the way society has developed. To understand why humans are the only species who have this ongoing relationship with symbols, we need to look inside our heads.

In your brain, there are two complete working halves. The left and right hemispheres of the human brain are both individually capable of keeping you alive and functioning even if one side of your head were destroyed. There is a more subtle purpose for this hemispheric independence, however. You have an evolutionary advantage in having two cerebral hemispheres. If this were not so, then humans would have evolved a less complex and a less biologically demanding, more unified brain. Current brain research shows that it is this twin-brained evolutionary development that has facilitated how we interact with symbols.[1]

Your two hemispheres communicate via a structure called the *corpus callosum*, which is a massive connecting cable made up of about 800 million neurons that link the hemispheres. During the latter half of the twentieth century, a radical treatment for epilepsy involved cutting this link, leaving the individual with two disconnected brains. Roger Sperry studied these patients and discovered that the two hemispheres are different and have evolved for different purposes.[2] He found that the right hemisphere loves symbols and metaphors, whereas the left hemisphere likes words. Many vertebrates and all birds have also evolved split brains.

Consciousness fulfills two conflicting functions, best understood in terms of how our attention works. To carry out delicate tasks, your brain needs to focus attention narrowly—say, to pick up a grain of corn instead of the piece of stone that lies next to it. But at the same time, your brain has to maintain a wide-open field of attention so it remains aware of predators. If you cannot concentrate, you will starve, and if you do not remain alert, you may get killed and eaten.

The evolutionary answer was to evolve two brains: a right brain that takes a wide overview, using symbols to compress information about the nature of surrounding reality, and a left brain that is able to concentrate on more detailed tasks. These two different ways of paying attention have made us amenable to the influence of symbols.

The result of this evolutionary survival quirk has given humans two systems of thinking: one that is articulate and one that responds to symbols. Your intellect analyzes, but your heart synthesizes. A symbol evokes understanding without needing to convey information.

The human left brain is unable to understand metaphor, narrative, or emotive symbols. We listen to stories, visualize symbols, and react emotionally to images with our inarticulate right hemisphere. Your left hemisphere concentrates its narrowly focused attention, while your right hemisphere stays alert to what is happening around you. Because of these differences, each hemisphere understands the world in a different way. The right hemisphere recognizes symbolic meaning and sees connections. The left hemisphere sees bits of the world that it often cannot link. The emotional response to ancient symbols happens in the right hemisphere. The way our brains work helps us to concentrate on a topic of interest and to ignore anything outside.[4] It gives us our hidden sense of the meanings of symbols, which we struggle to put into words.

Our right hemisphere has evolved to detect threats. It is good at spotting emotional changes and alerting us to potential problems. To some extent, we process language in both hemispheres, but each hemisphere interprets what it reads or hears in a different way. The left hemisphere is good with words, including syntax and grammar, but the right hemisphere understands context and metaphor. It is the right hemisphere that perceives visual symbols, although it is unable to explain them in words.

At this point, it is worth noting that the function of the corpus callosum—the wiring that connects the two hemispheres—is not to communicate information between the hemispheres but rather to inhibit one or other from acting. Our brain's evolutionary advantage stems from this fact: If the right hemisphere perceives a threat, it can turn off the focused attention of the left hemisphere and force you to become alert to your surroundings. Doing so is essential to avoid being eaten by predators. Likewise, the left hemisphere can stop the right hemisphere from prattling on and indulging its curiosity about everything around it, forcing you to focus on the tasks that are necessary to stay alive. But this means that when we try to use words to explain symbols, we encourage our left hemisphere to inhibit the right. This was why my students were not able to explain how the symbols affected them, although they were consistent in spotting the ones with powerful emotional messages.

SYMBOLS HAVE SEX APPEAL

A surprising side effect of the interaction between symbols and the right hemisphere of the human brain is that some symbols have an unexpected ability to stir sexual interest. The ancient symbols of farming were associated with sacred temples devoted to various goddess figures. The symbols of farming, as my survey showed, appeal to a basic instinct in both young men and young women.

Further tests showed that both men and women produced a strong galvanic skin response when they looked at these traditional shapes. In other words, the symbols made them sweat. When I followed up with additional tests, I found that their emotional response was one of attraction. I got a further clue when many students said that the ancient geometric symbols are sexy. They seem to tap into a deep emotional level of the human spirit.

Then I found something even more interesting: My daughter, who is a jeweler, turned some of these goddess images into pendants and bracelets. The feedback she got from the women who wore the pieces was that the symbols were extremely sexy.

Interestingly, ancient goddess symbols are sexy because they tap into the human sense of smell. Professor Martha McClintock, of the University of Chicago, published a groundbreaking study thirty years ago showing that the menstrual cycles of women living together tend to synchronize.

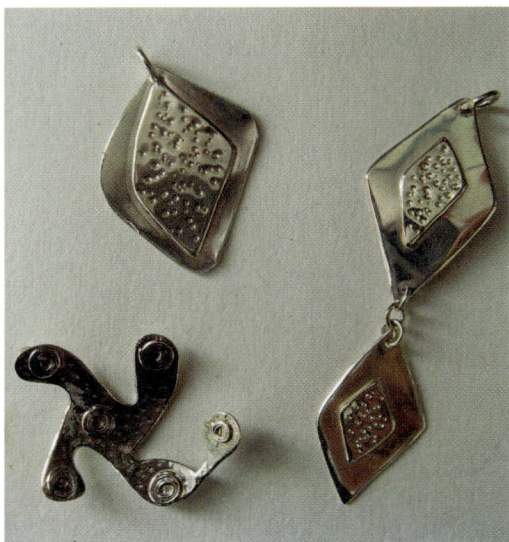

ANCIENT SYMBOLS TURNED INTO SEXY JEWELRY.
Courtesy of Delyth Lomas.

Subsequent brain scan research has shown that compounds known as *pheromones*, found in male and female sweat, trigger activity in the brains of people of the opposite sex. These subjectively odorless chemicals are sensed by two small pits—the vomeronasal organ (VNO)—high inside each nostril. Pheromones are known to trigger mating and other behavior in rodents. And they play a similar, if less frenetic, role in humans. Humans are sexually attracted to the scent of the fresh sweat of the opposite sex. And these ancient symbols trigger fresh sweat.

We have all seen the effect of pheromones on animals. A dog that urinates on a post is leaving behind pheromones to claim that territory. A female dog in heat releases pheromones that will attract male dogs from miles around. Ants leave behind pheromones to mark a fast trail to unsuspecting picnickers. Humans look at ancient symbols and sweat pheromones.

Pheromones are responsible for the physical chemistry that creates the "love at first sight" feeling humans sometimes experience. They deliver messages about a person's sexual state and play a role in helping us choose a mate whose genetic resistance to disease complements our own. This serves the evolutionary purpose of helping couples who will likely have healthy children recognize each other. This is why symbols that trigger the emission of human pheromones remain popular. They are inherently sexy.

I must issue a word of warning, however: You cannot simply rely on wearing the right symbols to make you sexy. Not all male pheromones are equally attractive. The male pheromone androstenone, for example, is not the same as androstenol. Androstenol is the scent produced by fresh male sweat and is attractive to females. Androstenone is produced by male sweat after exposure to oxygen (i.e., when less fresh) and is perceived as highly unpleasant by females. So men who believe that macho, sweaty body odor is attractive to women are deluding themselves. They need to constantly produce fresh sweat or change their clothes every twenty minutes to remove any trace of oxidized sweat. Generally, the female-repelling androstenone is the more prominent male body odor, as the fresh sweat odor of androstenol disappears quickly, unless constantly replenished. And that replenishment is something that sexy symbols can help with.

This is why my volunteers found these ancient symbols sexy. When a person sees one of these symbols, he or she exudes fresh sweat, which is sexually attractive to the right person. Claus Wedekind, a scientist at the University of Bern, did a series of tests to find out how humans use body odor to select mates. He asked a group of women to sniff T-shirts that had been worn by a group of unknown—and unwashed—men. All the women had to do was say which shirts smelled the best. The experiment was designed to find out if humans, like mice, use body odor to identify genetically appropriate mates. Female volunteers, like their rodent counterparts, were attracted to the genetically suitable men.

The ancient farming symbols that both males and females find attractive stimulate them to give off fresh, sexually attractive sweat. And so it is no wonder that these erotically charged symbols were venerated as sacred. The sexual attraction of these symbols has a firm biological basis both in the way our brains are wired and the way in which they stimulate us to emit sexual odorants.

THE INFLUENCE OF STONE SYMBOLS

The physiological sweat response to particular symbols is more than simple recognition. A shape can generate emotions to make us act quickly. Even simple organisms may identify a shape without needing to understand fully its true character. They just feel the fear. A good example of this can be seen in young birds, which, like humans, have split brains. A newly hatched chick can distinguish between the shape of hawk and the shape of goose by the shadows they cast on the ground beneath where they fly. The chick will try to hide from the silhouette of the hawk and ignore that of the goose (see right).

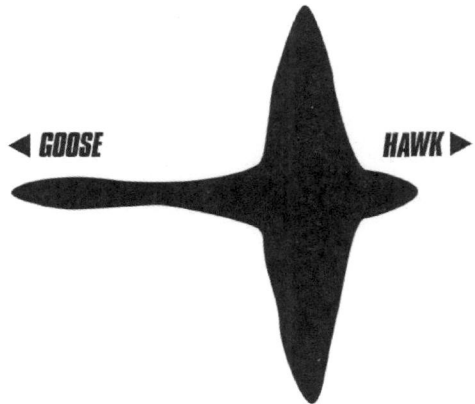

◀ *GOOSE*   *HAWK* ▶

Emotions are triggered without any thought on our part. Fear is triggered by seeing a snake long before the left hemisphere thinks the word *snake*. Symbolic shapes and smells trigger emotions without any need for judgment. Emotions are like smoke alarms. They go off because they detect particles in the air. So when we are in danger, we have a psychological mechanism in place that reacts to dangers and triggers bodily responses, just as there is a mechanism in a smoke alarm that sounds an alarm when it detect smoke particles. And that mechanism responds to symbols.

Freemasonry recognized this effect 500 years ago and set about sensitizing its members to the importance of certain symbols. It did this by distracting the verbal left hemisphere as it performed ritual actions, leaving the right hemisphere free to enjoy the emotional warmth of the symbol. It is no coincidence that the badge of Freemasonry echoes the oldest lozenge symbol ever drawn: the sexy chevron.

IT'S CERTAINLY NO COINCIDENCE THAT THE BADGE OF FREEMASONRY HARKENS BACK TO THE LOZENGE SYMBOL.

STONE SYMBOLS HAVE SACRED POWER

As humans settled down to farm and built towns and cities, symbols appeared on buildings. Stones were used for creating markers and for building large structures, and symbols were carved into them. During the late Neolithic period, before the symbols of writing appeared, the emotive symbols of farming could be found carved into the stone walls of chambers all over what is now Europe.

Perhaps some of the best examples of these stone-carved symbols can be seen in the Boyne Valley of Ireland at the three mounds of Newgrange, Knowth, and Dowth. These are massive human-made hills with rock-lined chambers constructed inside them. The rocks both inside the mounds and on the curbstones surrounding them are completely covered with examples of the sexy farming symbols that still excite modern men and women.

A traditional lozenge and spiral symbol of farming is carved on the curbstone at Newgrange. Archaeologist George Logan says:

> We do not know the nature of the ceremonies, but the various features, such as stone settings, must have served a related purpose. ... It may be assumed that part of the ritual involved exotic items, notable amongst which would have been the conical stone objects [counting tokens?] from Knowth and Newgrange. ... The rites could in part have concerned fertility, emphasizing the continuity of society.[5]

THIS CURBSTONE FROM THE NEWGRANGE COMPLEX SHOWS A NETWORK OF LOZENGE AND SPIRAL SYMBOLS USED BY EARLY FARMERS.

With the rise of cities, more and more symbols came to be carved into places of worship, and a particular class of stoneworkers—men known as *masons*—became skilled in shaping stones and carving these symbols. It is no coincidence that a group of medieval stonemasons realized that stone symbols could influence human minds. The stonemasons set out to study the symbols and the ways that people responded to them.

CHAPTER 5

HOW SYMBOLS CREATED FREEMASONRY

⟶ ◆ ⟵

SYMBOLS AND MYTHS WORK TOGETHER

During the mid-fifteenth century, in the land of Scotland, the aid of powerful emotive symbols was enlisted by an elite group of kings, priests, and would-be kings as tools to sustain political support. This means of manipulation had two important aspects: Emotive geometric symbols were carved into the stonework of prestigious buildings, where the people regularly assembled, and popular myths were recited about the significance of these symbols.

In the fifteenth century, Sir William Sinclair, a rich Scottish noble, accumulated more land than the king and wanted to seize the crown of Scotland. The Stuart kings had the Abbey of the Holy Rood, which housed the powerful symbol of the True Cross, but Sinclair had no symbolic building or venerated symbol to prove his right to rule. So Sinclair hired an architect, Sir Gilbert Haye, who was deeply versed in the power of myth and symbolism and commissioned him to build an ornate symbol-carved building to rival both the Holy Rood and the Abbey that housed it.

A group of stoneworkers became embroiled in this battle and saw firsthand the power that symbols had. When Sinclair's bid for power failed, these stoneworkers were put out of work, but a group of them came together in Aberdeen to study the power of symbols and to develop ways to sensitize individuals to their importance. This group of men—the first Freemasons—were deeply skilled in the ancient tradition of carving symbols into stone and creating places of public assembly. The symbols they studied created modern Freemasonry.

BUILDINGS ARE SYMBOLS

We saw in a previous chapter that around 5,000 or 6,000 years ago, before the arrival of the symbols of writing, humans built stone structures to hold religious assemblies. We can see from the ruins of those crude temples that their architects had discovered they could heighten their followers' sense of excitement if they carved emotive geometric symbols into the stone walls of the structures.

This newly discovered skill of shaping stones into emotive symbolic structures blossomed in ancient Egypt. There, the symbol of the triangle, which we saw so copiously carved into the walls of Newgrange, was written large and in the shape of the pyramid. Who could fail to be awestruck upon standing at the base of such a structure?

THE PYRAMID OF KHAFRE IN GIZA NEAR CAIRO, EGYPT, SHOWS HOW THE EGYPTIAN MASONS USED THE SYMBOL OF THE TRIANGLE IN THEIR PUBLIC STRUCTURES.

New skills in the working, moving, and shaping of stone were developed to create these massive chevron symbols. The Egyptians quarried stone, shaped it, lifted it into place, and bound it together. They invented the trade we now call *masonry*, but it was the Greeks who discovered a new group of symbols that would be used by future architects. For symbolic temples to stand firm, they had to be built according to certain rules of structure. These rules were revealed to humans by the symbols of geometry. Geometric symbols came into their own during the classical Greek period.

Every builder who worked with stone needed knowledge of the nature of the symbols of geometry, and over time, having this knowledge meant that bigger and more magnificent temples were built.

THE PARTHENON IN THE AKROPOLIS, ATHENS, BUILT BETWEEN 447 BCE AND 432 BCE, SHOWS HOW ANCIENT GREEK ARCHITECTURE USED THE SYMBOL OF THE PILLAR TO CREATE A POWERFUL PRESENCE FOR A BUILDING.

By the Middle Ages in Great Britain, this custom of constructing inspirational religious buildings had become the tradition of cathedral building. And at Canterbury, we can see the symbol of the triangle built into the facades.

The stonemasons who built these magnificent buildings were highly skilled craftsmen who used the symbols of geometry. The buildings that stonemasons spent their whole lives constructing were more than symbolic structures; emotive symbols were also incorporated into their facades. The Neolithic tradition of using emotive geometric symbols to inspire worshipers was manifest in the stonemasons' creations.

THIS AERIAL PHOTO OF CANTERBURY CATHEDRAL SHOWS HOW MASONS INCORPORATED THE SYMBOL OF THE TRIANGLE INTO THE FACADES.

In particular, the men who founded Freemasonry and established its study of symbology witnessed the power of one particular emotive geometric symbol: the cross. The evolution of this symbol had a great influence on the origins of Freemasonry.

HOW THE TRUE CROSS INSPIRED THE FIRST FREEMASONS

Without writing symbols, the Roman Empire could not have spread so far or lasted so long. Yet even after this great success, reading and writing were far from being universal. Only a few administrators, leaders, and priests within the Roman Empire were able to use these symbols.

The later Roman emperors, when they proclaimed themselves gods, created stone statues and busts to distribute throughout their lands. The realistic symbol of the god-emperor was intended to carry a religious idea and create an emotional state of mind in the vast number of illiterate individuals. This knowledge was not lost when Christianity became the official religion of the Roman Empire. The widespread recognition of the Latin cross provides a powerful example of how a symbol is capable of conveying an entire religious philosophy.

The cross of crucifixion, on which Jesus was put to death, was not an inspirational emotive symbol. It was a practical machine intended to cause pain. It did not have an upper section but rather a simple T-shape that was carefully crafted by the Romans to inflict tremendous pain with little effort. The individual to be punished had his arms either tied or nailed to the crosspiece (called the *patibulum*), and he was then forced to carry the crosspiece to a previously erected upright post. The crosspiece was lifted onto the upright (called the *stipe*), leaving him with his weight suspended by his arms. His heels were then nailed to the upright with his legs bent. His arms were fixed outward onto the crosspiece but left slightly bent. The victim's body was suspended from just three points, causing searing pain. Blood loss was minimal, and the victim remained fully conscious.

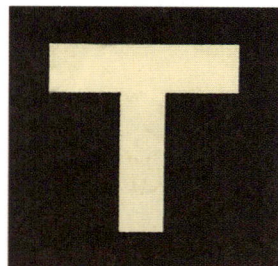

THE TAU CROSS

The victim's body weight worked against him, causing him to sag down and producing traumatic tension in the muscles of his arms, shoulders, and chest wall. The pain was indescribable, as the ribcage was drawn up and the chest was held in a position preventing exhalation. To avoid asphyxiation, the victim had no alternative but to push down on the wounds of his nailed feet to raise his body, so that his lungs could blow out and gasp in another chestful of air. The panic of not breathing was exchanged momentarily for the massive pain of standing on impaled flesh. The overall effect of repeating this vile dilemma was increased anoxia (shortage of oxygen), leading to agonizing cramps and a dramatically raised metabolic rate. Eventually, the legs cramped and failed, and the victim was no longer able to breathe. This could take days, which meant tremendous trauma for the victim—as was intended.

The cross of crucifixion was a Roman tool of torture and thus had no symbolic dimension. Its shape was never inspirational, unlike the powerful symbol of the True Cross. The symbol of the Latin cross is clearly different. It echoes a man with his arms outstretched to God and his head held high.

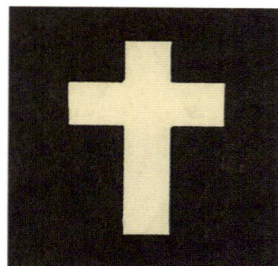

This powerful symbol of the Latin cross evolved into a badge of kingly power in the Middle Ages. It

THE LATIN CROSS

was exposure to this potent symbol and its accompanying myth that inspired the first Freemasons to begin a systematic study of the power of symbols.

An early queen of Scotland, St. Margaret, who married King Malcolm in 1069, had brought a piece of the True Cross with her as her dowry. Malcolm's descendants built a magnificent symbolic building, the Abbey of the Holy Rood, to house the True Cross. Today, the abbey stands behind Holyrood Palace and is a ruin.

A myth became attached to the symbol of the Holy Rood, as the fragment was known. As the story was told, King David was attacked by a stag while out hunting, and the Holy Rood materialized between him and the raging animal and saved his life. A symbol of a stag with a Latin cross was carved in stone at the entrance to the abbey. The same symbol now forms part of the entrance to Holyrood Palace, home of the kings of the Scots, which was built beside the ruins of the abbey. In the abbey's prime, pilgrims went there to venerate the fragment, listen to the recital of the myth, and give thanks to God for saving their king's life.

For the many generations of Scottish kings through James II, the symbol of the Holy Rood supported their god-given right to rule. However, as noted earlier, in the middle of the fifteenth century, Sir William Sinclair hired architect Sir Gilbert Haye to construct a building to rival the Abbey of the Holy Rood. The result was an ornate building called Rosslyn Chapel, which is steeped with symbolism and

THE FIRST FREEMASONS WORKED ON THE ORNATE ROSSYLN CHAPEL, IN SCOTLAND, WHICH IS COVERED IN CARVINGS RICH WITH SYMBOLISM. Engraved by J. Roffe, 1811, Elmes, James (1782–1862) (after) / Private Collection/The Bridgeman Art Library International

marinated in myth.[1] And the men who were to become the first Freemasons worked
on its construction.

After Sinclair's bid for the crown of Scotland failed, his estates were broken up,
his inspirational chapel fell into disrepair, and the stonemasons who had carved the
symbol-packed building were put out of work. A sizable group of them moved to
Aberdeen to work together on a large church dedicated to St. Nickolas.[2] These men
realized that they had stumbled on a great truth and set about trying to understand
what they had learned about symbols and myths. They had been shown symbols,
which they then carved. They had also been told poetic myths, which made sense of
the emotions the symbols evoked in their hearts. The stonemasons developed ways
of passing on this knowledge to their apprentice masons. They created the "peculiar
system of morality, veiled in allegory and illustrated by symbols" that has become
Freemasonry. The evidence for this can be seen in a piece of symbolic representation that they created: the first Masonic tracing board.

HOW SYMBOLS TAUGHT THE FIRST FREEMASONS

The activity of the first members of the Lodge of Aberdeen came to light only
when an early artifact of Masonic symbolism, known as the Kirkwall scroll, was carbon dated on July 21, 2000. The Kirkwall scroll is a hanging cloth made up of three
pieces of sailcloth sewn together and handpainted.

The carbon dating was reported in an article by Orkney journalist Kath
Gourlay that appeared in the London *Times* and the *Daily Telegraph*. The article said:

> The results of radiocarbon dating carried out on a rare wall hanging
> have shocked members of a Masonic lodge in the Orkney Islands,
> who have been told that their document is a medieval treasure worth
> several million pounds. ... Radio-carbon dating of the scroll points to
> the huge 18-ft sailcloth hanging as being fifteenth-century.[3]

But the issue of the age of the symbol-covered cloth was not straightforward.
There were two radiocarbon dates for the scroll: an older date for the center section
and a much more recent date for both outer sections.

The cloth was thought to be an early Masonic floorcloth from an eighteenth-
century London Masonic lodge. (A floorcloth is something like a carpet that has

been painted with symbols and is laid on the floor for a Masonic ritual to take place on it.) The floorcloth had been given to the lodge by a Mason named William Graham. He joined Lodge Kirkwall Kilwinning on December 27, 1785, and presented the scroll to the lodge a month later on January 27, 1786. For many years, it was generally believed that Graham had painted the floorcloth himself as a gift to the lodge he was joining. But the carbon dating ruled out this possibility for the center section.

Carbon dating revealed a 280-year difference between the age of the central strip and the two side strips. The outer strips had been cut from a single strip of material before being sewn to the outer edges of the central strip. If Graham had created the floorcloth, he would have had to obtain two strips of cloth—one new and the other 280 years old—and then cut the new cloth in two and sewn the two half-strips to the outside of the older cloth before starting to paint. Why bother? If he wanted a wider strip of canvas, he could have sewn the new strip to the old one. The radiocarbon evidence indicates that he added the outer strips to preserve the inner cloth. In a previous book, I showed that Graham disguised the older central section because it contained symbols that the Kirk of Scotland considered pagan. Many of them are ancient emotive symbols of farming.[4]

All the Masonic symbols that form the subject matter of the modern degrees of Freemasonry can be found on the Kirkwall scroll. Before the scroll was carbon dated, the accepted view was that the Freemasons developed rituals based on old craft guild mystery plays and then later added symbols to illustrate their rituals. The discovery of a complete set of ancient emotive symbols on a floorcloth dating to the earliest known Masonic lodge reveals a different explanation.

The poetic rituals and myths were attached to the symbols to help the Freemasons understand the symbols' meanings and to help them become sensitive to the emotive power the symbols project. Early on, Masons became aware of the importance and power of these symbols.

THE EMOTIONAL POWER OF SYMBOLS

As stated earlier, when the estates of William Sinclair were broken up in 1480, Gilbert Haye's workforce disbanded, and some of them went work in Aberdeen. The Burgh Council Minutes of 1483 contain the earliest written reference to a Masonic lodge anywhere in the world. The Lodge of Aberdeen was attached to the burgh church of St. Nicholas, which was being rebuilt at the time. In that lodge were a number of Masons who had worked on the powerful symbolism of Rosslyn Chapel. They took with them to Aberdeen a partial understanding of the innate power of symbols and set up a system of lodge governance to help teach this.[5]

It was the practice of all early Masonic lodges to draw symbols on the floor of the lodgeroom, and the Kirkwall scroll shows that this concept went back to the birth of Freemasonry. Bro. W. L. Wilmshurst, a Founder Master of my own lodge, wrote about the use of floorcloths. The symbols of the degree to be conferred were drawn on the floor of the lodge and later erased by the candidate. According to Wilmshurst:

> In earlier days, when the Craft was not a popular social institution but a serious discipline in a philosophic and sacred science, instruction was not treated casually. The Tracing Board was not, as now, a product of the Masonic furnisher's factory; it was the most revered symbol in the Lodge; it was a diagram which every Brother was taught to draw for himself, so that both his hand and his understanding might be trained in Masonic work. The literary records show that at each Lodge meeting the Tracing Board of the Degree about to be worked was actually drawn from memory with chalk and charcoal on the floor of the Lodge by the Master, who from previous practice was able to do this quickly and accurately. In advancing from West to East during the Ceremony, the Candidate took the steps of the Degree over the diagram. The diagram was explained to him as an integral part of the Ceremony, and, before being restored to his personal comforts, he was required to expunge it with a mop and pail of water, so that uninitiated eyes might not see it and that he might learn a first lesson in humility and secrecy.

The central strip of the Kirkwall scroll shows seven panels, each describing a step leading from the west to the east of the lodge, as it was unrolled from bottom to top. The lessons begin with the basic symbols of the Craft. The central, pivotal step shows a tomb, symbolizing the death of the ego, and the sequence progresses to an idyllic vision of the ecstatic bliss of the center, which is displayed using realistic hunting-type symbols. A continuity of vision is maintained—from the sun, the moon, and the stars and the vision of the rising of a lozenge-shaped all-seeing eye in the first step, to an ordered arrangement of the heavens, with the repeated symbols showing the stars rearranged as pillars around the moon as the center. This well-structured sky stands above a final scene of oneness with nature. Each scene in this floorcloth fits one of the seven spiritual steps to awareness that are still taught in esoteric Freemasonry.

The early Scottish Freemasons used just two simple ceremonies: a ritual of initiation and a procedure for becoming a Fellow of the Craft, which entitled one to become a Master of the Lodge. The Freemasons' records talk of them "having the Mason Word." They looked at symbols and tried to understand them, and they recited ritual poetry while they walked along the floorcloth, looking at the symbols.

The Kirkwall scroll, with its symbols, would have been unrolled during these ceremonies. In addition, the newly made Masons were exposed to the symbols' wordless, emotive messages as the members of the lodge recited their mythical stories.

Over time, many additional rituals have been added to the canon of Freemasonry, and each one helps Masonic candidates to learn more about particular symbols and their power. The first Masons chose well, as the panels they created show the main symbols that have since had enormous impact on the development of many societies.

THE CENTRAL STRIP OF THE KIRKWALL SCROLL.
Courtesy of www.tracingboards.com

The only group to have studied those symbols over many generations is the Freemasons. Over the last 500 years, the Masons have developed ways of sensitizing individuals to the significance of these symbols. Their way of teaching is odd. It involves reciting ritual. It involves "the art of memorie," because the rituals must be completely committed to memory—not read from books. (As noted earlier, Freemasons distrust the written word, viewing it as a potential tool of tyranny.) The teaching involves acting out myths, as well as telling and listening to heroic tales. And all of these actions take place in full view of the symbols that are being studied and talked about.

Yet the symbols are never explained in a straightforward manner. Because capturing their full import in words is impossible, the Craft has learned not to try. Instead, it uses metaphor and poetry to quiet the left hemisphere so that the right hemisphere can impart its understanding of the symbols.

The first Masons must have realized that certain groups of symbols work well together, and as Wilmshurst says, "Symbols always comprise so much more than can be verbally explained." With the first Freemasons came the first attempts to understand the power of symbols, to sensitize individuals to their messages, and to try to harness their power for the good of society.

HOW SYMBOLIC TEACHING SPREAD

The first Aberdeen Lodge of Freemasons were given a practical demonstration of the enhanced force created by combining myth and symbol by Sir Gilbert Haye, the architect of Rosslyn Chapel.[6] He took the story of the building of Solomon's temple as a way of harnessing the power of ancient symbols, such as St. Matthew's staff. The first Freemasons created a system of teaching that has continued to expand to the present day. When a candidate stands before the first-degree tracing board and listens to the rolling poetry of the traditional explanation of its landmarks, which is delivered from memory by a past master, he is immersed in the significance of the symbol and feels its meaning in a way no rational explanation can hope to emulate. During the ritual, the Freemason lives the symbol. The radiocarbon of the symbols is one of the secrets of Masonry that cannot be stolen or given away.

The continuity of teaching was apparent as Freemasonry spread south from Scotland—first to York and much later to London. The oldest tracing boards in Yorkshire date back to the early eighteenth century and are painted on wooden panels. They have not been carbon dated, so their exact age is unknown. But from their documented history, they are at least 300 hundred years old. Their images are similar to those of the Kirkwall scroll and were used for the same purposes.

CHAPTER 6

SYMBOLS CAN PENETRATE THE MIND OF GOD

---·•·---

A SYMBOL THAT ANALYZES EQUALITY

Immediately after the Restoration in 1660, in which the English monarchy returned to the throne, a group of Freemasons who had been sensitized to the significance of symbols by their ritual training tapped into a completely new set of symbols. These symbols unleashed a power that has completely changed the world. They made it possible to predict exactly the times and effects of many natural events. They made it possible to destroy the world. These symbols are nothing less than the words of a great cosmic language that lays bare the secrets the universe.

England suffered a devastating civil war in the seventeenth century. It began as an argument about the importance of the Stuart kings compared to their parliaments and ended with King Charles I being beheaded in public. During this turbulent period, symbolic science began. Somehow, in the middle of the bitter battle between king and parliament, the symbols of modern mathematical science appeared among humanity. England—a superstitious country that burned alive at least one hundred elderly women a year on the suspicion that they were causing disease by casting the "evil eye"—suddenly developed a critical mass of discerning mathematical scientists, who quickly became adept in the application of the symbols of science. This did not happen by chance. A symbol that was used by Masons to stand for equality and balance was rotated through "an angle of ninety degrees or the fourth part of circle" to reveal a whole new meaning. Today, it can be found on every computer keyboard: the equals sign (=).

The chain of events that led to recognition of this new symbol and exploration of its power began on November 28, 1660, at Gresham College, London. This was the first meeting of the Royal Society, whch was held after a public lecture by Christopher Wren. At this meeting, Freemason Sir Robert Moray brought together a group of men who were already trained to be alert to the import of symbols and who were inspired by the philosophical teaching of Freemasonry to study "the hidden mysteries of nature and science."[1]

The survivors of a civil war were not the most likely people to found modern science. After the death of Oliver Cromwell, England tottered on the brink of fresh conflict, until the controversial decision was made to invite the king to return. Meanwhile, Sir Robert Moray brought together the founding members of the new Royal Society, who had recently fought on opposite sides of the brutal civil war. His aims were to get them to solve the problems of geometry and military building and to strengthen King Charles II's weak navy. Moray offered his Brother Masons a chance to study interesting problems and an opportunity to earn the favor of the newly restored king. But the symbols of mathematics opened up a much wider prospect.

Inspired by Masonic discussion about how the "hidden mysteries of nature and science" could help you "better know your Maker," the founders of the Royal Society did more than simply solve a few military problems. They questioned the basic premises of religion and theology. Then they made contact with a group of symbols that enabled them to read and understand the plans of the Great Architect of the Universe.

John Wallis, who became the prophet of this new family of symbols, wrote about his links to the Craft and its role in the early meeting of the Royal Society. This Masonic environment was open to all symbols and helped him recognize and understand the power that was latent in the symbols of mathematics.

MASONIC SLIDE RULES AND EARLY ARITHMETIC

John Wallis, who became Savilian Professor of Geometry at Oxford in 1649, recognized that certain symbols could be used to stand for real things and then be manipulated to explain (or as scientists, say "to model") what was happening in the real world. When Wallis passed on this knowledge to his brethren in the Royal Society, he opened up a whole new range of possibilities.

In 1678, Wallis wrote a pamphlet about the meetings that led to formation of the Royal Society:[2]

> About the year 1645, while I lived in London (at a time when, by
> our civil wars, academic studies were much interrupted in both our
> Universities), beside the conversation of divers eminent divines as

to matters theological, I had the opportunity of being acquainted with divers worthy persons, inquisitive into natural philosophy, and other parts of human learning; particularly into what hath been called New Philosophy or Experimental Philosophy. We did by agreements, divers of us, meet weekly in London on a certain day and hour, under a certain penalty, and a weekly contribution for the charge of experiments, with certain rules agree amongst us to treat and discourse of such affairs. ... These meetings we held sometimes at Dr. Goddard's lodgings in Wood Street (or some other convenient place near), on occasion of his keeping an operator in his house for grinding glasses for telescopes and microscopes; sometimes at a convenient place (The Bulls Head) in Cheapside, and (in term time) at Gresham College at Mr. Foster's lectures (then the Astronomer Professor there) and, after the lecture ended repaired, sometimes to Mr. Fosters lodgings, sometimes to some other place not far distant.

Our business was (precluding matters of theology and state affairs) to discourse and consider of Philosophical Enquiries. ... About the year 1648/9 some of our company being removed to Oxford (first Dr. Wilkins on his appointment by the Protector as Warden of Wadham College, then I and soon after Dr. Goddard) our company divided. Those in London continued to meet there as before (and we with them, when we had occasion to be there) and those of us at Oxford, ... continued such meetings in Oxford and brought these studies into fashion there.[3]

The "Philosophical Enquiries" Wallis mentions are the formal Masonic interests in the secret science of symbols and how they give insight into the hidden mysteries of nature. Wallis was about to release what had formally been a totally hidden power. He had formed the habit of discussing his ideas at Masonic meetings in which the purpose was to sensitize the brethren to the import of symbols. There was no better venue or audience for his ideas at that time. This sensitization prepared Wallis for a great step forward by opening his mind to a new family of symbols. They were more powerful than either the symbols of counting or the symbols of writing, although they drew on properties inherent in both. These were the symbols of mathematical equality, or as we know them today, the symbols of algebraic equations.

As a boy, Wallis was fascinated by the symbols of counting. These symbols introduced the idea to him that symbols could potentially manipulate reality. In later life, he said about the experience, "Mathematics, at that time with us, were scarce looked on as academical studies, but rather mechanical—as the business of traders, merchants, seamen, carpenters, surveyors of lands and the like."[4]

Wallis's first encounter with representative symbols was at the hands of a Freemason. As a private pupil, he was taught by Freemason and astrologer William Oughtred, the man who invented the slide rule. (The slide rule reduced multiplication and division to a simple mechanical manipulation of symbolic number positions, making it much easier to calculate the positions of the stars when casting a horoscope.) Wallis lived in Oughtred's house in Albury and received instruction in arithmetic. As a young man, Wallis

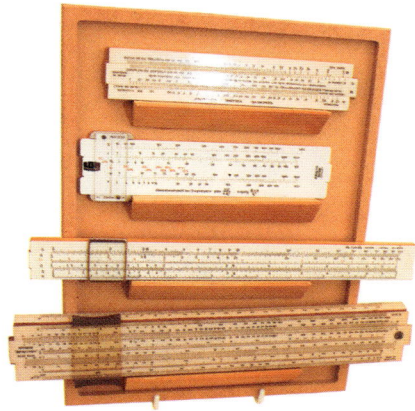

SLIDE RULE INVENTOR WILLIAM OUGHTRED WAS A MEMBER OF AN EARLY LODGE OF SPECULATIVE FREEMASONS. Jack Cox - Travel Pics Pro/Alamy

moved to Cambridge, where he became a Fellow of Queen's College. When he married Susanna Glyde in 1645, he gave up his fellowship and he moved to London to become secretary to the clergy of Westminster Abbey. There, he renewed his friendship with his old tutor and was introduced to Oughtred's fellow Freemasons. Wallis must have been pleased to find that there were men who shared his same interests and could guide him toward deeper understanding of many symbols.

William Oughtred was a member of an early lodge of speculative Freemasons and the inventor of the slide rule. In addition, he was the author of a book on arithmetic, *Clavis Mathematicae*. Oughtred introduced Wallis to the Masonic way of studying symbols. Wallis writes in his autobiography that he was so inspired by the inherent logic of Oughtred's book that he mastered its ideas within a couple of weeks. Before Wallis, no one had realized the great power inherent in the symbol of equality and the Masonic philosophy of balance and harmony that it symbolized.

WHY EQUATIONS ARE A MYSTERY

An incredible mystery is hidden within the simple equations that we all learn in school. Albert Einstein was so impressed by the knowledge opened up by the symbolic theory of equations that he wrote:

> We are in the position of a little child entering a huge library filled with books in many languages. The child knows someone must have written those books. It does not know how. It does not understand the languages in which they are written. The child dimly suspects a mysterious order in the arrangements of the books, but doesn't know what it is. ... We see a universe marvelously arranging and obeying certain laws, but only dimly understand these laws. Our limited minds cannot grasp the mysterious force that moves the constellations.[5]

The symbolic power of equations comes from two key factors. The first is that a symbol can be used to represent something that is real, such as the speed at which a stone falls to the ground or the number of gulps of trapped air a man can take in a diving bell without running out of oxygen. (These are actual problems considered by members of the early Royal Society.) The second factor is that the equality described by an equation is total, absolute, and uncompromising.

The equals sign first appeared in a book written by Robert Recorde, who became a fellow of All Souls College, Oxford, in 1510.[6] A Welshman from Tenby, Recorde was a dedicated educationalist who wrote school textbooks about arithmetic and geometry in English, which was unusual for the time. He first used a symbol to stand in for the words "is equal to" in his 1557 book *Whetstone of Witte*. This how he described the equals symbol:

WHEN MATHEMATICIAN JOHN WALLIS BEGAN TO DISCOVER THE POWER OF THE EQUALS SIGN, HIS FREEMASON PAST REVEALED IT AS TWO PILLARS TURNED HORIZONTALLY. Tony Lilley/Alamy

To avoide the tediouse repetition of these woordes: is equalle to: I will settle as I doe often in woorke use, a paire of paralleles, or gemowe lines of one lengthe: =, bicause noe .2. thynges, can be moare equalle.[7]

When John Wallis began to discover the full power of the equals symbol, he had the benefit of Masonic training to sensitize him to the two parts of Recorde's revelation. Freemasonic sensitization suggested that this symbol looked like the two pillars turned horizontally and meant "is equal to."

The Masonic ritual, Wallis would have learned, says this about the instrument known as a *level*:

The Level is to lay levels, and prove horizontals.

The Level demonstrates that we are all sprung from the same stock, partakers of the same nature, and sharers in the same hope; and although distinctions among men are necessary to preserve subordination, yet ought no eminence of situation make us forget that we are Brothers; for he who is placed on the lowest spoke of fortune's wheel is equally entitled to our regard; as a time will come and the wisest of us knows not how soon when all distinctions, save those of goodness and virtue, shall cease, and Death, the grand leveller of all human greatness, reduces us to the same state.

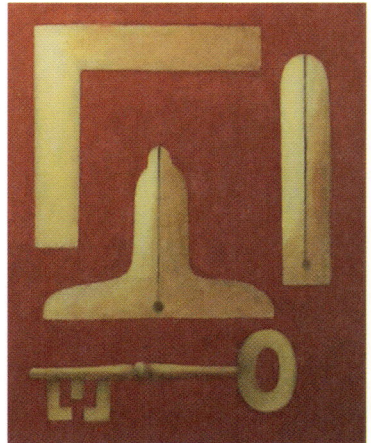

AMONGST THE MOST UBIQUITOUS FREEMASON SYMBOLS, THE LEVEL TEACHES EQUALITY. Copyright Angel Millar. Reprinted with permission

The Level being an emblem of equality, points out the equal measures the Senior Warden is bound to pursue in conjunction with the Master in the well ruling and governing of the Lodge.

The Level teaches equality.

When an Apprentice Mason moved from this degree to that of Fellowcraft, he first had to acknowledge the power of another symbol. The ritual describes it as follows:

> First, the Master asks the Junior Warden: "Bro. Junior Warden, are you a Fellowcraft Freemason?"
>
> He replies, "I am, Worshipful Master. Try me and prove me."
>
> The Master responds, "By what instrument in architecture will you be proved?"
>
> The Junior Warden replies, "The square."
>
> The Master counters, "What is a square?"
>
> And the Junior Warden replies, "An angle of ninety degrees, or the fourth part of a circle."

At the time Wallis began to study the symbols of algebra, the equals sign was hardly known and thus little used. However, he likely recognized both the level and the rotations of the fourth part of a circle, and the juxtaposition of these symbols gave him a great insight. In 1656, he wrote a book called *Arithmetica Infinitorum*, where he drew on this relationship between the level and the square to work out the value of pi (π, a number that relates the diameter of a circle to its circumference). He was intrigued by the challenge of figuring out this transcendental property of a circle from a series of counting symbols laid out in a logical order.

In his *Treatise on Algebra*, Wallis explained how symbols can reveal matters that are otherwise inaccessible to human understanding. He said that a symbolic equation had the power to uncover the mechanisms of nature. The term he chose for accessing this hidden power was *algebra*, an Arabic word that means "to bring together."

Wallis had read how this word was used by Mohammad ibn-Musa al-Khwarizmi around the year 830 CE in a book titled *The Science of Bringing Together and Opposing*. Al-Khwarizmi's book was about Wallis's first love: the symbols of counting. As a native of what is now Iraq and had once been Sumer, Al-Khwarizmi was a son of a land whose rulers had grown rich on the influence of counting symbols. He explained how symbols of counting could be used to deduce facts. For example, if one starts with ten tons of grain and eats half a ton a month for six months, then he or she will have seven tons left in storage. Wallis took this simple idea of counting imaginary practical events and discovered it could be used to manipulate any type of number symbol.

In his *Treatise on Algebra*, Wallis discovered ways to evaluate equations that would later be used by Sir Isaac Newton in his fundamental work on physics.

THE GREAT ARCHITECT

The newly formed Royal Society was a potent package. It brought together a lively group of thinkers who had been presensitized to symbols, and it gave them money, encouragement, and a journal to share knowledge. Without this freedom to study the works of the Great Architect of the Universe (the symbolic term Freemasons use for the power that governs the cosmos), Newton's ideas would never have been published. Less than a generation earlier, Galileo had been persecuted for daring to suggest that the earth might revolve around the sun. Yet only fifty years later, Newton was able to write about knowing the mind of God through the symbolic equations that the Great Architect used to control the movements of the heavens.

Today, all Freemasons recite a formal statement of the Galileo heresy as part of the ritual of being admitted to the Fellowcraft degree. Someone who wishes to become a Fellowcraft Freemason must admit in front of the whole lodge that the earth goes around the sun. This is a permanent memorial to the work of Bro. Sir Robert Moray, who put into practice his Masonic oath to "study the hidden secrets of Nature and Science in Order to better know his Maker." By doing so, he encouraged the study of symbols as an extension of human reasoning.

The tools Newton discovered grew from an alliance between the Masonic symbols of geometry and the newly discovered analytic symbols of algebra. Newton said of this insight into the mind of God:

> Have we any idea of the substance of God? We know him only by his most wise and excellent contrivances of things, and final causes; we admire him for his perfections; but we reverence and adore him on account of his dominion; for we adore him as his servants; and a god without dominion, providence, and final causes is nothing else but Fate and Nature. Blind metaphysical necessity, which is certainly the same always and everywhere, could produce no variety of things. All that diversity of natural things which we find suited to different times

and places could arise from nothing but the ideas and will of a Being necessarily existing. Thus, the diligent student of science, the earnest seeker of truth, is led, as through the courts of a sacred Temple, wherein, at each step, new wonders meet the eye, till, as a crowning grace, they stand before a Holy of Holies, and learn that all science and all truth are one which hath its beginning and its end in the knowledge of Him whose glory the heavens declare, and whose handiwork the firmament showeth forth.[8]

This comment by Newton shows that he felt the symbols of mathematics, which enabled him to understand the movements of the heavens, are thoughts that come directly from the Great Architect of the Universe, not something invented. The Royal Society's study of "the hidden mysteries" led to the success of physics and widespread application of its laws.

But we should never forget it was Masonic training that sensitized Wallis to a deeper meaning within the symbol of the two pillars and made it possible for him to see within Recorde's rotated symbol of equality a new symbol that would gave him a route into the mind of God. What is less well known, however, is that certain symbolic teaching that Newton received from other Freemasons guided him, as well.

SYMBOLS ARE THE KEY TO THE MIND OF GOD

Sir Isaac Newton was an alchemist, a keen student of the mystical architecture of King Solomon's temple, and the man who discovered the system of scientific symbol manipulation that has dominated technological thinking for the last 400 years. Not everyone is aware of his alchemical, hermetic, and esoteric interests or how they helped him reveal the full power of the new symbolism he saw emerging from the writings of John Wallis.

When Newton first went to Cambridge University as an undergraduate, he seemed odd to his fellow students. He had no interest in socializing and spent all his time thinking and making notes about algebraic symbols. When the Black Death swept through Cambridge, Newton's degree studies were interrupted, and he spent a year at his home in Lincolnshire to avoid catching the plague, sitting and thinking in solitary isolation.

Newton's notebooks show that during his first term at Cambridge, he bought a copy of Freemason William Lily's book *Christian Astrology*. He struggled to understand it because it involved two branches of symbolic reasoning known as *geometry* and *trigonometry*. This pushed him to study the writings of Lily's fellow Mason, John Wallis. Newton's student notes show that Wallis became an early inspiration: "About the beginning of my mathematical studies, the works of our celebrated countryman, Dr. Wallis, fell into my hands."[9]

Wallis inspired Newton's interest in arithmetic, alchemy, astrology, and methods of arithmetic calculation. After reading Wallis, Newton felt inspired to look at the works of Euclid. (Euclid's Propositions form part of the ritual explanation of certain symbols that Freemasonry teaches, and myths about Euclid form a key part of the Masonic canon.) Reading Wallis also inspired Newton to read and absorb the symbolic ideas in Oughtred's *Clavis Mathematicae*.

Many people think that Newton became a Freemason when he joined the Royal Society in 1671. This seems likely, as the organization was dominated by speculative Freemasons. However, I have been unable to find any record of an initiation, even though Newton's notebooks show that his interest in symbolic thinking grew rapidly after mixing with men from the Royal Society.

Newton first met with the Royal Society in 1664, while he was still a student. From then on, he took a special interest in Solomon's temple, writing more notes about this than he did about mathematics or science.[10] Solomon's temple is a subject of special interest to Freemasons, because it is provides the underlying myth used in the Masonic method of sensitizing members to the hidden meanings of symbols and the power of symbolic buildings. Masonic myth says Solomon's temple was inspired by God, whom the Freemasons call the *Grand Geometrician of the Universe* in this ritual instance.

Newton became a Fellow of Trinity College, Cambridge, in 1667, and the Lucasian Professor of Mathematics two years later. Between 1673 and 1683, he gave a series of lectures on algebra and the theory of equations, but much of

TEMPLE DE SALOMON. III. *Rois, chap.* VI.

SIR ISAAC NEWTON TOOK A SPECIAL INTEREST IN SOLOMON'S TEMPLE, WRITING MORE NOTES ABOUT THIS THAN HE DID ABOUT MATH OR SCIENCE. Mary Evans Picture Library/Alamy

his spare time was taken up studying in Solomon's temple, as he tried to understand the method of thinking used by the Grand Geometrician.[11] His work on equations extended Wallis's use of the equals symbol but was not published until 1707 in a book called *The Universal Arithmetic*.

During 1692, Newton corresponded with Wallis and discussed ideas about a form of symbolic representation that he turned into his greatest work on the reality of nature.[12] The method of symbolic manipulation he discovered is now known as *calculus*, but then, it was called the method of *fluxions*. It combined the symbolic visualization system of Euclid with Wallis's representation of physical quantities as algebraic symbols. Newton drew on the Masonic idea of God as the Grand Geometrician of the Universe to bring Euclid's system of graphic symbols together with the mathematical analysis made possible by algebraic symbols. He published this work during 1687 as *Principia Mathematica*.

Newton's work was a landmark step toward humans' understanding the universe. As the *Standford Encyclopedia of Philosophy* explains:

> No work was more seminal in the development of modern physics and astronomy than Newton's *Principia*. Its conclusion that the force retaining the planets in their orbits is one in kind with terrestrial gravity ended forever the view dating back at least to Aristotle that the celestial realm calls for one science and the sublunar realm, another. ... The ultimate success of Newton's theory of gravity made the identification of the fundamental forces of nature and their characterization in laws the primary pursuit of physics.[13]

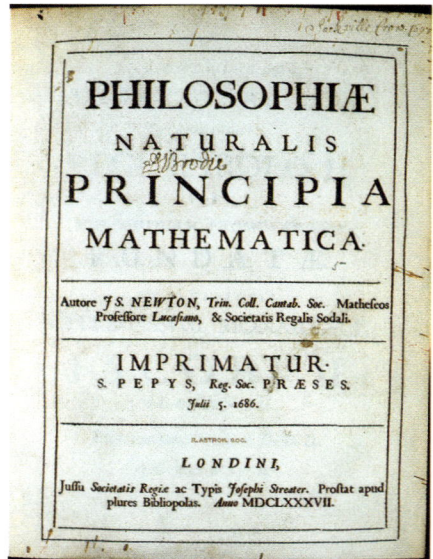

NEWTON'S PRINCIPIA DEMONSTRATED HIS
UNMATCHED UNDERSTANDING OF SECRET SYMBOLS.
The Print Collector/Alamy

Newton's discovery of the hidden secrets of the symbol of equality gave a totally new view of how the universe is controlled and ordered. The French mathematician Lagrange described the *Principia* as "the greatest production of the human mind," and said he felt dazed at such an illustration of what man's intellect might be capable. In describing the effect of his own writings and those of Laplace it was a favorite remark of his that Newton was not only the greatest genius that had ever existed, but he was also the most fortunate, for as there is but one universe, it can happen but to one man in the world's history to be the interpreter of its laws.[14]

Newton's understanding came from his study of Masonic symbolism. The innate power of the symbols to influence human minds can be seen by the way this Masonic knowledge affected the thought processes of others as Newton shared it. In particular, there was a dispute between the German philosopher Gottfried Leibnitz and Newton about who discovered calculus.

What is less well known is that both Newton and Leibniz were exposed to the same symbolic teaching by the Freemasons of the Royal Society: Newton through his association with Wallis and his reading of Lily and Oughtred, and Leibniz through a protracted correspondence with Bro. Sir Robert Moray, the Freemason who founded the society. The symbolic mix of geometric insight and algebraic analysis that is the calculus appeared simultaneously to these two men, as if it had been fully formed in another place and was just waiting for a chance to manifest in the human mind.

Masonic teaching offers a means of accessing the place where symbols are eternally present. This place is called by some physicists the *Platonic heaven* and is derived from Plato's discovery of the perfect forms.

THE HEAVEN OF PURE SYMBOLS

Wallis, Lily, and Oughtred introduced Newton to a tradition that has since become common among modern scientists. Wallis and Newton discovered the power of mathematics by exploring the consequences of symbolic relationships. They believed that pure symbols arose from the mind of God, existed before the world began, and would endure long after the world had passed into oblivion. Newton wrote down his explanation of this idea in the *Principia*:

The most beautiful system of the sun, planets, and comets, could only proceed from the counsel and dominion of an intelligent and powerful being. And if the fixed stars are the centres of like systems, these, being formed by the like wise counsel, must be all subject to the dominion of one; especially since the light of the fixed stars is of the same nature with the light of the sun, and from every system light passes into all the other systems; and lest the systems of fixed stars should, by their gravity, fall on each other, he hath placed those systems at immense distances from one another.

This being governs all things, not as the soul of the world, but as Lord over all; and on account of his dominion he is wont to be called the Lord God or Universal Ruler, for God is a relative word, and has a respect to servants; and Deity is the dominion of God not over his own body, as those imagine who fancy God to be the soul of the world, but over servants. The Supreme Being is eternal, infinite, absolutely perfect, omnipotent and omniscient. ... We know him only by his most wise and excellent contrivances of things and final causes.[15]

Implicit in this eternal worldview is the idea that for a mathematical theorem to be discovered, it must already exist before any human thinks about it. As mentioned previously, this idea of a transcendental world of absolute symbolic forms was proposed by the Greek philosopher Plato (427–347 BCE).

Plato believed that we have genuine knowledge of truth, goodness, and beauty as well as equality, even though we perceive only imperfect instances in the real world. He called things of this sort *Platonic forms* and defined them as abstract entities that exist independently of the sensible world. Ordinary objects are imperfect and changeable, but they faintly copy the perfect and immutable forms. Many of the Platonic shapes—such as the square, the equilateral triangle, the circle, the pentangle, and the heptangle—appear in the Masonic set of symbols.

Plato claimed that all souls have knowledge of these suprasensible realities and that they cannot possibly have obtained through any bodily experience. He believed this knowledge must be something that the human soul learns prior to birth. This implies that Platonic symbols have an independent and eternal existence. It is this vision of Platonic perfection that drives all physicists and is at the heart of many systems of scientific research that have been developed in the twentieth century.

Roger Penrose, a committed scientific Platonist, writes about this idea:

> The Platonic viewpoint is an immensely valuable one. It tells us to be careful to distinguish the precise mathematical entities from the approximations that we see around us in the world of physical things. Moreover, it provides us with the blueprint according to which modern science has proceeded. Scientists will put forward models of the world—or, rather, of certain aspects of the world—and these models may be tested against previous observation and against the results of carefully designed experiment.
>
> If the model itself is to be assigned any kind of "existence," then this existence is located within the Platonic world of mathematical forms. Of course, one might take a contrary viewpoint: namely that the model is itself to have existence only within our various minds, rather than to take Plato's world to be in any sense absolute and "real." Yet, there is something important to be gained in regarding mathematical structures as having a reality of their own. For our individual minds are notoriously imprecise, unreliable, and inconsistent in their judgments. The precision, reliability, and consistency that are required by our scientific theories demand something beyond any one of our individual (untrustworthy) minds. In mathematics, we find a far greater robustness than can be located in any particular mind. Does this not point to something outside ourselves, with a reality that lies beyond what each individual can achieve?[16]

The Platonist philosophy of eternal and perfect symbols that underlies the scientific method of answering questions about reality gives rise to the term *research* (i.e., "re-search"). As a scientist, when Penrose conducts research, he is repeating a search that any individual could repeat independently to discover a truth about the symbolic nature of reality that could be found by anyone prepared to interact with the Platonic symbols.

This concept of research was formalized during World War II, when scientists working for the Allies—in particular, Leo Szilard and Albert Einstein in the United States[17] and Neils Bohr in the United Kingdom—realized that a weapon of immense destructive power already existed within the realms of symbolic Platonic truth. The implication of this thought was that a frightful weapon was sitting somewhere, waiting to be used by the first bold searcher to discover it and to let it help win the war. That searcher could be on either side, as basic work on nuclear instability had been carried out for the Nazis by Werner Heisenberg but ignored by Adolf Hitler. In the United Kingdom, work on material preparation for a ballistic-impact uranium bomb was already well underway at the Nobel explosive works in Porth Madog, North Wales, under the secret patronage of the MAUD committee.[18] But it was a real fear, shared by Einstein and Neils, that this fearsome weapon was sitting unprotected in the heaven of the Platonic symbols, just waiting to be accessed and used.

Szilard and Einstein wrote to President Franklin D. Roosevelt urging him to devote all the United States' scientific talent to searching for this atom bomb. They warned that the consequences of Hitler getting to it first would be catastrophic.[19] Roosevelt, himself a Freemason, took their warning seriously and set up the Manhattan Project. It brought together the organizational and logistic skills of General Leslie Groves and the inspired scientific leadership of Dr. J. Robert Oppenheimer in the remote desert site of Los Alamos, New Mexico. The result was two symbolic discoveries: two different types of atom bomb, one based on uranium (Little Boy) and one based on a previously unknown Platonic element, plutonium (Fat Boy). Both bombs worked and were deployed over Japanese cities to bring about the end of World War II.

Nobody today questions the idea that there are symbolic scientific entities just waiting in the Platonic heaven to be discovered by explorers who know how to reach that realm. The atomic bomb is harrowing proof of this.

CHAPTER 7

THE SECRET SYMBOL OF POLITICAL STABILITY

THE PILLARS THAT INSPIRED REPUBLICANISM

Without the inspirational Masonic symbol of the two pillars, no truly democratic government would have emerged or succeeded. The symbol of the two pillars has inculcated political stability in the minds of the people who view it from the earliest times down to today. It is no coincidence that this iconic picture of George Washington, the first president of the United States, shows him standing in front of one pair of pillars and between another pair.

BRO. GEORGE WASHINGTON APPEARS BETWEEN A PAIR OF TWO PILLARS AND IN FRONT OF ANOTHER PAIR OF PILLARS. Library of Congress

This pattern of pillars is echoed by the repeated use of the number 1 on the front of a dollar bill.

Each pair of 1s represents a pair of pillars. The upper pair is conjoined by the United States of America, and George Washington is between the lower pair. Even the symbol of the dollar currency was written as an S with two pillars inscribed on top of it. Many current computer fonts now show the dollar symbol as $, but even this simplified computer font shows an S split into two equal and opposite halves—a less blatant form of the two pillars. The parallel lines of the two pillars implies stability.

This symbol of two equal and opposite pillars has influenced three of the world's enduring democratic societies. It appeared as the symbol of England's first elected ruler, Oliver Cromwell, who was a member of Parliament for Huntingdon and Lord Protector of the Commonwealth of Great Britain.

Just as George Washington was depicted a hundred years later, Cromwell stands between two pillars.

The fundamental statement of the aims of the French Revolution, the "Declaration of the Rights of Man and of the Citizen," states that the rights of humans are universal: valid at all times and in every place.

ENGLAND'S FIRST ELECTED RULER, OLIVER CROMWELL, APPEARS BETWEEN TWO PILLARS IN THIS (1658) ENGRAVING, THE EMBLEM OF ENGLAND'S DISTRACTIONS.
Private Collection /The Bridgeman Art Library International

THE DECLARATION OF THE RIGHTS OF MAN AND THE CITIZEN, ISSUED BY THE REVOLUTIONARIES OF FRANCE, IS FRAMED BY THE SYMBOL OF THE TWO PILLARS. Musee de la Ville de Paris, Musee Carnavalet, Paris, France/Giraudon/The Bridgeman Art Library International

What does this symbol represent, and why has it figured so strongly in these iconic images from three of the most important democracies of Western civilization?

To understand the symbol's meaning, we need to look at its history—and fortunately, its history is well documented. This is one of the key symbols that has been preserved, studied, and applied by Freemasons. It represents one of the most important ideas behind the emergence of democracy.

The concept behind the symbol is that there are two powerful forces that rule a state, and if either of them is too dominant, the state will become unbalanced and tyrannical. Both pillars must work together for a society to be stable. Let us return to the symbol's beginnings in Freemasonry in fifteenth-century Aberdeen, Scotland.

THE PILLARS THAT FORMED FREEMASONRY

We saw early Masonic versions of this symbol on the Kirkwall scroll, dating from around 1480, and it was in two different versions. The first version showed the two pillars separate and standing apart, as they appear in the foreground of the image of George Washington and in the image of Oliver Cromwell.

The other form of this image on the Kirkwall scroll (see page 77) showed the two pillars conjoined by a keystone.

These two versions of the pillar symbol were being used in Masonic rituals 200 years before Cromwell claimed it as an icon to support his political aims.

We can find the same symbols in Masonic images preserved in a Masonic lodge in Yorkshire. They date from the time of the French Revolution and the American Revolutionary War.

THE SYMBOLS THAT TAUGHT GEORGE WASHINGTON

George Washington knew about the Masonic meaning of the symbol of the two pillars, because both forms were embroidered on the apron he wore to attend Masonic meetings. Washington was introduced to Freemasonry by a Yorkshire Freemason, Lord Fairfax. Young George got his first job as a surveyor working for Fairfax, who was a major landowner in Virginia. Members of the Fairfax family were active patrons of the Masonic Grand Lodge of York and were familiar with the Old Yorkshire Masonic symbols shown earlier. The family also took a great interest in the local Masonic lodges of Virginia, and when George Washington was old enough, the family encouraged him to join.

Washington was initiated into the Fredericksburg Lodge No. 4 on Saturday, November 4, 1752. He became a Fellowcraft Mason on the first Saturday of March 1753, and on Saturday, August 4, 1753, he was made a Master Mason by the Fredericksburg Lodge. In 1779, he was offered the Office of General Grand Master Mason of the United States but declined it because of his military commitments.

A French Freemason, the Marquis de Lafayette, joined Washington's army in 1777 and became his close friend. In 1784, Lafayette presented Bro. Washington with a gift: a Masonic apron embroidered by his wife, which Washington wore with enormous pride.[1] Here is proof that Washington was fully aware of the power of the symbol of the two pillars. Lafayette chose the symbols on the apron to inspire Washington in working toward the difficult tasks that lay ahead in the growing dispute over English rule of the American colonies.

But what had Freemasonry taught Washington about this symbol?

THE MASONIC MEANINGS OF THE TWO PILLARS

Freemasonry teaches that the symbol of the two pillars has two conjoined meanings, both of which are illuminated by a ritual recitation of a traditional myth. The first meaning is expressed through the names given to the two pillars that stood outside Solomon's temple. The left-hand pillar is associated with the power of the king.

The ritual says:

> Boaz was the name of the left-hand pillar which stood at the porchway or entrance of King Solomon's Temple. It was named after the great grandfather of David who was a Prince and Ruler in Israel and represents the force of temporal power as expressed through the actions of the king.

The right-hand pillar is associated with the power of the priest. The ritual says:

> Jachin was the name of the right-hand pillar that stood at the entrance or porchway of King Solomon's Temple. It was named after the Great High Priest who officiated at the dedication of the Temple. It represents the power of the priest and the benevolent force of religion.

When the two pillars are brought together, they take on an additional layer of meaning. They can be symbolically linked by a keystone, a lintel, or by the Royal Arch of the Heavens. But when conjoined, the ritual says of them:

The two great Pillars which were placed at the Porch or Entrance of
King Solomon's Temple have a separate and conjoint significance. The
former denotes "strength," the latter "to establish," and when conjoined "stability," for God hath said "In strength will I establish My
word in this Mine house that it will stand fast forever."

The two pillars represent two forces that act on society. These are the secular force of the king, who rules, protects the people, and governs the land, and the
spiritual force of the priest, who guides the people's religious and spiritual life. The
double-pillar symbol represents the great power for stability that flows from these
two forces when they work together. If either becomes too powerful, society will
lurch into either religious or secular despotism, neither of which is desirable.

This same symbol appears in a slightly different form in a myth told about the
patriarch Enoch:

Masonic ritual tells this story of Enoch:

Enoch, the son of Jared, was the sixth in descent from Adam.
Filled with the love and fear of God, he strove to lead men in the way
of honor and duty. In a vision, the Deity appeared to him in the visible
shape of a pure golden triangle, and said to him, "Enoch, thou hast
longed to know my true name: arise and follow me, and thou shalt
know it."

Enoch, accepting his vision as an inspiration, journeyed in search
of the mountain he had seen in his dream, until, weary of the search,
he stopped in the land of Canaan, then already populous with the
descendants of Adam, and there employed workmen; and with the
help of his son Methuselah, he excavated nine apartments, one above
the other, and each roofed with an arch, as he had seen in his dream,
the lowest being hewn out of the solid rock. In the crown of each
arch he left a narrow aperture, closed with a square stone, and over
the upper one he built a modest temple, roofless and of huge unhewn
stones, to the Great Architect of the Universe.

Upon a triangular plate of gold, inlaid with many precious gems, he engraved the ineffable name of God, and sank the plate into one face of a cube of agate.

None knew of the deposit of the precious treasure; and, that it might remain undiscovered, and survive the Flood, which it was known to Enoch would soon overwhelm the world in one vast sea of mire, he covered the aperture, and the stone that closed it and the great ring of iron used to raise the stone, with the granite pavement of his primitive temple.

Then, fearing that all knowledge of the arts and sciences would be lost in the universal flood, he built two great columns upon a high hill—one of brass, to resist water, and one of granite, to resist fire. On the granite column was written a description of the subterranean apartments; on the one of brass, the rudiments of the arts and sciences.

The Masonic myth continues to say that one of the pillars was found by the Jews and the other by the Egyptians. It claims that an elite group of Freemasons was created to protect the Jewish pillar and its teachings, and the secret meaning of the pillars is said only to survive within Freemasonry. This knowledge is displayed in Masonic lodges as two freestanding pillars.

THE PILLARS THAT ESTABLISHED ANCIENT EGYPT

Ancient Egyptian society lasted for 4,000 years. Its longevity and prosperity grew around the power of the symbol of the two pillars, which became the base on which the dynasties of the Pharaohs were founded and sustained.

The Nile River in Egypt supported small, isolated groups of nomadic hunters from about 30,000 BCE on, as *Homo sapiens* spread out of Africa. Farming-related symbols began to appear and spread west from Anatolian villages. The symbols of counting and writing took root as the early Egyptians developed proto-kingdoms and created boundaries that they protected against intruding hunter-gatherers.

In this tense environment, the symbol of the two pillars became increasingly important. It was a symbol of cooperation and engendered the realization in its observers that unity was more effective than aggression. The lozenge and spiral symbols of farming had developed from patterns of shadows cast by two pillars.

As the farming villages turned into towns and then into cities, these mono-lithic pillars became a strong emotive symbol. This symbol helped create groups of harmonious communities, which gradually coalesced into two kingdoms known as Upper and Lower Egypt. By 3100 BCE, they had become a combined kingdom. Although Upper and Lower Egypt were conjoined by a single divine and absolute ruler, in many ways, they remained separate kingdoms. A pillar symbol stood at the center of each kingdom. To explain the myths behind the pillars, we must go back to the early symbolic history of Egypt.

The rulers of Egypt began as kings, with priests assisting them in their relation-ships with the gods. But they grew into pharaohs, who were half gods and half kings, and they ruled by the divine right of their godly parentage. Each king was a partly divine son of god, and when he died, he joined his forefathers to become a full god.

The sky goddess Nut had five children, the eldest of whom was Osiris. Symbolically, Nut was the sky, and her arms and legs were pillars that held up the heavens. She touched the land at the four cardinal points of the horizon. One of her legs was planted in Heliopolis and was the great pillar of Lower Egypt. Her other leg stood in Upper Egypt at the city of Nekheb. But the actual ground of the two Egypts was the province of Geb, the god of the earth, from whose clay humanity was formed. Geb was the lover of Nut, and their union gave birth to the first king of the Two Lands of Egypt.

The children of Nut and Geb were part sky and part land. The people of the Two Lands believed that Osiris, Nut and Geb's eldest son, had become their first king. He was part man and part god. Osiris married his sister Isis, who was part woman and part goddess, establishing a tradition that would be followed by the future kings of Egypt.

Osiris ruled wisely, but his brother Set became jealous of his success and mur-dered him in the night, while the darkness hid that act from their mother's sight. Set cut Osiris into pieces and then threw them into the Nile. When light returned, Isis was distraught, as Osiris had not produced an heir. So with Nut's oversight, Isis located the pieces of Osiris's body and reassembled them. She called on her father, Geb, to breathe a last short moment of life into the human part of her husband. As Osiris's reassembled body quivered with a brief flash of life, Isis lowered herself onto his phallus and took his seed into her. While Osiris quivered with ecstasy, his mother reached down and took him in her hands. Then she stood upright, her legs planted firmly in the center of each kingdom, and lifted him to the stars, where she made him the ruler of the kingdom of the dead.

Isis gave birth to a son named Horus, who became the next king of the Two Lands. He challenged Set to battle. Horus won the fight, but his eye was gouged out. His grandmother, the goddess Nut, whose pillar legs straddled the Two Lands, took his eye and cradled it in her hands in the sky above his combined kingdoms. So Horus's single, all-seeing eye floated above the two pillars that joined his kingdoms. Nothing was hidden from his sight. From that time on, the pharaoh was believed to be the earthly incarnation of Horus until his death, when he, too, would be lifted by Nut to the stars.

The twin pillars of Heliopolis and Nekheb reminded the people of the presence of the goddess Nut and her role in supporting the Pharaoh. Her legs, planted firmly in each major city, linked the earthly half-god pharaoh to his future destiny as a full god in the starry sky. And this symbolism reminded the pharaoh's subjects of his overarching power and his all-seeing eye.

These symbolic pillars were important to both of the countries, even though they shared a single king. Lower Egypt was larger and more prosperous than Upper Egypt, but the security, stability, and wealth of Egypt arose from both states working together. The two pillars linked and unified the two lands, and the people believed that as long as both were intact, their conjoined kingdom would prosper.

The civilization of Egypt did prosper, and the symbol of the two pillars was displayed outside their temples to remind the people of the divine source of wealth and power. The king would pass between the legs of the sky goddess as he entered the temple and remind his people of his divine right to rule.

But how did this symbolism come to pass into the symbolic teachings of Freemasonry? To answer that question, we need to look more closely at the mythical Grand Masters of Freemasonry at the time of the construction of King Solomon's temple. And a key player in this story was a Phoenician king famed for his building skills: Hiram, King of Tyre.

THE PILLARS AND THE CONCUBINES

The Phoenicians occupied a narrow strip of land on the eastern coast of the Mediterranean. It was about 200 miles long but only 5 to 15 miles wide, extending to the mountains of Lebanon. The Phoenicians did not have a unified state but formed a group of city-kingdoms. Around 1800 BCE, the Egyptians invaded and took control for approximately 400 years. Then the raids of the Hittites against Egypt gave the Phoenician city-kingdoms an opportunity to rebel, and by 1100 BCE, the Phoenicians were again independent. But the Egyptian political symbol of the two pillars had taken root in the temple of Tyre, the richest of the Phoenician cities.

After breaking free of the Egyptians, the Phoenicians continued to build temples characterized by a porchway or entrance flanked by two pillars, in a style similar to the temples in Egypt. King Hiram's city of Tyre had just such a temple, with two pillars at its entrance, long before King Solomon built one.

Hiram was an extremely successful king and a builder of historic proportions. At the beginning of his reign, the main port of Tyre stood on the mainland. But this builder king realized that an island lying less than one-half mile (800 meters) from shore would form a highly defensible stronghold and provide a fully integrated docking system for his fleet. The King of Tyre was a superb engineer. He was far better suited than King Solomon to be an early Grand Master of Freemasonry, and his important place in Masonic ritual was well earned. But how much was he helped by the power of the two pillars?

In 1923, a French expedition discovered the stone coffin of Hiram, King of Tyre. It contained a Phoenician inscription around the edge of the lid written in the linear alphabet.[2] The inscription told the story of a king who was the earthly representative of a goddess and through his congress with her became a god himself. The inscription claims he was the lover of Baalat, the powerful Phoenician goddess whose symbol of two pillars marked the entrance to her temple.

The Phoenicians of Tyre worshiped a trinity of gods consisting of El, the father god; his wife, Baalat; and their son, Baal. El was the mightiest of the three. He would see and punish all evil deeds. His only failing was his infidelity to his wife, Baalat. He was fond of impregnating any human female who took his fancy, and to do so, he would disguise himself as a passing stranger. To make sure El could satisfy his desires, all Phoenician woman had a religious duty to make themselves sexually available to passing strangers around the spring and autumn equinoxes. They would sit between the symbolic pillars at the front of Baalat's temples and offer themselves for money.

It was the rule that the women had to charge the strangers for sex and then turn over the money to Baalat, the long-suffering wife of El and the mother of Baal. While El had his wicked way with all the women of the lands he ruled, the women charged him for his pleasure and donated the money to placate his deceived wife. She in turn took their human king as her lover, using the body of a priestess as her proxy, and made the king a god. So all were satisfied, and passing strangers looking for a bit of fun knew to look between the two pillars for women keen to carry out their duty of religious fornication.

Baalat was widely worshiped in Tyre, where her two pillars stood before the entrance of the Temple Hiram, built in her honor. She took Hiram, King of Tyre and Grand Master of Freemasonry, as her lover, as she did every Canaanite king, and made him into a living but mortal god.

Hiram was not just a king; he was also the consort and lover of the goddess whose symbol was the two pillars. When Hiram was asked by Solomon to design and build a temple for the God of the Jews in Jerusalem, what could have been more natural than to suggest that it should have two pillars at its entrance? This living god of Tyre, whose power came from the symbolic pillars of the goddess who was his lover, built the temple. And he provided the craftsmen to build the two great pillars that stood at the porchway or entrance to King Solomon's temple.

THE PILLARS THAT INFLUENCED THE ENGLISH CIVIL WAR

By the mid-seventeenth century, the symbol of the two pillars was firmly embedded in the ritual teaching of Freemasonry. As mentioned earlier, Oliver Cromwell used this symbol to rally support for his cause. However, the symbol was also used by his opponents.

The seventeenth-century illustration below shows how the kingly and priestly pillars were used to try to bolster the right to rule of an anointed king. But the king in the illustration is not a king of Israel; rather, he is a king of England.

James VI of Scotland was an enthusiastic Mason, became a member of the Lodge of Scoon and Perth in 1601, and was well known for introducing Masonic symbolism and rituals into his court.[3] His son, King Charles I, tried to use the Masonic pillar symbol but made a critical change in the keystone. The king is shown in the role of guarantor of the good behavior of both pillars. By identifying himself as the keystone that locks them together, Charles took on the role that God filled for Solomon and David. Charles was making a symbolic statement that he ruled both church and state by divine rright. It would also prove his undoing and cause his beheading.

In this engraving of Charles I, he hovers in godlike dominance above the conjoined pillars. The left-hand pillar is labeled "The Church" and is surmounted by the figure of Truth. The right-hand pillar is labeled "The State" and is surmounted by the figure of Justice. The two pillars are linked by the sharing of a Masonic handshake.

THIS SEVENTEENTH-CENTURY ETCHING SHOWS KING CHARLES I OF ENGLAND, WHO EVENTUALLY WAS EXECUTED DURING THE ENGLISH CIVIL WAR, USING THE SYMBOL OF THE TWO PILLARS AS A POLITICAL TOOL.

Charles wanted a monarchical despotism, in which the temporal power of the king brooked no spiritual challenge and no democratic restraint. His misuse of this symbol reveals that he saw himself in the role of an absolute arbiter with no need for God to ensure fair play. Charles was corrupting the Freemason symbol that had been passed to him. But the symbol had greater resources than Charles realized, and it fought back in supporting his chief opponent. This was Cromwell, who is depicted standing between the pillars and beneath the dove of blessing, symbolizing God as the keystone conjoining the pillars and balancing the forces of disruption. This symbol carried the day with the common people.

THE PILLARS THAT SUPPORT THE U.S. PRESIDENTS

For the symbol of the two pillars to work its hidden influence on the mute right hemisphere of the human brain, it must be kept before the eyes of the people. It has been used in banknotes, currency symbols, iconic images, and stone carvings.

George Washington used the iconic image of him standing between the pairs of pillars and also placed the symbol in the written representation of the currency, but he also made sure that it could reinforce the position of the president. To ensure that the symbol's emotional impact would continue to work in the new republic, Washington made sure that two sets of pillars were built into the entrance of the White House in Washington, DC, when he approved James Hoban's design.

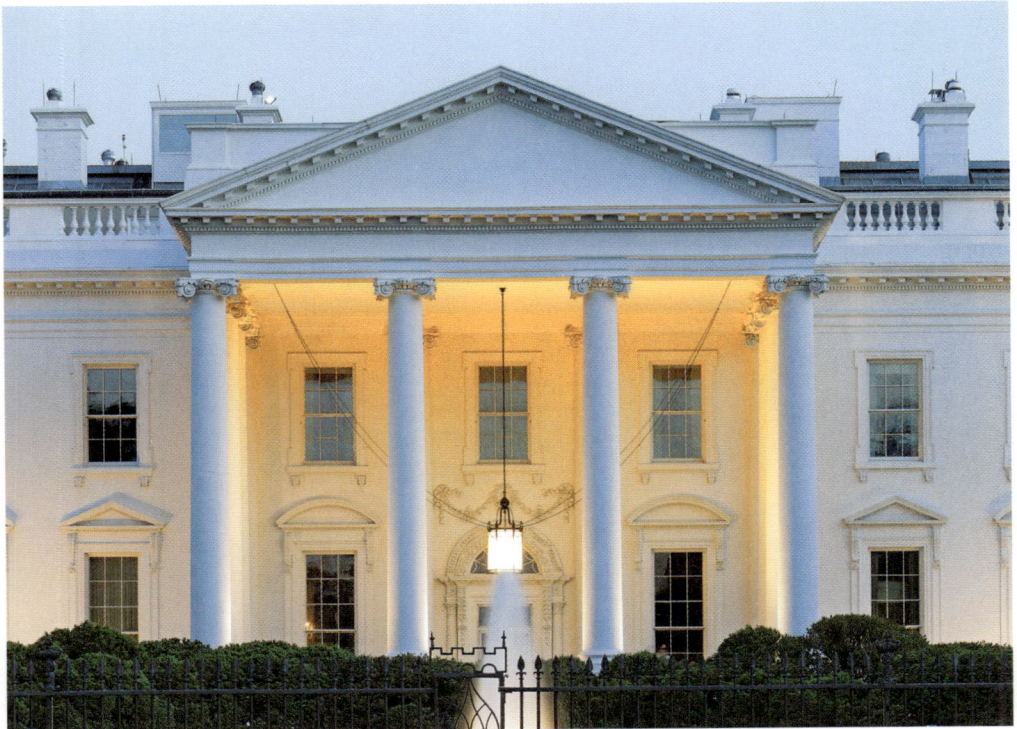

THE NORTH FACE OF THE WHITE HOUSE SHOWING TWO PAIR OF PILLARS AND AN UPWARD POINTING TRIANGLE. THIS DESIGN WAS APPROVED BY BRO. GEORGE WASHINGTON.

The two outer pillars, linked by the triangular arch pointing to the heavens, are the pillars of balance and stability, while the inner pillars are the pillars of knowledge.

When a U.S. president stands before this symbolic entrance, the symbols continue to work their magic by creating a mood of emotional stability and confidence. The portico of the White House symbolizes the separation of church and state. Each remains separate and strong and is able to limit the excesses of the other. Because neither can become powerful enough to become despotic, freedom is maintained and society prospers.

THE PILLARS THAT RECONCILED ENGLAND AND THE UNITED STATES

Freemasons have long recognized that the symbol of the two pillars works to stabilize societies. Here is an instance of how Masons used two pillars, which had stood outside the temple of Heleopolis in ancient Egypt for 4,000 years, to help reconcile England and the United States after the American Revolutionary War.

Heliopolis was one of the largest cities in ancient Egypt and the home of one of the binding pillars of the Two Lands. At its center stood a massive temple known as the Great House. It was built around 2000 BCE and had two pillars at its entrance. Around 13 BCE, the Roman Emperor Augustus moved those pillars to Alexandria and reconstructed them. There they stayed until 1301 CE, when one fell on its side and the other slipped sideways during an earthquake. The pillars were never properly reset and remained uncared for until 1878 CE. That year, both fallen pillars were procured by British and American Freemasons. The two pillars, which had once represented the unity of the two lands of ancient Egypt, were shipped away and

CLEOPATRA'S NEEDLE IN NEW YORK CITY'S CENTRAL PARK.

intended to play a new role: to bind together two other states.

Bro. Dr. Erasmus Wilson paid £10,000 to carry one pillar from Egypt and erect it in London. After being transported on a specially designed cigar-shaped container ship named the *Cleopatra*, the pillar arrived in July 1878. It was established with a public Masonic ceremony conducted by Bro. Wilson on September 12, 1878.[4]

In New York, Bro. William Hulbert persuaded Bro. William J. Vanderbilt to pay for the other pillar's transport to the United States. Its carriage was overseen by Bro. Henry H. Gorringe of Anglo Saxon Lodge No. 137 of New York City. The pillar was transported onboard the steamship *Dessoug* and arrived in New York in 1880. Grand Master Mason of the state of New York,

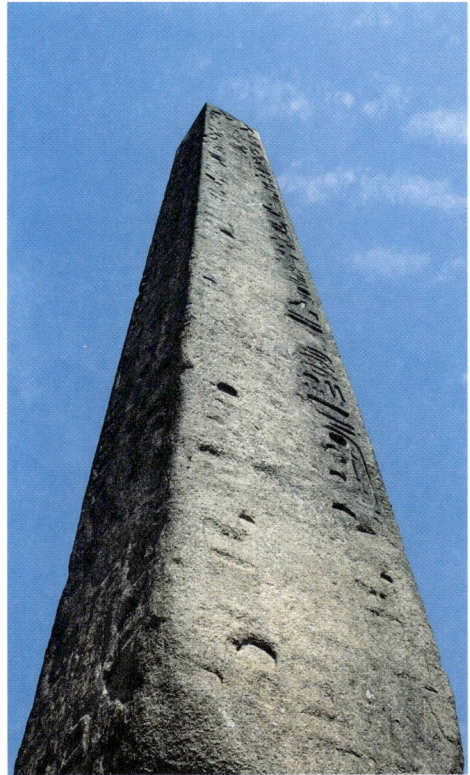

CLEOPATRA'S NEEDLE IN LONDON. THE TWO OBELISKS WERE INTENDED TO HELP RECONCILE ENGLAND AND THE UNITED STATES AFTER THE AMERICAN REVOLUTIONARY WAR.

the Most Worshipful Jesse B. Anthony, presided as the obelisk was set in place with full Masonic ceremony on October 2, 1880, in Graywacke Knoll, Central Park. Over 9,000 Masons in full Masonic regalia paraded up Fifth Avenue from 14th Street to 82nd Street, and over 50,000 spectators lined the parade route. The benediction was presented by the Grand Chaplin of New York Masons, the Right Worshipful Louis C. Gerstein.

In this way, the brethren of the two oldest Masonic-inspired states in the world reinstated an ancient symbol of stability to bind them together again.

A PRESENT-DAY SYMBOL TO STRENGTHEN THE EURO

Perhaps the most recent use of a currency symbol incorporating the parallel lines of the two-pillar symbol can be seen in the Euro symbol (€). In it, the two pillars are shown horizontally. This is the statement made about the Euro by the European

Commission at its launch: "Inspiration for the € symbol itself came from the Greek epsilon (Є)—a reference to the cradle of European civilization—and the first letter of the word Europe, crossed by two parallel lines to 'certify' the stability of the euro."[5]

THE EURO SYMBOL INCORPORATES THE TWO PILLARS IN ITS MATHEMATICAL FORM AS AN EQUALS SIGN.

CHAPTER 8

MASONIC SYMBOLS THAT CHANGED THE U.S. CONSTITUTION

THE SYMBOLIC SOLUTION TO THE CORRUPTION OF POWER

When a group of British colonists met in Williamsburg, Virginia, on May 15, 1776, they were seething under what they perceived was arbitrary autocratic rule by a distant king. They realized that when absolute power was vested in a single authority, it was easily abused. They decided such abuse needed to be challenged and abolished.

There were eighteen Freemasons amongst the fifty-six signees of the Declaration of Independence, and they were well versed in the use of Masonic symbols. These same symbols had been shown to prevent abuses of power like those that provoked the writing of the Declaration.[1] Only when this symbolic system of checks and balances was written into the U.S. Constitution did this secret method become public knowledge.

The opening lines of the Declaration say:

> When, in the course of human events, it becomes necessary for one people to dissolve the political bands which have connected them with another, and to assume among the powers of the earth, the separate and equal station to which the laws of nature and of nature's God entitle them, a decent respect to the opinions of mankind requires that they should declare the causes which impel them to the separation.

By stating that there are substantial causes to break away from the established system of rule (and these causes are listed in full detail later in the document), the Declaration of Independence offered a way toward a new, more open system of government. The key statement that followed drew on the Platonic symbolic view that there are certain *self-evident truths* that must be considered when a group of people decide to govern themselves. These self-evident truths had been taught by Freemasonry for the previous 300 years. As stated in the Declaration:

We hold these truths to be self-evident, that all men are created equal, that they are endowed by their Creator with certain unalienable rights, that among these are life, liberty, and the pursuit of happiness. That to secure these rights, governments are instituted among men, deriving their just powers from the consent of the governed. That whenever any form of government becomes destructive to these ends, it is the right of the people to alter or to abolish it, and to institute new government, laying its foundation on such principles and organizing its powers in such form, as to them shall seem most likely to effect their safety and happiness.

THERE WERE EIGHTEEN FREEMASONS AMONG THE FIFTY-SIX SIGNERS OF THE DECLARATION OF INDEPENDENCE.

This statement was truly revolutionary. The founders of United States understood that to declare independence, they had to establish an intellectual basis for self-government. Among those founders was a sizeable minority trained in the Masonic method of sensitization to symbols and privy to the Masonic teaching that a combination of symbols could be used to prevent the sort of abuses they all objected to in British rule. These symbols are the square, the level, and the plumb rule.

These three symbols are assigned to the three officers who rule a Masonic lodge. There is an overall Master, but he is supported by two other officers who look after different aspects of governance. The Master makes the rules, the Senior Warden enforces them, and the Junior Warden makes sure they are applied fairly. There is no absolute ruler within a lodge, although the Master takes the lead. The three officers work together to fulfil the duties of governing the lodge, and each displays one of these three symbols on his collar of office. And most importantly for the United States' founders, the Master is elected by the members.

The Declaration of Independence from Great Britain, adopted on July 4, 1776, drew on another basic Masonic symbol for its *reason d'etre*: the symbol of the ballot box, used for the secret ballot to elect all potential candidates for Freemasonry and all potential Masters.

The route the British colonies in North America followed from declaring their independence to establishing a constitutional government is one of the great journeys in the history of democratic societies. But what is not always recognized is that it was a road inspired by the Masonic symbols of democratic government, including the three symbols that enforce the sharing of power. The use of these symbols by the United States' founders ultimately produced the most influential national constitution ever written. The symbols embedded in the Constitution keep it a living, flexible document.

HOW SYMBOLS CAN SEPARATE POWERS

The Freemasons of the Lodge of Aberdeen realized that they had stumbled on a great truth of the human condition: symbols change the way people think and act. The Masons worked together to understand what they had discovered. The first thing they did was to display the most important symbols on a floorcloth, so that they could point out these images and sensitize their apprentices to them. Second, the Masons made sure that the message of the symbol was shared between the

Master and his apprentice. They did this by creating and memorizing pieces of ritual poetry that the lodge members recited to the apprentice while he stood gazing at the symbols. Poetic and metaphorical language was used to quiet the left hemisphere, thereby allowing the right hemisphere to respond to the symbol. This is why Freemasons talk about the sincerity and impact they feel after listening to what, at first hearing, seems to be disconnected couplets of poetic and mythical nonsense.

To make sure that such a system worked, the first Freemasons of Aberdeen created a calm atmosphere. They achieved this by giving symbols of office to the men who ran their meetings. As noted earlier, symbols can convey messages that are beyond the scope of words, and these symbols remind everyone of his place, role, and responsibilities within the group.

Each lodge is ruled by a Worshipful Master, and he is assisted by a Senior Warden and a Junior Warden. Each has a role in governing the lodge, and this is marked by a symbol of office and a ritual, metaphorical, and poetic explanation.

The Master's role is to employ and instruct his brethren in Freemasonry. As the sun rises in the east to open and enliven the day, so is the Worshipful Master placed in the east to open the Lodge. The Master wears the symbol of the square.

The square teaches us to regulate our lives and actions according to the Masonic line and rule and to harmonize our conduct in this life to make us acceptable to that Divine Being from whom all goodness springs and to whom we account for all our actions. The square sym-

THE SQUARE

bolizes the importance of adjusting rectangular corners of buildings and the need to bring rude matter into due form; the level symbolizes the importance of laying levels and proving horizontals; and the plumb rule symbolizes the importance of adjusting uprights while fixing them on their proper bases.

The Senior Warden's role is to mark the setting sun. As the sun sets in the west to close the day, so is the Senior Warden placed in the west to close the lodge by his Worshipful Master's command. The Senior Warden wears the symbol of the level.

As an emblem of equality, the level points out the equal measures the Senior Warden is bound to pursue in conjunction with the Worshipful Master in ruling and governing the Lodge. The level demonstrates that we are all sprung from the same stock, partakers of the same nature, and sharers in the same hope. And although distinctions among men are necessary to preserve subordination, no eminence

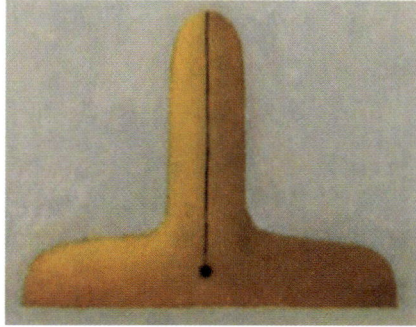

THE LEVEL

of situation should make us forget that we are brothers. He who is placed on the lowest spoke of fortune's wheel is equally entitled to our regard. A time will come, and the wisest of us knows not how soon, when all distinctions, save those of goodness and virtue, shall cease, and death, the grand leveler of all human greatness, will reduce us to the same state.

The Junior Warden's role is to mark the sun at its meridian and to call the brethren from labor to refreshment and from refreshment to labor, that profit and pleasure may be the mutual result. The Junior Warden wears the symbol of the plumb rule.

The plumb rule is an emblem of uprightness and points out the integrity of the measures the Junior Warden is bound to pursue in conjunction with the Worshipful Master and the Senior Warden in governing the lodge. One of the Junior Warden's duties is to examine visitors to prevent an unqualified person from gaining admission to Masonic assemblies and innocently leading the brethren to violate their obligations. The infallible plumb rule, which, like Jacob's ladder, connects Heaven and Earth, is the criterion of rectitude and truth. It teaches us to walk justly and uprightly before God and man, turning neither to the right nor the left from the path of virtue. Likewise, it teaches us not to be an enthusiast, persecutor, or slanderer of religion, neither bending toward avarice, injustice, malice, revenge, nor the envy and contempt of mankind, but giving up every selfish propensity that might injure others. To steer the

THE PLUMB RULE

bark of this life over the seas of passion, without quitting the helm of rectitude, is the highest level of perfection that human nature can attain. And as the builder raises his column by the level and perpendicular, so every Mason should conduct himself toward this world, to observe a due medium between avarice and profusion, to hold the scales of justice with equal poise, to make his passions and prejudices coincide with the just line of his conduct, and, in all his pursuits, to have eternity in view.

HOW MASONIC SYMBOLISTS INFLUENCED JAMES MADISON

Dr. Brent Morris, a historian and physicist, sums up the support that Freemasons gave to the fledgling U.S. republic:

> In addition to the signers of the Declaration of Independence, the Articles of Confederation, and the Constitution, thirty-three general officers of the Continental Army were Freemasons. Benjamin Franklin, Ambassador to France during the American Revolution, had been Deputy Provincial Grand Master of Pennsylvania. Paul Revere, whose "midnight ride" has been immortalized, went on to become Grand Master of Massachusetts. The Americans' cause of freedom attracted supporters for other countries, including two of Washington's general officers: the Marquis de Lafayette and Friedrich W. A. von Steuben. The "father of the American Navy," Admiral John Paul Jones, was a craftsman, as was, alas, General Benedict Arnold, the traitor.[2]

The idea of checks and balances is always associated with James Madison, the fourth president of the United States, who was not a Freemason. As Professor J. C. Stagg, the editor-in-chief of the *Papers of James Madison Project* and professor of history at the University of Virginia says:

> Madison led the Virginia delegation to the Philadelphia meeting, which began on May 14, 1787, and supported the cry for General Washington to chair the meeting. Madison's "Virginia Plan" became the blueprint for the constitution that finally emerged, eventually earning him the revered title, "Father of the Constitution." Having

fathered the document, Madison worked hard to ensure its ratification. Along with Alexander Hamilton and John Jay, he published the Federalist Papers, a series of articles arguing for a strong central government subject to an extensive system of checks and balances.[3]

Madison's inspiration for the system of checks and balances is often reported to have come from Charles Montesquieu, a French political theorist, and John Jay, who worked with him on the Federalist Papers and went on to become the first chief justice of the United States. Although Madison was not a Freemason, both Montesquieu and Jay were, as was the chairman of the meeting, Bro. George Washington.

Charles de Secondat, Baron de la Brède et de Montesquieu, is said to be the ideological founder of the U.S. Constitution. Montesquieu argued that despotism could be prevented by the separation of the powers of the king and church, as portrayed by the symbol of the two pillars.

Another key thinker about Masonic symbolism who influenced Madison was George Washington. William Pierce, a delegate from Georgia, wrote short character sketches of each of the delegates. This is what he said about Bro. Washington:

> General Washington is well known as the Commander-in-chief of the late American Army. Having conducted these states to independence and peace, he now appears to assist in framing a Government to make the People happy. Like Gustavus Vasa, he may be said to be the deliverer of his Country; like Peter the Great, he appears as the politician and the States-man; and like Cincinnatus he returned to his farm perfectly contented with being only a plain Citizen, after enjoying the highest honor of the Confederacy, and now only seeks for the approbation of his Country-men by being virtuous and useful. The General was conducted to the Chair as President of the Convention by the unanimous voice of its Members. He is in the fifty-second year of his age.[4]

Madison's own writing makes it clear that he had thought through the ideas that had been put forward by Masonic philosophers such as Montesquieu.

Montesquieu's ideas were based on the Masonic symbol of center, which is two pillars standing on either side of a circle.

WHY THREE PILLARS OF STATE UNDERPIN THE U.S. CONSTITUTION

It became the custom in every lodge for the members to elect by ballot a new Master each year at the Feast of St. John. The Master had to be an experienced craftsman and skilled in the knowledge of the symbols and how to teach them. He presided over the lodge by virtue of his possession of peculiar secrets that were not yet within the comprehension of the junior brethren. Today, in speculative lodges,

the Master still passes through a special Ceremony of Installation, during which secrets specific to the Master's role are communicated to him. He must be a Brother who is well qualified by years of service as a member and officer of the lodge, so that he can govern his brethren with wise understanding and sensitivity to the meanings and applications of symbols.

When the new Master and his Junior and Senior Wardens are installed into their positions, each is given a collar bearing the symbolic badge of his office (the square, the level, and the plumb rule, respectively) and also custody of a symbolic pillar. The pillars are known by the names Wisdom, Strength, and Beauty, and each symbolize the responsibilities of each officer.

As each officer is given his symbolic pillar, he is told about its nature and why the governing powers must be split into three.

THE THREEFOLD SPLIT OF POWER TRADITIONALLY FOUND IN MASONIC LODGES, WHICH IS REPRESENTED AS THREE PILLARS IN THIS TRACING BOARD, WOULD PROVIDE INSPIRATION FOR THE FOUNDING FATHER'S THREE BRANCHES OF AMERICAN GOVERNMENT. From the collection of the Chancellor Robert R Livingston Masonic Library of Grand Lodge, New York, N.Y.

Q: Why do three Rule a Lodge?

A: Because there were but three Grand Masters who bore sway at the
   building of the first Temple at Jerusalem, namely, Solomon King of
   Israel, Hiram King of Tyre, and Hiram Abif.

The newly installed Master is given custody of the Pillar of Wisdom. He is
said to represent King Solomon, whose wisdom conceived the idea of building the
temple. The Senior Warden is given custody of the Pillar of Strength. He is said to
represent King Hiram of Tyre, whose strength and careful application of the laws
of geometry built the temple and made it stand firm and true. The Junior Warden is
given custody of the Pillar of Beauty. He is said to represent Hiram Abif, the architect of the temple who made the structure beautiful to behold and who died rather
than reveal and compromise the secret rules that underpinned the way the building
was created.

The ritual explains the role of these symbolic pillars in conducting a Masonic
lodge in a series of questions and answers:

Q: What supports a Freemason's Lodge?

A: Three great pillars.

Q: What are they called?

A: Wisdom, Strength, and Beauty.

Q: Why Wisdom, Strength, and Beauty?

A: Wisdom to contrive, Strength to support, and Beauty to adorn.

Q: Moralize them.

A: Wisdom to conduct us in all our undertakings, Strength to support
   us under all our difficulties, and Beauty to adorn the inward man.

Q: Illustrate them.

A: The Universe is the Temple of the Deity whom we serve; Wisdom,
   Strength and Beauty are about His throne as pillars of His works,
   for His Wisdom is infinite, His Strength omnipotent, and Beauty
   shines through the whole of the creation in symmetry and order.
   The Heavens He has stretched forth as a canopy; the earth He
   has planted as a footstool; He crowns His Temple with Stars as
   with a diadem, and with His hand He extends the power and glory.

The Sun and Moon are messengers of His will, and all His law is concord. The three great pillars supporting a Freemason's Lodge are emblematic of those Divine attributes, and further represent Solomon King of Israel, Hiram, King of Tyre and Hiram Abif.

Q: Why those three great personages?

A: Solomon, King of Israel, for his wisdom in building, completing, and dedicating the Temple at Jerusalem to God's service; Hiram, King of Tyre, for his strength in supporting him with men and materials; and Hiram Abif for his curious and masterly workmanship in beautifying and adorning the same.

Q: As we have no noble Order of Architecture known by the names of Wisdom, Strength, and Beauty, to which do they refer?

A: The three most celebrated, which are the Ionic, Doric, and Corinthian.

A PAINTING BY PAUL ORBAN SHOWING THE 1880 CORNERSTONE-LAYING CEREMONY FOR THE EGYPTIAN OBELISK IN CENTRAL PARK IN NEW YORK CITY. From the collection of the Chancellor Robert R Livingston Masonic Library of Grand Lodge, New York, N.Y.

When James Madison realized the practical limitations of the two-pillar symbol that Washington had used to provide stability to the new republic and that had inspired the political philosophy of Montesquieu, he worked with Bro. John Jay to strengthen it. The threefold split of power that had traditionally been used to govern Masonic lodges since the beginning of the Craft in Aberdeen gave him his answer.

The Pillar of Wisdom would inspire the elected bodies (the Senate and the House of Representatives), so that they would frame the laws with wisdom. The Pillar of Strength would inspire the role of the president and the executive officers, so that they would lead the country for the good of all its people and all its states. The Pillar of Beauty would inspire the Supreme Court, which would not allow the U.S. Constitution to be perverted into the tyranny that had so often befallen earlier methods of government.

As Brent Morris points out:

> There have been over one hundred Justices of the United States
> Supreme Court, at least thirty-four of whom were Masons. (The exact
> number is imprecise because eighteenth-century records are scanty
> and incomplete.) These jurists are the final "line of defense" against
> those who would challenge freedom. Their sworn duty is to preserve
> the Constitution against all enemies, domestic and foreign. It takes
> a special bravery to make unpopular decisions to protect liberty. The
> first Chief Justice, John Jay, was a Mason, as were six others to hold
> that position. John Blair, Jr. and John Marshall were Grand Master of
> Virginia, and Earl Warren was Grand Master of California.[5]

These symbolic powers have stood the test of time and made the U.S. Constitution the living and flexible document it is today.

CHAPTER 9

HOW SYMBOLS AND MANKIND TOOK A GREAT LEAP TOGETHER

MASONS AND THE APOLLO SPACE PROGRAM

From its very beginnings, Freemasonry has been aware of the significance of the symbols of the heavens. The top panel of the Kirkwall scroll, the oldest record of Masonic symbolic teaching, shows the moon and seven planets in its top right-hand corner.

It is no coincidence that the first man on the moon was the son of a Freemason and the second, an active Freemason. The vice president who recommended to President Kennedy to commit the United States to reaching the moon was a Freemason, the administrator of the Apollo Moon Landing Program was a Freemason, and the manager of the Apollo Program Command and Service Modules was a Freemason.

On May 25, 1961, President John F. Kennedy delivered a speech before a joint session of Congress on the subject of urgent national needs. He made a statement that would result in a Masonic symbol traveling to the moon and back:

> With the advice of the Vice President, who is Chairman of the National Space Council, we have examined where we are strong and where we are not, where we may succeed and where we may not. Now it is time to take longer strides—time for a great new American enterprise—time for this nation to take a clearly leading role in space achievement, which in many ways may hold the key to our future on earth. ... I believe that this nation should commit itself to achieving the goal, before this decade is out, of landing a man on the moon and returning him safely to the earth. No single space project in this period will be more impressive to mankind, or more important for the long-range exploration of space; and none will be so difficult or expensive to accomplish. ... In a very real sense, it will not be one man

going to the moon—if we make this judgment affirmatively, it will be an entire nation. For all of us must work to put him there.[1]

John F. Kennedy was not a Freemason and had not undergone any program of sensitization to symbols. But his vice president, Lyndon B. Johnson, was initiated on October 30, 1937, in Johnson City Lodge No. 561 in Johnson City, Texas. Johnson remained an Apprentice, but all Masonic Apprentices are taught about the symbolic importance of the moon. James Edwin Webb, the administrator of the National Aeronautics and Space Administration (NASA) from 1961 to 1968, was a member of University Lodge No. 408 in Chapel Hill, North Carolina. Kenneth S. Kleinknecht, manager of the Apollo Program Command and Service Modules, was a member of Fairview Lodge No. 699 in Fairview, Ohio. Neil Armstrong Sr., the father of Neil Armstrong, the first man on the moon, was an officer of the Grand Lodge of Ohio. Edwin E. "Buzz" Aldrin, the co-pilot of *Apollo 11* and the second man on the moon, is a member of Clear Lake Lodge No. 1417 in Seabrook, Texas.[2] The first moon landing had considerable involvement from Freemasons not because of some Masonic conspiracy but because all Freemasons have been sensitized to a powerful inspirational force associated with the symbol of the moon.

WHY THE MOON IS A POWERFUL SYMBOL

The moon is an important inspirational symbol in Freemasonry and is described by the ritual as one of the three lesser lights that guide the path of a candidate for Masonic truth. (The three great lights are the square, the compasses, and the Volume of the Sacred Law). The ritual, which was taught to all the Masons involved in the Apollo program, describes the moon as follows:

> **Q:** How are the three lesser lights situated?
>
> **A:** East, South, and West.
>
> **Q:** For what purpose?
>
> **A:** To show the due course of the Sun, which rises in the East, gains its meridian lustre in the South, and sets in the West; likewise to light men to, at, and from labor.
>
> **Q:** Why is there no light in the North?

A: The Sun being then below our horizon, darts no ray of light from that quarter to this our hemisphere.

Q: What do those three lesser lights represent?

A: The Sun, Moon, and Master of the Lodge.

Q: Why the Sun, Moon, and Master?

A: The Sun to rule the day, the Moon to govern the night, and the Master to rule and direct his Lodge.

MORE THAN SIMPLY A SYMBOL OF HOPE IN A WORLD OF DARKNESS, MOONLIGHT PLAYED A ROLE IN MANY LODGES' CEREMONIES—AND STILL DOES. Courtesy of NASA

Q: Why are the Master and officers of a Freemason's Lodge compared to those grand luminaries?

A: As it is by the benign influence of the Sun and Moon that we, as men, are enabled to perform the duties of social life, so it is by the kind care and instruction of the Worshipful Master and his officers, that we, as Masons, are enabled to perform those duties the Craft requires of us.

But there is much more to the symbolic teaching given to an Entered Apprentice about the heavens. Here are the ritual myths that are recited while images of the moon are displayed on the walls of the temple and on various tracing boards or floorcloths (such as the Kirkwall scroll). The ritual says:

The Universe is the Temple of the Deity whom we serve; Wisdom, Strength and Beauty are about His throne as pillars of His works, for His Wisdom is infinite, His Strength omnipotent, and Beauty shines through the whole of the creation in symmetry and order. The Heavens He has stretched forth as a canopy; the earth He has planted as a footstool; He crowns His Temple with Stars as with a diadem, and with his hand He extends the power and glory. The Sun and Moon are messengers of His will, and all His law is concord. The Sun and Moon

were created one to rule the day, and the other to govern the night.
They were ordained for signs and for seasons, for days and years.
Besides the Sun and Moon, the Almighty was pleased to bespangle the
ethereal concave with a multitude of Stars, that man might contemplate thereon, and justly admire the majesty and glory of His creator.

The moon the law of nature does display, reflecting but a faint and glimmering
ray. Faith, that aspiration toward the infinite, was represented by the sun; hope by
the moon, and charity by the bright morning star.

Freemasonry teaches that the moon is a source of hope in a world of darkness.
When the sun sets and the awful hour of disappearing light saps our strength, we
can rely on the moon to reflect the light of truth into our darkest hours. The moon
was more than just a symbol of hope amid a dark world to early Freemasons. In the
days before streetlights and public transportation, many lodges met by the light of
the full moon, because it made traveling from lodge to home easier. Some lodges,
such as the Yorkshire Lodge of the Three Graces, still meet on the evening of the
full moon. They are known as moon lodges. Some lodges went further and carried
the symbolic involvement with moonlight as far as having an aperture in the roof
of the temple to allow the light of the full moon to shine into the ceremonies. The
ritual speaks of the importance of meeting by moonlight:

Our ancient brethren met always at night, when the moon was full;
and the more perfectly to remain unknown, allowed no light but hers.

Even in the modern days of electric lighting, some old Yorkshire moon lodges
still insist on illuminating the three-degree ceremony with moonlight.

The ritual draws poetic attention to the need to let the symbols speak to the
heart. It does not try to explain but speaks in allegory, saying:

Listen and learn. Interpret our symbols for yourself. In every rough ashlar of marble is hidden the perfect cube. One is the symbol, the other
its meaning. The sun and moon in our lodges are the truth, and the
reflection of the truth in doctrine. Allegory, the mother of all dogmas,

is the substitution of the impression for the seal, of the shadow for the reality. It is the falsehood of the truth, and the truth of the falsehood.

And of course, the Greek name for the sun was *Apollo*. This name was also chosen for NASA's project to land men on the moon.

HOW SYMBOLS ASSISTED PROJECT APOLLO

The name *Apollo* and the role of the symbol of the sun have a long and distinguished history within Freemasonry. The symbol of the sun appears on the top left of the Kirkwall scroll.

The ritual that is recited while this symbol is displayed clearly links the symbol of the sun with the symbol Delta (Δ, depicting the sun above being formed of two interlaced deltas) and with the symbol of the moon. It says:

> The Delta is emblematic of the Sun, Moon, and Stars, in this sense: Those in the highest sphere of life have the largest province wherein to do good, but those of an inferior degree will be as eminently distinguished if they move regularly and prove useful members of society. The highest is he who performs his part best, not he who fills the most exalted position: for the Moon, although reflecting her light from the Sun, evidently sets forth the glory of The Great Architect; and the flowers of the field declare His power equally with the Stars of the firmament.

The name *Apollo* is significant in another sense, as well. The oldest university lodge in the world was established at Oxford University in 1818, and it took the symbolic name of the sun god: Apollo. The crest of the lodge shows the sun god in a suitably Masonic pose.

Tom Wolfe, writing in the *New York Times* in 2009, pointed out that the United States' real motive in pursuing the Apollo project was fear of the Soviet Union's supremacy in rocket science. But the appeal of a flight to the moon was exactly the symbolic enterprise that would engage any symbol-sensitized Freemason.

The rockets that had lifted the Soviets' five-ton manned ships into orbit were worth thinking about. They were clearly powerful enough to reach any place on Earth with nuclear warheads. But that wasn't what was on President Kennedy's mind when he summoned NASA's administrator, James Webb ... to the White House in April 1961. The president was in a terrible funk. He kept muttering: "If somebody can just tell me how to catch up. Let's find somebody—anybody. ... There's nothing more important." He kept saying, "We've got to catch up." Catching up had become his obsession. He never so much as mentioned the rockets. ... There was no way we could catch up with the Soviets when it came to orbital flights. A better idea would be to announce a crash program on the scale of the Manhattan Project, which had produced the atomic bomb. Only the aim this time would be to put a man on the Moon within the next ten years. Barely a month later Kennedy made his famous oration before Congress: "I believe that this nation should commit itself to achieving the goal, before this decade is out, of landing a man on the Moon and returning him safely to Earth."

Just as scientists Leo Szilard and Albert Einstein had convinced President Franklin D. Roosevelt that the atom bomb was sitting in the Platonic realm waiting to be revealed, so Webb was able to convince Vice President Johnson that the machine to fly to the moon was also a Platonic reality, revealed by Newton's physics, just waiting to be built. If the United States did not build it first, then the Soviets would, and Bro. James Webb was up for the challenge. As NASA's own website says:

> For seven years after President Kennedy's May 25th, 1961, lunar landing announcement, through October 1968, James Webb politicked, coaxed, cajoled, and maneuvered for NASA in Washington. As a long-time Washington insider, he was a master at bureaucratic politics. In the end, through a variety of methods, Administrator Webb built a seamless web of political liaisons that brought continued support for and resources to accomplish the Apollo Moon landing on the schedule President Kennedy had announced.[3]

And a key part of that success was the powerful symbols he drew on to support him.

In this logo are brought together the Delta, the sun (in the name *Apollo*), the moon, the stars, and the spiral path that leads to the throne of the Great Architect. This path provides the route by which the ritual says we may "ascend to that Grand Lodge above [the source of the Platonic perfect forms] where the world's Great Architect lives and reigns forever."

As the Apollo project successfully reached Mission 8, it became clear that the first moon landing could be the mission of Apollo 11. The two ones that make up the figure 11 echo the symbol of the two pillars that were so successful in supporting the fledgling United States on the dollar bill. But the flight badge of the *Apollo 11* mission shows an eagle landing on the moon and bearing in its talons a sprig of acacia, which is the Masonic symbol of eternal life. The significance of this symbol was noted by Tom Wolfe, who is not a Freemason but who wrote:

> The Earth we live on is a planet that is in orbit around the Sun. The Sun itself is a star that is on fire and will someday burn up, leaving our solar system uninhabitable. Therefore we must build a bridge to the

THE NUMERIALS OF THE APOLLO II MISSION ECHO THE TWO PILLARS, AND THE EAGLE IS SHOWN WITH A SPRIG OF ACACIA, THE MASONIC SYMBOL OF ETERNAL LIFE, IN ITS TALONS.

stars, because as far as we know, we are the only sentient creatures in the entire universe. When do we start building that bridge to the stars? We begin as soon as we are able, and this is that time. We must not fail in this obligation. We have to keep alive the only meaningful life we know of.[4]

HOW SYMBOLS HELPED PUT MAN ON THE MOON

In November 1969, *New Age Magazine* (which is now known as the *Scottish Rite Journal*) published a special edition celebrating the success of Project Apollo and praising the Masons involved in its success. Writing in that issue, Bro. Kenneth Kleinknecht, the manager of the Apollo Program Command and Service Modules and also a Project Mercury member of Fairview Lodge No. 699, said:

> Note how many of the astronauts themselves are Brother Masons:
> Edwin E. Aldrin, Jr.; L. Gordon Cooper, Jr.; Donn F. Eisle; Walter M.
> Schirra; Thomas P. Stafford; Edgar D. Mitchell, and Paul J. Weitz.
> Before his tragic death in a flash fire at Cape Kennedy on January 27,
> 1967, Virgil I. "Gus" Grissom was a Mason, too. Astronaut Gordon
> Cooper, during his epochal *Gemini V* spaceflight in August of 1965,
> carried with him an official Thirty-third Degree Jewel and a Scottish
> Rite flag. Via the lunar plaque, the Masonic insignia and flag, and the
> Masonic astronauts themselves—Masonry *already* is in the space age.
> Can we doubt Freemasonry and its spiritual relevance to the modern
> era when even its material representatives have today made historic
> inroads into the infinite expanses of outer space?[5]

But that's not the end of the story. There is a Masonic Grand Lodge that has established jurisdiction over the symbol of the moon.

> On July 20, 1969, two American Astronauts landed on the moon
> of the planet Earth, in an area known as Mare Tranquilitatis, or
> "Sea of Tranquility." One of those brave men was Brother Edwin
> Eugene (Buzz) Aldrin, Jr., a member of Clear Lake Lodge No. 1417,

AF&AM, Seabrook, Texas. Brother Aldrin carried with him the
Special Deputation of then Grand Master J. Guy Smith, constitut-
ing and appointing Brother Aldrin as Special Deputy of the Grand
Master, granting unto him full power in the premises to represent the
Grand Master as such and authorize him to claim Masonic Territorial
Jurisdiction for The Most Worshipful Grand Lodge of Texas, Ancient
Free and Accepted Masons, on The Moon, and directed that he
make due return of his acts. Brother Aldrin certified that the Special
Deputation was carried by him to the Moon on July 20, 1969.[6]

Bro. Aldrin carried a Masonic flag to the moon. The flag is now in the Museum
of the Supreme Council Scottish Rite in Washington, DC. Here is a photograph of
it showing a sprig of acacia within the circle to the left of the symbol of the eagle:

THIS IS THE MASONIC FLAG WHICH BRO. BUZZ ALDRIN CARRIED TO THE MOON AND BACK TO SET UP THE MOON
AS A MASONIC PROVINCE OF THE GRAND LODGE OF TEXAS. NOTICE, AGAIN, THE EAGLE AND THE SPRIG OF
ACACIA SYMBOLS.

On the basis of this symbolic authority, the Grand Lodge of Texas has since warranted a new lodge that is authorized to hold Masonic meetings and teach the philosophy and symbology of Freemasonry on the moon. Here is the statement made on the lodge's website:

> Tranquility Lodge 2000 is based in Texas under auspices of The Grand Lodge of Texas until such time as the Lodge may hold its meetings on the Moon. Our meetings are held quarterly at various cities in Texas, with the annual meeting being held in Waco each July.
>
> Providing support and assistance to Masonic Organizations and to other worthy organizations who help make life better for all living on the Earth requires the support of all worthy Freemasons around the World. Your Membership in Tranquility Lodge 2000 helps in providing that assistance while offering Fraternal Brotherhood with Good Men of like mind.[7]

From the stonemasons of Aberdeen to the rocket scientists at NASA, the teaching and symbols of Freemasonry remain the same. Each Brother knows that Freemasonry is a peculiar system of morality, veiled in allegory and illustrated by symbols.

PART TWO

A PRACTICAL INTRODUCTION TO MASONIC SYMBOLOGY

THIS SECTION PROVIDES AN OVERVIEW OF THE ancient Masonic teaching about symbology. The method of teaching is to reveal the symbol as part of the lodge decoration, by wearing it as badge or token, or by drawing it on a tracing board. As the Masonic Candidate is shown the symbol, ritual statements are made about it that help him understand its purpose and become sensitized to its emotional power.

The aim of this part of the book is to illustrate the symbols alongside the ritual statements, as they have traditionally been taught to Freemasons for the last 500 years. The ritual poetry that sensitizes each candidate to the power of the symbol follows each image.

For each symbol, I have also added a personal view on how I interpret it. I do not intend this viewpoint to be a prescription for others as they consider the meaning of the symbol. As I have emphasized throughout this book, capturing the full significance of the symbols using words is difficult. The box labeled "Robert Lomas's Personal View" that appears at the end of each ritual definition should be considered a general description of how the symbol speaks to me. The symbol may have a different meaning for you. Neither of us is right or wrong.

SYMBOLS OF THE FIRST DEGREE

W HEN EACH SYMBOL IS INTRODUCED TO A NEW FREEMASON, A series of poetic ritual statements are made about its purpose and function so that the Brother may learn how to apply the emotional importance of the symbol to his own soul. The Brother memorizes and repeats the ritual description of the symbol as he looks at the image. Often the recitation takes place as a formal series of ritual questions and answers. I have omitted the prompting questions.

The Square

The square is used to adjust rectangular corners of building and to assist in bringing rude matter into due form. It teaches us to regulate our lives and actions according to the Masonic line and rule and to harmonize our conduct in this life so as to be acceptable to the Divine Being, from whom all goodness springs and to whom we must be accountable for all our actions.

With the assistance of the square, rude matter is brought into due form. Using the square, the brethren are able to resolve any animosities that may arise among them, so that the business of Masonry may be conducted with harmony and decorum.

Thus, the square teaches morality and how to regulate our actions.

A COMPOSITE METAL SQUARE DECORATED WITH THREE ROWS OF RHINESTONES AND ATTACHED TO A MASTER'S COLLAR FROM FRANCE. From the collection of the Chancellor Robert R Livingston Masonic Library of Grand Lodge, New York, N.Y.

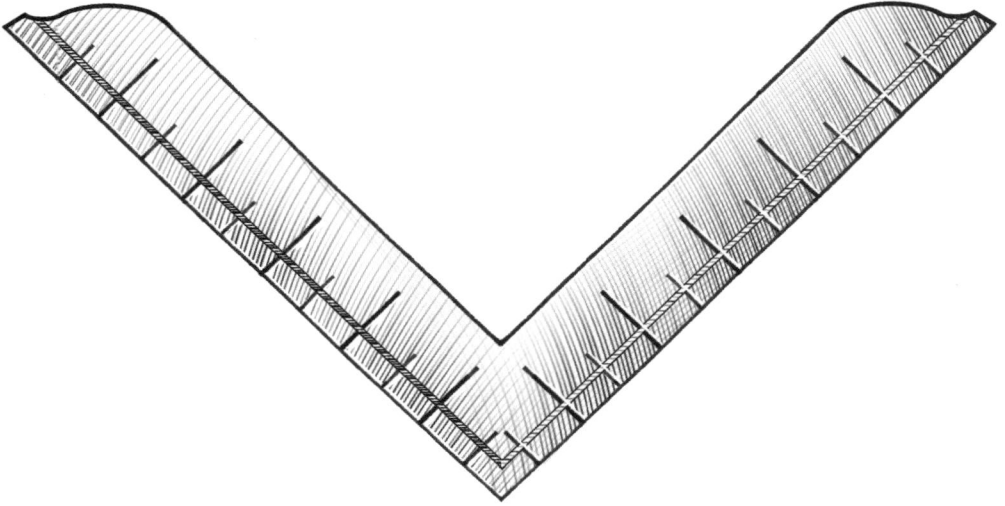

Robert Lomas's personal view

THE SQUARE IS A SYMBOL THAT MEASURES THE ACCURACY OF A RIGHT ANGLE. TWO SQUARES MAKE UP A TRIANGLE, AND FOUR SQUARES FORM THE ANGLE SUBSUMED BY THE CENTER OF A CIRCLE. THE SQUARE IS ONE OF THE PERFECT PLATONIC SHAPES AND CAN BE MADE USING STICKS OF THREE, FOUR, OR FIVE UNITS IN LENGTH. SUCH A TRIANGLE ALWAYS FORMS A RIGHT ANGLE.

THE TASK OF THE MASON IS TO SHAPE THE ROUGH-HEWN STONE OF HIS SOUL INTO A SMOOTH AND PERFECT CUBE. THE CUBE IS THE THREE-DIMENSIONAL REPRESENTATION OF THE SOUL IN ALL ITS ASPECTS. THESE ASPECTS ARE SYMBOLIZED BY THE FOUR SQUARES AT THE CENTER OF A CIRCLE AND COMPRISE THE EMOTIONS, THE INTELLECT, THE SPIRIT, AND THE SOUL OF THE MASTER MASON. TOGETHER, ALL FORM THE FOURTH PART OF THE COMPLETE CIRCLE OF THE COMPLETE MASON.

THE CRAFT SQUARE IS AN APPROXIMATION OF A TRIANGLE WITH ITS APEX DOWN AND ITS BASE UPWARD. THIS TRIANGLE IS AN ANCIENT SYMBOL OF THE MIND OR INTELLECT OF MAN AND IS KNOWN AS THE WATER TRIANGLE.

The Level

The level is used to lay levels and prove horizontals. It demonstrates that we have all sprung from the same stock, partake of the same nature, and share in the same hope. Although distinctions among men are necessary to preserve subordination, no eminence of situation should make us forget that we are brothers. He who is placed on the lowest spoke of Fortune's wheel is equally entitled to our regard. A time will come (and not even the wisest of us knows how soon) when all distinctions—save those of goodness and virtue—shall cease, and Death, the grand leveler of all human greatness, will reduce us to the same state.

The level, as an emblem of equality, points out the equal measures the Senior Warden is bound to pursue in conjunction with the Master in ruling and governing the lodge.

The level teaches equality.

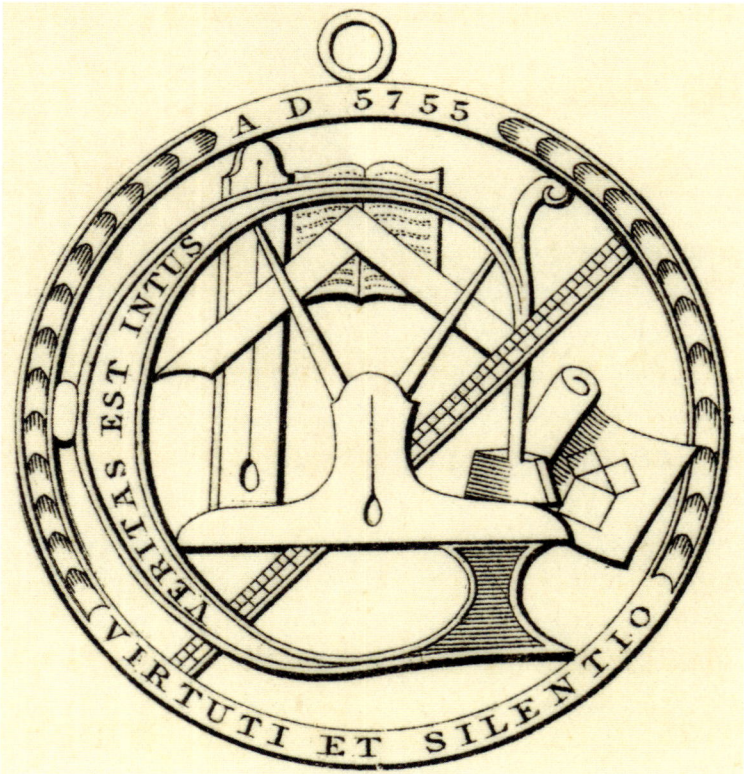

MASONIC SEAL, FROM "THE HISTORY OF FREEMASONRY, VOLUME III," PUBLISHED BY THOMAS C. JACK, LONDON, 1883/PRIVATE COLLECTION/KEN WELSH/THE BRIDGEMAN ART LIBRARY INTERNATIONAL

Robert Lomas's personal view

THE LEVEL IS A WORKING TOOL THAT IS GIVEN TO THE MASON TO HELP BRING INTO BALANCE AND EQUALITY OF APPLICATION THE SENSES, THE EMOTIONS, AND THE MIND, SO THAT THEY ALL PLAY AN EQUAL PART IN THE INTERACTION OF THE SOUL WITH THE MYSTERY OF THE CENTER. THE FLOOR OF THE LODGE, AS SHOWN IN THE FIRST-DEGREE TRACING BOARD, IS A LEVEL EXPANSE OF ALTERNATING BLACK AND WHITE SQUARES. THESE SQUARES REPRESENT THE GOOD AND THE BAD EXPERIENCES WE HAVE IN OUR DAILY LIVES.

OUR TASK, IF WE ARE TO LEARN WISDOM, IS TO RISE ABOVE THIS DUALISM. WE MUST RE-ADJUST OUR CONSCIOUSNESS TO A LEVEL OF OUTLOOK THAT SEES BEYOND THEM. WE MUST ALSO LEARN TO MASTER OUR LOWER NATURE AND BODILY TENDENCIES TO STAND DETACHED FROM THE IN-EVITABLE FLUCTUATIONS OF FORTUNE AND EMOTION TO WHICH THEY ARE SUBJECT AND TO REGARD LIFE'S UPS AND DOWNS, WHITES AND BLACKS, AS BEING OF EQUAL EDUCATIONAL VALUE TO US.

The Plumb Rule

The plumb rule is used to adjust uprights while fixing them on their proper bases. The infallible plumb rule—which, like Jacob's ladder, connects Heaven and Earth—is the criterion of rectitude and truth. It teaches us to walk justly and uprightly before God and man, turning neither to the right nor the left from the path of virtue. Moreover, using the plumb rule teaches us not to be an enthusiast, persecutor, or slanderer of religion, neither bending toward avarice, injustice, malice, revenge nor the envy and contempt of mankind but giving up every selfish propensity that might injure others. To steer the bark of this life over the seas of passion, without quitting the helm of rectitude, is the highest level of perfection that human nature can attain. And as the builder raises his column by the level and perpendicular, so should every Mason conduct himself toward this world, to observe a due medium between avarice and profusion, to hold the scales of justice with equal poise, to make his passions and prejudices coincide with the just line of his conduct, and to have eternity in view in all his pursuits.

The plumb rule teaches the justness and uprightness of life and actions.

All squares, levels, and perpendiculars are true and proper signs by which to know a Mason. You are therefore expected to stand perfectly erect, your feet formed in a square, and your body thus considered an emblem of your mind.

The square, level, and plumb rule are called "movable jewels" because they are worn by the Master and his Wardens and transferable to their successors on nights of Installation.

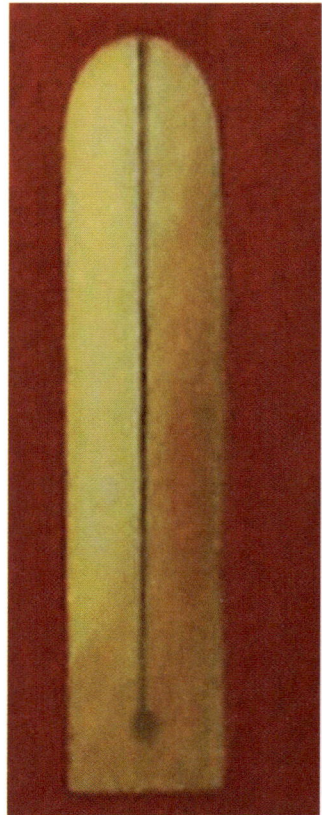

PLUMB RULE TAKEN FROM A MODERN INTERPRETATION OF THE SECOND-DEGREE TRACING BOARD. Copyright Angel Millar. Reprinted with permission

Robert Lomas's personal view

THE PLUMB RULE IS A SYMBOL OF THE SILVER CORD THAT EXTENDS FROM THE MYSTICAL CENTER TO THE SOUL OF THE INDIVIDUAL MASON. THE PLUMB RULE ALWAYS FORMS A RIGHT ANGLE WITH THE LEVEL CHORD TO THE CIRCUMFERENCE, WHERE THE BRETHREN DWELL IN DARKNESS AS THEY AWAIT THE RISING OF THE BRIGHT MORNING STAR AND THE COMING OF THE LIGHT OF WISDOM. THE PLUMB RULE PROVIDES THE MEANS BY WHICH A MASON CAN DETERMINE THE DIRECTION OF THE CENTER, EVEN AS ITS MYSTERY REMAINS AS DARKNESS VISIBLE.

The Altar

The altar is a double cube formed from a rough ashlar into a perfect six-sided form. The altar is a symbol of how your mind will be when made perfect in all its parts. The concealed underside resting on the earth stands for the hidden, submerged depths of your subconscious. The four sides facing the four quarters of the lodge signify your elementary human nature brought into a balance as a harmonious four-square foundation stone for a spiritual building.

A SILK APRON WITH SILK FRINGE AND PAINTED SYMBOLS. From the collection of the Chancellor Robert R Livingston Masonic Library of Grand Lodge, New York, N.Y.

The upper side of the altar is exposed to the light of the bright morning star. On its surface rest the three great lights of Masonry. This is the reverse of the concealed underside and represents the consciousness of a purified personality turning away from mundane interests and facing toward the source of light. From the altar, a ladder of innumerable steps leads to the firmament and then to infinity.

You must be an altar made from Earth—the builder of it, the offering upon it, the priest who serves it. And then you must ascend the great spiritual ladder to achieve union with the center beyond the heavens.

Robert Lomas's personal view

THE ALTAR REPRESENTS THE MASON'S PERSONALITY WHEN IT HAS BEEN MADE PERFECT IN ALL ITS PARTS. THE ALTAR IS A DOUBLE CUBE WITH A SIX-SIDED FORM. ITS CONCEALED UNDERSIDE STANDS FOR THE HIDDEN, SUBMERGED DEPTHS OF THE UNCONSCIOUS MIND. THE FOUR SIDES FACING THE QUARTERS OF THE LODGE SYMBOLIZE THE HUMAN SOUL WHEN IT HAS BEEN MOLDED INTO A BALANCED, HARMONIOUS FOUR-SQUARE FOUNDATION FOR LOFTIER WORK. ON THE EXPOSED UPPER SIDE REST THE THREE GREAT EMBLEMATIC LIGHTS. THE ALTAR REPRESENTS THE CONSCIOUSNESS OF THE PURIFIED PERSONALITY TURNED TOWARD THE HEIGHTS IN ASPIRATION FOR UNION WITH THE SOURCE OF LIGHT.

The Volume of the Sacred Law

Your first and most serious contemplation should be of the Volume of the Sacred Law (VSL). Consider it as the unerring standard of truth and justice, and regulate your actions by the divine precepts it contains. Upon considering it, you will be taught the important duties you owe to God, to your neighbor, and to yourself:

- To God, by never mentioning his name without the awe and reverence that are due from the creature to his creator; by imploring his aid on all your lawful undertakings; and by looking to him in every emergency for comfort and support

- To your neighbor, by acting with him upon the square, by rendering him every kind of office that justice or mercy may require, by relieving his distresses and soothing his afflictions, and by doing to him as, in similar cases, you would wish he should do to you

- And to yourself, by such prudent and well-regulated course of discipline that may best contribute to the preservation of your corporeal and mental faculties in their fullest energy, thereby enabling you to exert the talents with which God has blessed you, as well as to his glory as to the welfare of your fellow creatures

THE VOLUME OF THE SACRED LAW REPRESENTS THE MASON'S OWN VIEW OF THE ORDER OF THE UNIVERSE. Copyright and reproduced by permission of The Library and Museum of Freemasonry, London and Painton Cowen

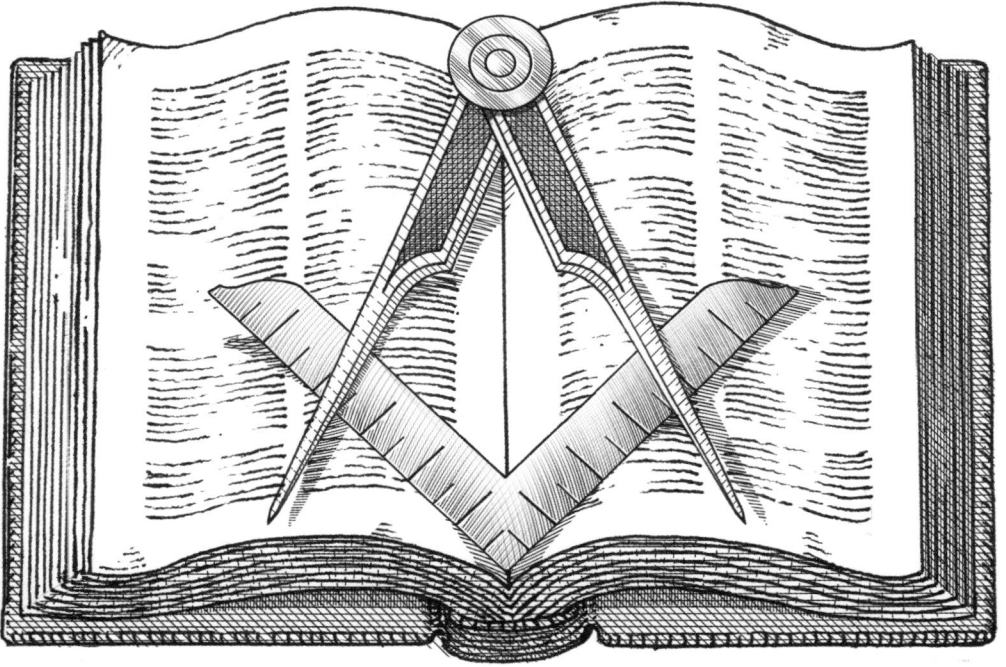

Robert Lomas's personal view

THE VSL REPRESENTS THE MASON'S OWN VIEW OF THE ORDER THAT UNDERLIES THE NATURE OF
THE UNIVERSE. THE ACTUAL VOLUME CONSIDERED TO HOLD THIS TRUTH WILL VARY ACCORDING
TO THE BELIEFS OF THE INDIVIDUAL MASON. SYMBOLICALLY, AS THE VSL IS OPENED, A CHRISTIAN
SEES IT AS THE BIBLE, A JEW SEES IT AS THE TORAH, A MOSLEM SEES SIT AS THE KORAN, AND A
PHYSICIST SEES IT AS THE *PRINCIPICIA MATHEMATICA*. SOMETIMES, A BROTHER WILL ASK FOR HIS
PARTICULAR VOLUME TO BE OPENED ALONGSIDE A LODGE BIBLE. MORE OFTEN, THE INDIVIDUAL
VIEWS THE PARTICULAR BOOK THAT IS OPENED AS A SYMBOL OF THE INNER TRUTH CONTAINED
IN HIS OWN VOLUME. THE WRITTEN WORD IS THE EMBLEM AND EXTERNAL EXPRESSION OF THE
UNWRITTEN ETERNAL WORD, THE LOGOS OR SUBSTANTIAL WISDOM OUT OF WHICH EVERY LIVING
SOUL HAS EMANATED AND THAT IS, THEREFORE, THE GROUND OR BASE OF HUMAN LIFE.

The Compasses

The compasses are to keep us in due bounds with all humankind, particularly our brethren in Freemasonry. The compasses belong to the Master, in particular, as the chief instrument used in forming architectural plans and designs. This symbol is peculiarly appropriate to the Master as an emblem of his dignity, as he is the chief, head, and governor of the lodge.

The compasses and square, when united, regulate our lives and actions.

THE POINTS OF THE COMPASSES SYMBOLICALLY TRACK CANDIDATE'S PROGRESS. Copyright and reproduced by permission of the Library and Museum of Freemasonry, London and Painton Cowen

Robert Lomas's personal view

THE COMPASSES ARE A SYMBOL OF THE FUNCTIONAL ENERGY OF THE SPIRIT. THIS FIERY ENERGY IS THE SPIRIT OF A MASON—A GOOD OR EVIL FORCE, ACCORDING TO HOW IT IS SHAPED. IT IS SHOWN AS THE SHAPE CALLED THE *FIRE TRIANGLE* (A TRIANGLE WITH IS APEX UPWARD AND BASE DOWNWARD), WHICH IS HOW THE COMPASSES ARE PLACED WHEN THE LODGE IS OPEN. THERE IS AN INTERACTION BETWEEN THE SQUARE AND COMPASSES.

IN THE FIRST DEGREE, THE POINTS OF THE COMPASSES ARE HIDDEN BY THE SQUARE. IN THE SECOND DEGREE, ONE POINT IS SHOWN. IN THE THIRD, BOTH ARE EXHIBITED. THE IMPLICATION IS THAT AS THE CANDIDATE PROGRESSES, THE INERTIA AND NEGATIVITY OF HIS SOUL BECOME INCREASINGLY TRANSMUTED AND SUPERSEDED BY THE POSITIVE ENERGY AND ACTIVITY OF THE SPIRIT. THE FIRE TRIANGLE GRADUALLY PREVAILS OVER THE WATER TRIANGLE, SIGNIFYING THAT THE DEVELOPING MASON IS BECOMING A MORE VIVIDLY LIVING AND SPIRITUALLY CONSCIOUS BEING.

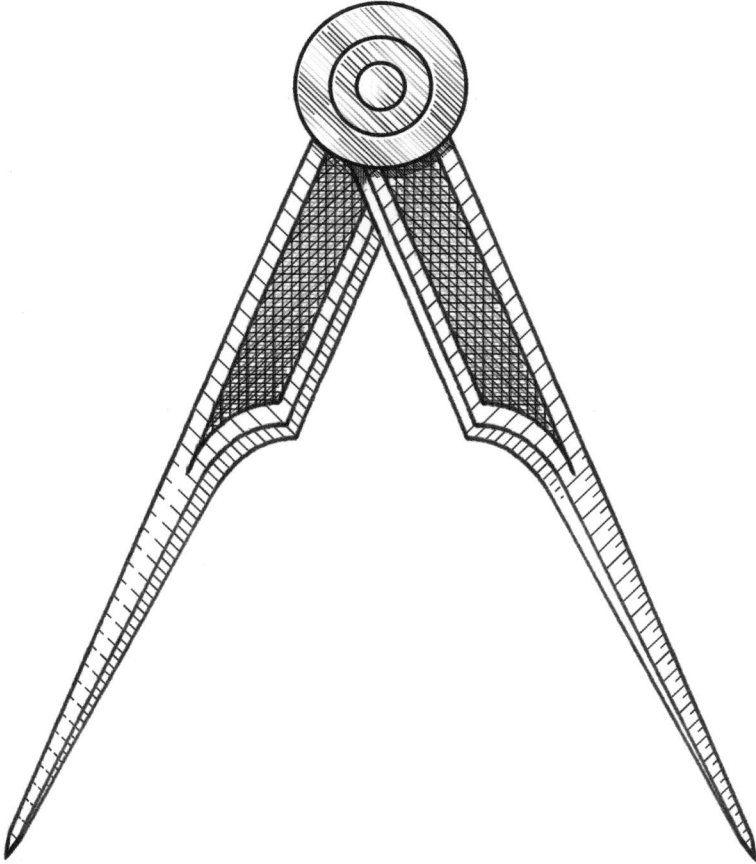

The Sun

The sun is to rule the day. Masonic lodges are situated due east and west, because the sun, the glory of the Lord, rises in the East and sets in the West. All places of divine worship—as well as Masons' regular, well-formed, constituted lodges—are or should be so situated.

The sun rises in the East, gains its meridian luster in the South, and sets in the West. Likewise, the brethren labor with this pattern of the light. The sun enlightens the earth, and by its benign influence, it dispenses its blessings to humankind in general.

The sun's white light is invisible until it passes through a prism, which decomposes it into seven constituent colors, three of which are primary. When the spiritual light of the center falls on the prism of the human spirit, its sevenfold properties begin to manifest, and of these, three are primary. Masonry calls them *wisdom*, *strength*, and *beauty*.

As the sacred laws are the center of the whole universe and control it, so the sun is the center and lifegiver of the solar system. As such, the sun controls and feeds the planets circling around it, just as a vital, immortal principle exists at the secret center of an individual human life: the soul.

A FREEMASON FORGED THROUGH THE TOOLS OF HIS LODGE, 1754 (COLORED ENGRAVING), ENGLISH SCHOOL/ BIBLIOTHEQUE NATIONALE, PARIS, FRANCE/ARCHIVES CHARMET /THE BRIDGEMAN ART LIBRARY INTERNATIONAL

Robert Lomas's personal view

THE MASONIC SUN SYMBOLIZES THE MASON'S SOUL—THAT LARGE SPIRITUAL AREA IN EACH OF US THAT IS NOT SUBJECT TO TIME AND SPACE BUT LIVES IN THE DAYLIGHT BEYOND THE DARK PRISON OF THE MUNDANE PERSONALITY. THE DEATHLESS SOUL IS THE PERMANENT, INCORRUPTIBLE PRINCIPLE IN EVERY HUMAN BEING. THE SOLAR BODY ENDURES BUT THE PRESENT CHARACTER. EACH OF OUR DOMINANT TENDENCIES IS THE NET PRODUCT OF ALL OUR FORMER ACTIVITIES. WE ARE TODAY WHAT WE HAVE MADE OURSELVES IN THE PAST, AND WE MAY BE ASSURED THAT OUR FUTURE DESTINY IS BEING MOLDED BY OUR PRESENT CONDUCT AND THOUGHT.

The Moon and the Stars

The moon is to rule the night. The universe is the temple of the deity whom we serve. The heavens, God has stretched forth as a canopy; the earth, he has planted as a footstool. He crowns his temple with stars as with a diadem, and with his hand, he extends the power and glory. The sun and the moon are messengers of God's will, and all his law is concord.

The moon is a satellite moving with and illumining the earth. So in us, the reasoning mind is a satellite moving with and enlightening the body, but it has no light in itself and shines only by reflection from the superior solar luminary.

Those two grand luminaries, the sun and moon, were created to rule the day and to govern the night, respectively. They were ordained for signs and for seasons, for days and for years.

Besides the sun and moon, the Great Architect was pleased to bespangle the ethereal concave with a multitude of stars, on which man, whom God intended to make, might contemplate and justly admire the majesty and glory of his creator.

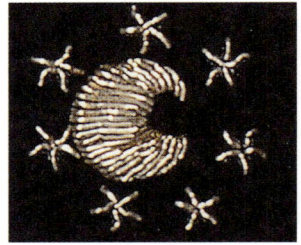

THE LIGHT CAST BY THE MOON AND THE STARS IS OF GREAT SIGNIFICANCE. Copyright and reproduced by permission of the Library and Museum of Freemasonry, London and Painton Cowen

Robert Lomas's personal view

THE MOON, SURROUNDED BY THE STARS, SYMBOLIZES THE NATURAL REASON OR LOWER CARNAL MIND THAT HUMANS SHARE WITH ALL INTELLIGENT CREATURES. IT SYMBOLIZES OUR REASONING OR INTELLECTUAL FACULTIES, AND JUST AS THE MOON REFLECTS THE LIGHT OF THE SUN, IT SHOULD REFLECT THE LIGHT COMING FROM THE HIGHER SPIRITUAL FACULTY AND TRANSMIT IT INTO OUR DAILY ACTIONS. IN THE PERSONAL HEAVENS OF A MASON, METAPHYSICAL FORCES ARE AT WORK. IN EACH OF OUR MAKEUP, THERE EXISTS A FIELD OF VARIOUS FORCES THAT DETERMINES OUR INDIVIDUAL TEMPERAMENTS AND TENDENCIES AND THUS INFLUENCES OUR FUTURE. TO THOSE FORCES HAVE ALSO BEEN GIVEN THE NAMES SUN, MOON, AND PLANETS. MOREOVER, THE SCIENCE OF THEIR INTERACTION AND OUTWORKING WAS THE ANCIENT SCIENCE OF ASTROLOGY, WHICH IS ONE OF THE LIBERAL ARTS AND SCIENCES RECOMMENDED FOR STUDY BY EVERY MASON AND THE PURSUIT OF WHICH BELONGS IN PARTICULAR TO THE STAGE OF A FELLOW OF THE CRAFT.

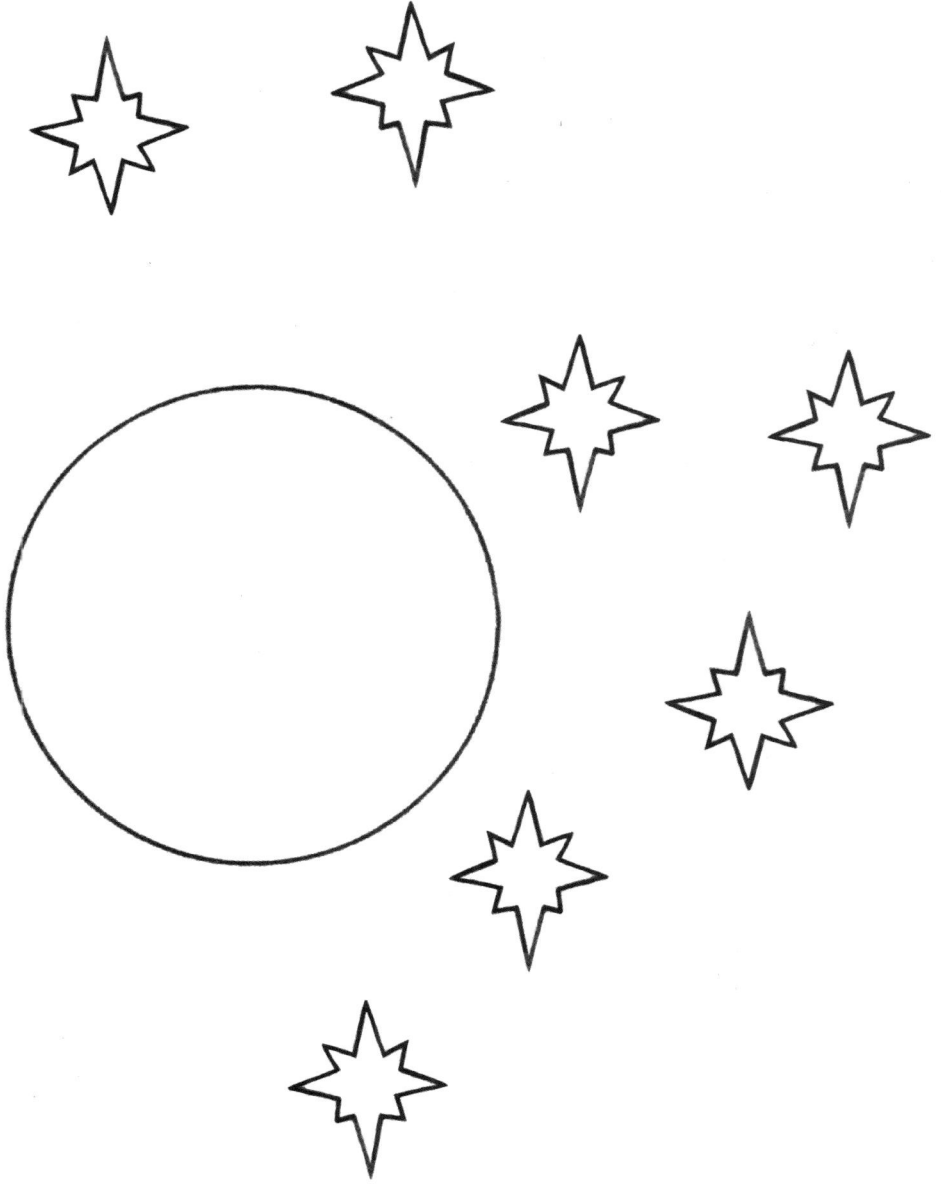

The Northeast Corner

In the erection of all stately and superb edifices, it is customary to lay the first, or foundation, stone in the northeast corner of the building. You, being newly admitted into Freemasonry, are placed in the northeast corner of the lodge to represent that stone, and from the foundation laid during Installation, you may raise a superstructure that is perfect in all its parts and honorable to the builder.

ARTIST PETER WADELL'S "THE AGE OF REASON MADE MANIFEST," SHOWING MASONIC SYMBOLISM IN THE MAP OF DC, AT THE FREEMASON PAINTING EXHIBIT AT THE HEXAGON. Photo by Chris Maddaloni/Roll Call/Getty Images

Robert Lomas's personal view

THE SUN IS IN THE NORTHEAST CORNER OF THE TRACING BOARD. LIKEWISE, IT IS IN THE NORTH-EAST CORNER OF THE LODGE THAT THE NEW MASON IS PLACED AS A FOUNDATION AND ENJOINED TO BUILD A PERFECT SUPERSTRUCTURE. THE SOUL, OR SOLAR BODY, IS THE SUPERSTRUCTURE RE-FERRED TO, AND IT IS BUILT UP FROM OUR PERSONALITY IN THE PHYSICAL WORLD, WHICH SERVES AS ITS FOUNDATION STONE. WHATEVER WE DO OR THINK USING OUR PHYSICAL BODY BUILDS SOMETHING FRESH INTO OUR SOUL, EITHER STRENGTHENING OR WEAKENING IT, CLARIFYING OR CLOUDING IT. SO A MASON ASPIRES THAT ALL HIS THOUGHTS, WORDS, AND ACTIONS MAY ASCEND PURE AND UNPOLLUTED INTO HIS SOLAR BODY, SINCE THAT IS THE PERMANENT RECEPTACLE IN WHICH ALL OUR ACTIVITIES ARE GATHERED UP AND PRESERVED.

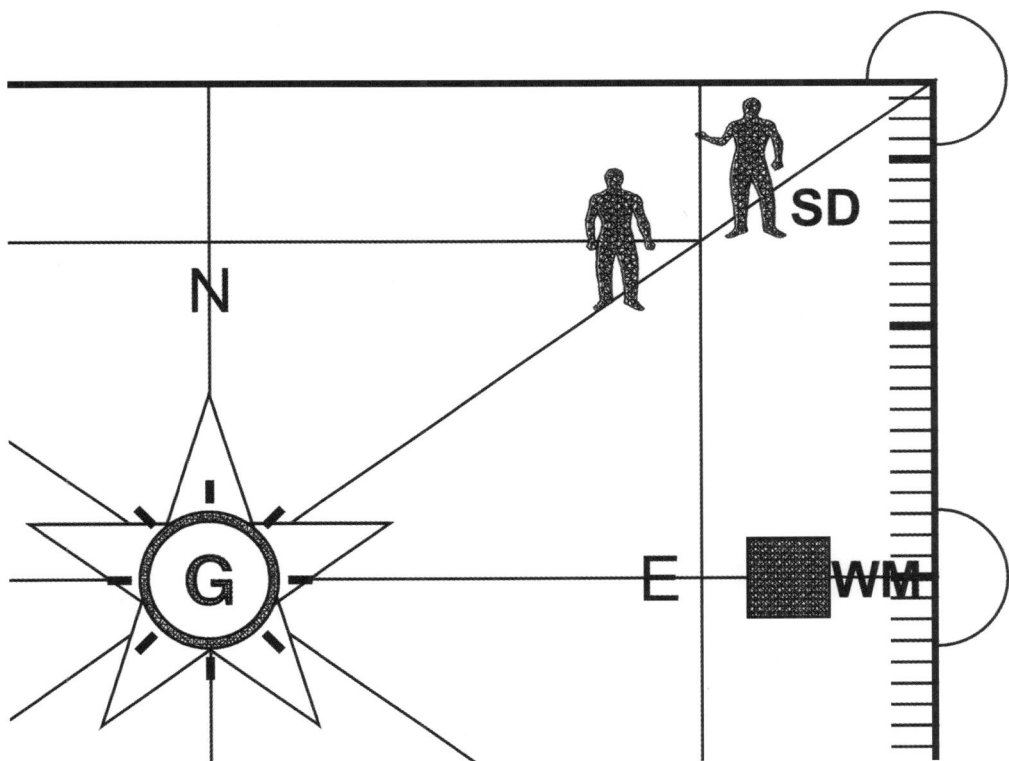

The Glory at the Center

When our ancient brethren were in the middle chamber of the temple, their attention was peculiarly drawn to certain Hebrew characters that are now depicted in a Fellow of the Craft's lodge by the letter G in the center of a blazing star. The letter G denotes God, the Grand Geometrician of the Universe, to whom we must all submit and whom we should all humbly adore.

Let us remember, wherever we are and whatever we do, that God is with us. His all-seeing eye ever beholds us, and while we continue to act as faithful Fellows of the Craft, may we never forget to serve him with fervency and zeal.

A GRAND MASTER'S JEWEL THAT WAS SCULPTED BY BRO. GUTZON BORGLUM, WHO ALSO MADE MOUNT RUSHMORE. From the collection of the Chancellor Robert R Livingston Masonic Library of Grand Lodge, New York, N.Y.

Robert Lomas's personal view

IN THE FIRST-DEGREE TRACING BOARD, THE CHECKERED PAVEMENT AND THE FIRMAMENT REPRESENT A MASON'S PHYSICAL AND MENTAL FACULTIES, BUT IN THE EAST, THERE IS A SYMBOL THAT TRANSCENDS BOTH. IT IS THE SPIRITUAL ESSENCE THAT IS THE ULTIMATE ROOT OF A MASON'S BEING AND AFFILIATES HIM WITH THE CENTER. THIS ULTIMATE SPIRIT IS BEYOND DESCRIPTION USING WORDS AND LANGUAGE, AS IT HAS NO FORM. IN THE BOARD, IT IS ONLY SUGGESTED AS A BLAZING STAR IN THE EAST AND BY A FORMLESS, BLINDING BRIGHTNESS THAT SUFFUSES THE EAST AND OUTSHINES THE LIGHT OF THE SUN, THE MOON, AND THE STARS, WHICH ARE BUT SUBORDINATE LUMINARIES AND INSTRUMENTS TO ITS SUPREME LIGHT.

THIS CENTER IS THE SUPREME SPIRITUAL ESSENCE IN US. THE GLORY AT THE CENTER IS THE GOAL OF ALL MYSTICAL ATTAINMENT IN MASONRY, COMPRISING THE UNION OF OUR INDIVIDUAL CONSCIOUSNESS WITH THE SHARED CONSCIOUSNESS OF THE UNIVERSE.

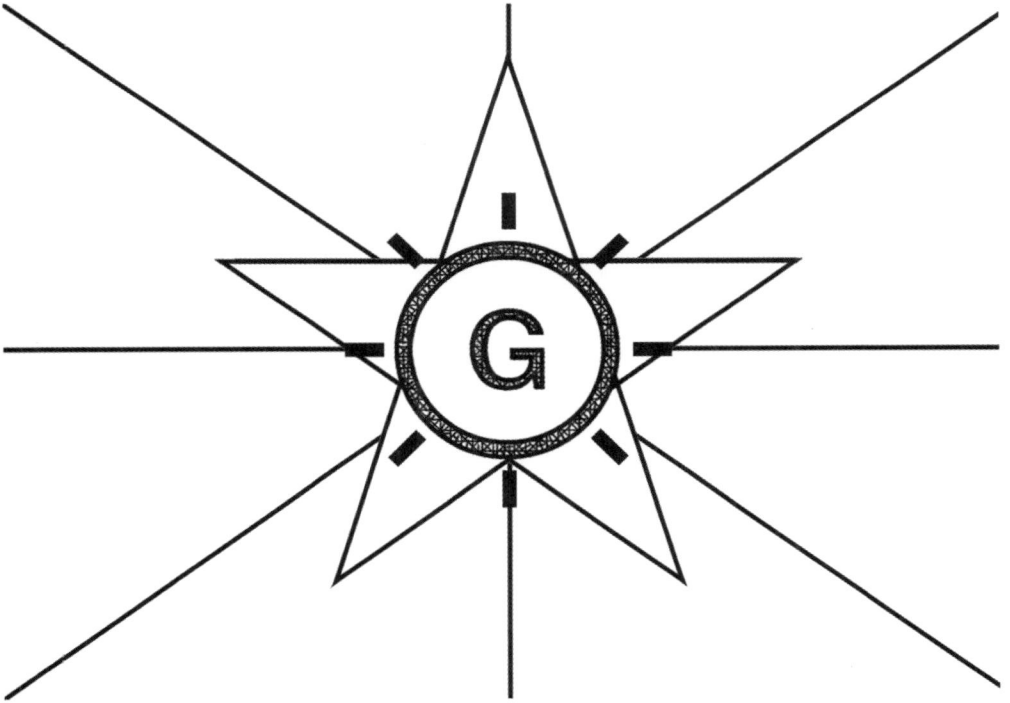

The Left-Hand Pillar

Boaz was the name of the left-hand pillar that stood at the porchway or entrance of King Solomon's temple. It was named after the great-grandfather of David, who was a prince and ruler in Israel, and represents the force of temporal power, as expressed by the rule of the king.

PAINTED LEATHER APRON WITH SILK EDGING AND FABRIC BACKING.
From the collection of the Chancellor Robert R Livingston Masonic Library of Grand Lodge, New York, N.Y.

Robert Lomas's personal view

THE LEFT-HAND PILLAR THAT STOOD BEFORE SOLOMON'S TEMPLE SIGNIFIES THE POWER OF A KING OR A PRINCE TO RULE OVER HIS PEOPLE. IT IS ONE OF TWO PILLARS THAT CAN BE CALLED PAIRS OF OPPOSITES, AS NEITHER IS COMPLETE WITHOUT THE OTHER. THE CHECKERED FLOOR SHOWS THAT EVERYTHING IN LIFE IS DUAL AND CAN ONLY BE KNOWN BY CONTRASTING IT TO ITS OPPOSITE. THE TWO IN COMBINATION PRODUCE A METAPHYSICAL THIRD, WHICH IS A SYNTHESIS OF PERFECT BALANCE. THUS, WE HAVE GOOD AND EVIL, LIGHT AND DARKNESS, ACTIVE AND PASSIVE, POSITIVE AND NEGATIVE, YES AND NO, OUTSIDE AND INSIDE. NEITHER IS COMPLETE WITHOUT THE OTHER, AND TAKEN TOGETHER, THEY FORM STABILITY, JUST AS MORNING AND EVENING UNITE TO FORM THE COMPLETE DAY.

THE FIRST PILLAR IS THE TEMPORAL POWER OF AN EARTHLY RULER, BUT IT ALONE IS NOT ENOUGH TO ENSURE STABILITY. FOR THAT, WE NEED ANOTHER PILLAR WHOSE SYMBOL WE MEET ELSEWHERE IN THE CRAFT.

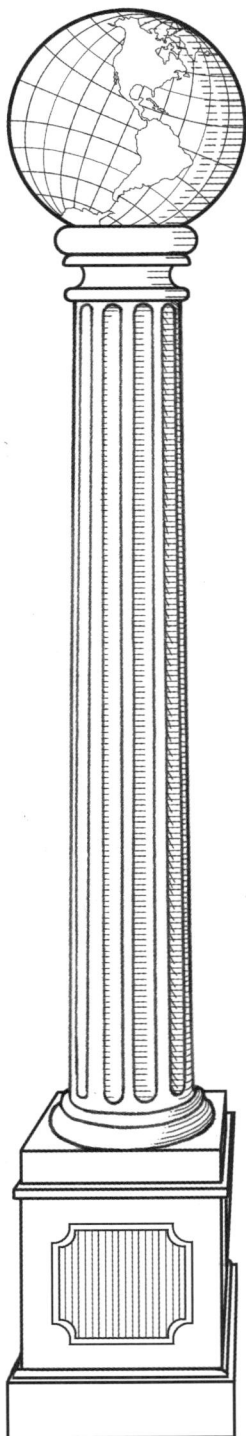

The Master of the Lodge

The Master represents the eternal spirit of wisdom from above. He is enthroned in the East, so that through him, that spirit may flow into every part of the lodge. For as the lodge is the image of the soul of man, so the Master is the image of the divine spirit that quickens that soul. He is the head and directing intellect of the assembled brethren.

The Master is distinguished by the square, turned downward, which is the representative of the Great Architect. The Master may shape into the divine likeness all below him who have been entrusted to his care, whether in his lodge or in his own being, of which the lodge is a symbol.

The sun is to rule the day, the moon is to govern the night, and the Master is to rule and direct his lodge.

Robert Lomas's personal view

THE MASTER OF THE LODGE SYMBOLIZES THE ETERNAL SPIRIT OF WISDOM. HE SITS ON A THRONE IN THE EAST, SYMBOLIZING THE RISING OF THE SUN TO BRING LIGHT AND WISDOM TO HIS BRETHREN. THE LODGE IS A MODEL OF THE SOUL OF A MASON, AND THE MASTER IS THE HEAD AND DIRECTING INTELLECT OF THE ASSEMBLED BRETHREN AND HENCE THE SOUL OF THE MASON. WITHOUT THE LIGHT AND WISDOM IN HIS SPIRIT, THE SOUL OF A MASON IS DARKNESS AND HIS BODY OF FLESH, WORTHLESS. UNTIL THE SOUL AND THE BODY ARE BROUGHT TOGETHER IN HARMONY, THE SPIRIT CANNOT GROW AND FLOURISH. THE GREAT ARCHITECT HAS JOINED THESE THREE TOGETHER AND APPOINTED THE SPIRIT AS A WISE MASTERBUILDER, SYMBOLIZED BY THE MASTER OF THE LODGE TO RULE OVER SOUL AND BODY. AND FROM THESE IMPERFECT, CORRUPTIBLE MATERIALS, A MASON WILL LEARN HOW TO SHAPE HIMSELF TO BECOME A LIVING STONE IN THE IMMORTAL TEMPLE OF HUMANITY.

The 24-Inch Gauge

A working tool of an Entered Apprentice Freemason is the 24-inch gauge, used to measure our work. But because Masons are speculative, we also apply this tool to our morals. In this sense, the 24-inch gauge represents the twenty-four hours of the day—part to be spent in prayer to almighty God, part to be spent in labor and refreshment, and part to be spent in serving a friend or Brother in time of need.

A PAINTING BY PAUL ORBAN SHOWING THE INITIATE RECEIVING THE FIRST WORKING TOOL, THE 24-INCH GAUGE. From the collection of the Chancellor Robert R Livingston Masonic Library of Grand Lodge, New York, N.Y.

Robert Lomas's personal view

THE 24-INCH GAUGE IS A SPIRITUAL TOOL TO HELP A MASON BALANCE HIS DAILY TIME AMONG THREE DUTIES, WHICH DO NOT NECESSARILY INVOLVE EQUAL AMOUNTS OF TIME BUT ALL HAVE EQUAL VALUE. THIS ANCIENT PRACTICE OF THE CRAFT IS SOMETHING MODERN JARGON CALLS "ESTABLISHING A BALANCE BETWEEN WORK AND LIFE."

THESE ARE THE THREE IMPORTANT THINGS FOR WHICH YOU, AS A MASON, SHOULD MAKE TIME:

- YOUR SPIRITUAL TRANQUILITY, TO ENSURE YOU ARE AT PEACE WITH YOURSELF AND HAVE TIME TO THINK AND REFLECT
- YOUR MATERIAL PURSUITS AND THE CARE OF YOUR PERSON AND FAMILY, TO ENSURE THAT YOU PUT ENOUGH EFFORT INTO WORK TO SUPPORT YOURSELF AND YOUR DEPENDENTS
- YOUR ALTRUISTIC RESPONSIBILITY TO THOSE LESS HAPPILY PLACED THAN YOURSELF—OR THE WORK OF CHARITY—WHICH SHOULD ALWAYS BE DONE BY STEALTH, AS IT IS DONE FOR THE BENEFIT OF THE RECIPIENT, NOT THE AGGRANDIZEMENT OF THE DONOR

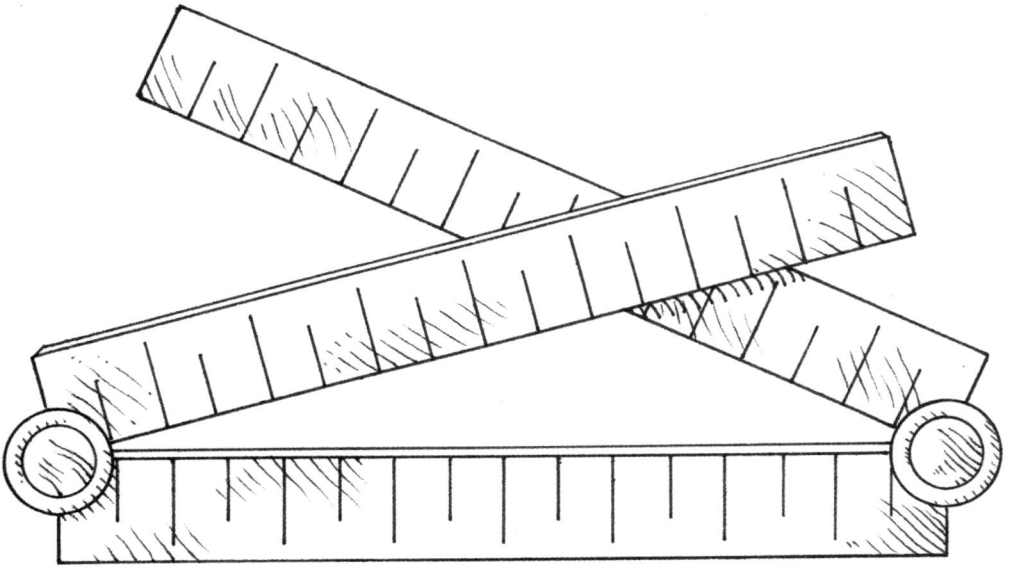

The Common Gavel

A working tool of an Entered Apprentice Freemason is the common gavel, which is used to knock off all superfluous knobs and outgrowths. But as we are Free and Accepted Masons, we apply this tool to our morals as well. In this sense, the common gavel represents the force of conscience. It should be used to keep down all vain and unbecoming thoughts that might obtrude during any of the aforementioned periods, allowing our words and actions to ascend unpolluted to the throne of grace.

A RELIC GAVEL MADE OUT OF WOOD FROM THE USS CONSTITUTION AND THE USS KEARSARGE AND WRAPPED WITH BANDS OF SILVER FROM A WATCH FOUND ON THE USS TALLAPOOSA. From the collection of the Chancellor Robert R Livingston Masonic Library of Grand Lodge, New York, N.Y.

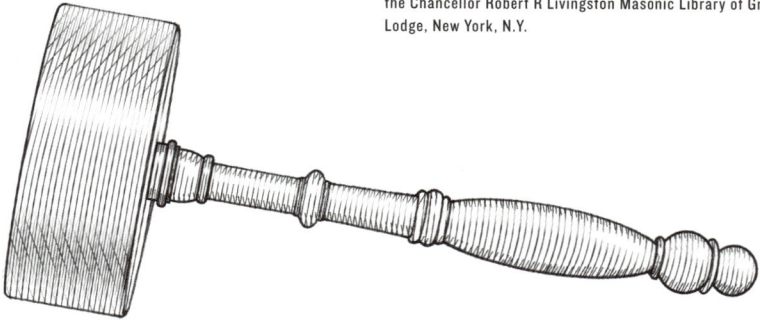

Robert Lomas's personal view

THE MASTER'S GAVEL CONTROLS THE LODGE, AND ITS KNOCKS CREATE ORDER AND OBEDIENCE WITHIN THE LODGE, WHICH IS A SYMBOL OF THE MASON'S SOUL. A MASON LEARNS THAT HIS BODY AND HIS SOUL ARE LEVEL GROUND, UPON WHICH HE IS TO BUILD AN ALTAR IN THE SHAPE OF HIS OWN SPIRITUAL LIFE. HE SHOULD ALLOW NO DEBASING HABIT OF THOUGHT OR CONDUCT TO DEFILE THIS WORK. AS AN APPRENTICE, THE MASON IS GIVEN THE COMMON WOODEN GAVEL TO HELP HIM SMOOTH THE ROUGH ASHLAR OF HIS IMPERFECT SOUL AND TO SHAPE IT TO BECOME THE PERFECT SYMBOL OF THE CUBICAL ALTAR THAT STANDS AT THE CENTER OF HIS OWN CONSCIOUSNESS. THE COMMON GAVEL IS A SYMBOL OF THE FORCE OF CONSCIENCE, AND BY LEARNING TO USE IT SKILL-FULLY, YOU WILL LEARN TO CONTROL YOUR ANGER AND INTOLERANCE.

The Chisel

A working tool of an Entered Apprentice Freemason is the chisel, which is used to smooth and prepare the stone and to make it fit for the hands of the more expert workman. But as we are Free and Accepted, or speculative, Masons, we apply these tools to our morals. In this sense, the chisel points out to us the advantages of education, by which means alone we are rendered fit members of regularly organized society.

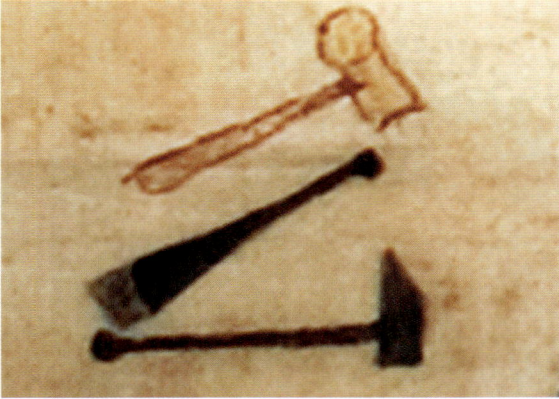

A SILK APRON HAND-PAINTED WITH NUMEROUS MASONIC SYMBOLS.
From the collection of the Chancellor Robert R Livingston Masonic Library of Grand Lodge, New York, N.Y.

Robert Lomas's personal view

THE CHISEL IS A SYMBOL OF EDUCATION, BECAUSE WHEN IT IS DRIVEN BY THE FORCE OF THE COMMON GAVEL, IT IS ABLE TO CHIP AWAY THE ROUGH EXTERIOR OF A FRESHLY QUARRIED STONE AND REVEAL THE PERFECT CUBE HIDDEN WITHIN. EDUCATION SHAPES A MASON'S INTELLECT, DEVELOPS AND EXPANDS HIS MIND, BROADENS HIS PERSPECTIVE, AND MAKES HIM A MORE CIVILIZED HUMAN BEING. THE DISCIPLINE OF STUDY AND LEARNING IS A GOOD HABIT TO ACQUIRE, AND AS MASONS, WE ARE ALL ENCOURAGED TO MAKE A DAILY STEP IN MASONIC KNOWLEDGE.

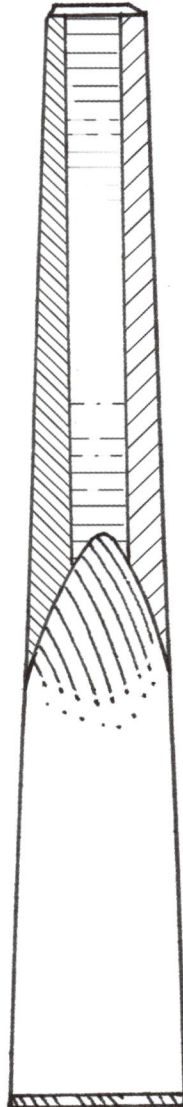

The Form of the Lodge

The form of the lodge is a parallel epipedon in length from east to west, in breadth between north and south, in depth from the surface of the earth to the center, and even as high as the heavens. A Masonic lodge is described of this vast extent to show both the universality of the science and the boundless nature of a Mason's charity, save the bounds of prudence.

Robert Lomas's personal view

THROUGHOUT THE RITUALS AND LECTURES, REFERENCES TO THE LODGE ARE NOT TO THE BUILDING IN WHICH WE MEET. THAT BUILDING IS BUT A SYMBOL ITSELF. THE REAL LODGE IS THE MASON'S OWN INDIVIDUAL PERSONALITY, AND WHEN THE MASONIC SYMBOLS ARE INTERPRETED IN THIS LIGHT, THEY REVEAL A NEW ASPECT OF THE CRAFT. NAMELY, WHEN WE TALK OF A BUILDING, WE ARE REFERRING TO THE SPIRIT OF A MASON.

THIS MEANS THAT EACH MASON IS A LODGE. JUST AS A MASONIC LODGE IS AN ASSEMBLY OF BRETHREN MEETING TO REFLECT ON THE MYSTERIES OF THE CRAFT, SO EACH HUMAN CONSCIOUS-NESS IS A COMPOSITE STRUCTURE OF VARIOUS PROPERTIES AND FACULTIES PUT FORTH BY OUR MIND FOR THE HARMONIOUS INTERACTION AND FOR WORKING OUT THE PURPOSE OF LIFE. EVERY-THING IN MASONRY IS SYMBOLIC OF HUMANKIND—ITS HUMAN CONSTITUTION AND SPIRITUAL EVO-LUTION. YOUR FIRST ENTRY INTO A LODGE IS SYMBOLIC OF YOUR FIRST ENTRY INTO THE SCIENCE OF KNOWING YOURSELF.

THE FOUR SIDES OF THE LODGE HAVE FURTHER SIGNIFICANCE. THE EAST SIDE OF THE LODGE REPRESENTS SPIRITUALITY, AND THE WEST SIDE REPRESENTS NORMAL RATIONAL UNDERSTAND-ING. MIDWAY BETWEEN THESE EXTREMES IS THE SOUTH SIDE, THE MEETING PLACE OF THE SPIRITUAL INTUITION AND THE RATIONAL UNDERSTANDING, WHICH SYMBOLIZES ABSTRACT INTEL-LECTUALITY AND KNOWLEDGE. THE NORTH SIDE IS THE SIDE OF IGNORANCE, WHICH IS ACCESSIBLE BY THE LOWEST MODE OF PERCEPTION: OUR PHYSICAL SENSATIONS.

THUS, THE FOUR SIDES OF THE LODGE SYMBOLIZE THE FOUR POSSIBLE WAYS OF GAINING KNOWLEDGE ABOUT YOURSELF.

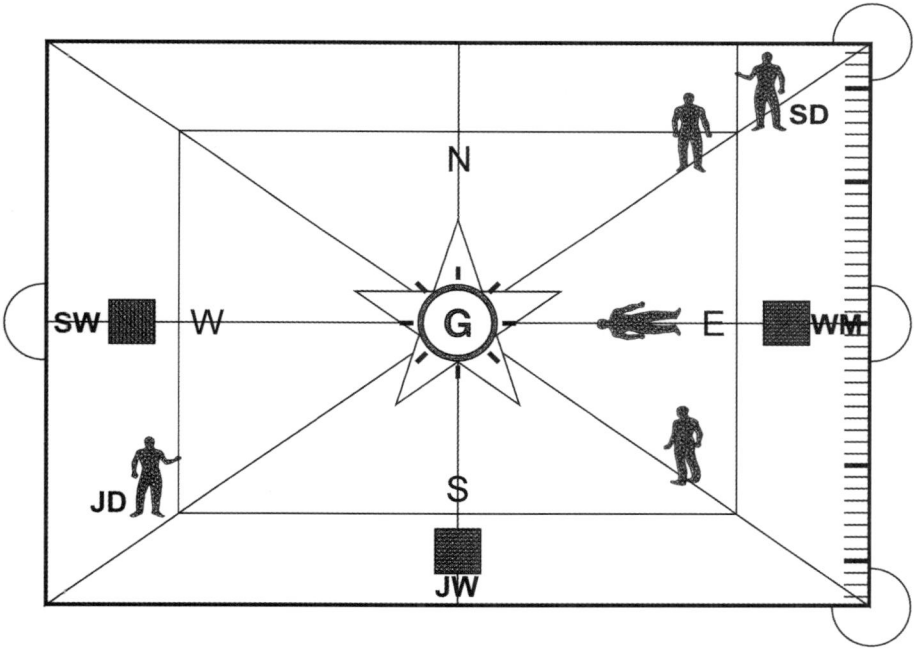

The Pillar of Wisdom

The column's capital is adorned with volutes, and its cornice has dentils. The famous Temple of Diana at Ephesus, which took more than 200 years to build, was composed of this order. Both elegance and ingenuity were displayed in the invention of this column. It was modeled after a beautiful young woman, echoing her elegant shape and flowing hair.

This column is also known as the Pillar of Wisdom. To have wisdom is to contrive, and wisdom should conduct us in all our undertakings. The universe is the temple of the deity whom we serve, and wisdom is the first pillar of his throne.

AN IONIAN GREEK-STYLE SANDSTONE COLUMN.

Robert Lomas's personal view

THE IONIAN PILLAR IS A SYMBOL THAT IS PLACED IN THE EAST OF THE LODGE. FROM ITS SUMMIT FLOWS THE FOUNTAIN OF WISDOM, DIVIDING ITSELF INTO ACTIVE AND PASSIVE PROPERTIES TO INDICATE THAT IN THE BUILDING UP OF THE SOUL, THE RIGHT HAND OF ACTION MUST BE BALANCED BY THE LEFT HAND OF UNDERSTANDING, AND THE MIND AND THE HEART MUST LABOR EQUALLY AND ASPIRE TOGETHER. THE ELEGANT SYMMETRICAL SHAPE OF THE PILLAR INCORPORATES THIS DUALITY IN ITS FORM.

THE PILLAR OF WISDOM IS IN THE CARE OF THE MASTER OF THE LODGE TO INSPIRE HIM TO STRIVE TO ADJUST AND HARMONIZE THE DIFFERENT ELEMENTS OF HIS LODGE, THAT THEY MAY BE AS BRETHREN DWELLING TOGETHER IN UNITY IN ONE HOUSE.

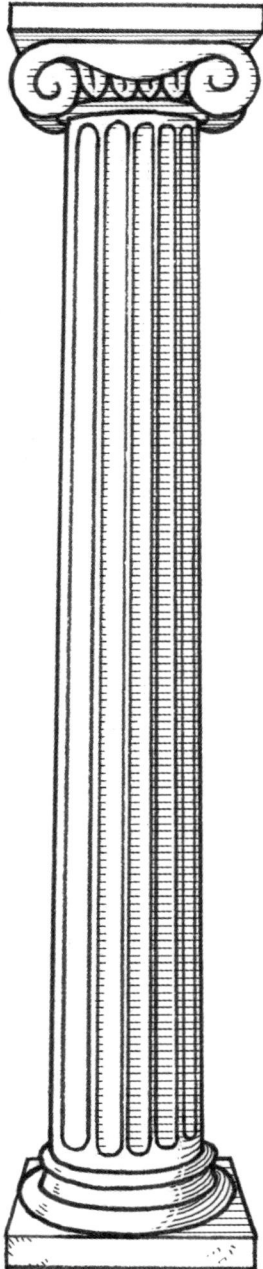

The Pillar of Strength

This Doric column has no ornamentation except moldings on the base, or capital. Its frieze is distinguished by triglyphs and metopes, and its cornice, by mutules. As the most ancient of all the orders, the Doric retains more of the primitive hut style than any of the rest. The triglyphs in the frieze represent the ends of the joists, and the mutules in its cornice represent the rafters.

The composition of this order is both grand and noble. Because it was formed after the model of a muscular, full-grown man, delicate ornaments are repugnant to its characteristic solidity. It therefore succeeds best in the regularity of its proportions, and it is used principally in warlike structures, where strength and noble simplicity are required.

This column is also known as the Pillar of Strength. Strength is to support us under all our difficulties. The universe is the temple of the deity whom we serve, and strength is the second pillar of his throne.

THE MOST FAMOUS TEMPLE IN THE DORIC ORDER IS THE PARTHENON ON THE ACROPOLIS IN ATHENS.

Robert Lomas's personal view

THE DORIC PILLAR IS PLACED IN THE WEST OF THE LODGE. ITS STRENGTH AND PLAINNESS SYMBOLIZE THE ENDURING SUBSTANCE OF THE SOUL. THE PILLAR STANDS UPRIGHT BEFORE THE LODGE HAS BEEN OPENED, SYMBOLIZING THE STRENGTH NEEDED TO FACE THE WORLD'S HARDSHIPS AND THREATS. BUT ONCE THE LODGE HAS BEEN OPENED, THE PILLAR IS LOWERED, AS THE CORPORATE MIND OF THE OPEN LODGE NO LONGER NEEDS ITS PROTECTION. AS THE SUN SETS IN THE WEST TO CLOSE THE DAY, SO THE SENIOR WARDEN LOWERS THE PILLAR OF STRENGTH TO CLOSE THE LODGE. AS THE PILLAR IS LOWERED, THE BRETHREN REMEMBER THE SPLENDOR THAT HAS SHONE ON IT. THEY ALSO REFLECT THAT THE SOUL GROWS TO PERFECTION YET LOOKS FORWARD TO THAT TIME WHEN IT WILL RISE BEYOND DUALITY AND CHANGE AND PASS INTO THE ENDURING UNITY OF THE CENTER.

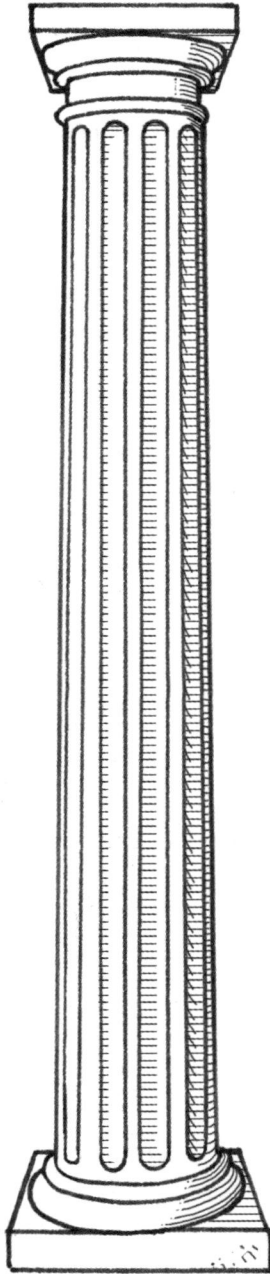

The Pillar of Beauty

The capital of this column is adorned with two rows of leaves and eight volutes that sustain the abacus. This order is used chiefly in stately structures.

Calimachus was inspired to create the capital of this column from the following remarkable circumstance: While accidentally passing by the tomb of a young lady, he saw a basket of toys that had been left there by her nurse. The basket was covered with a tile and placed over an Acanthus root. As the leaves grew up, they encompassed the basket until they overgrew the tile, met with an obstruction, and bent down. Calimachus set about imitating the figure. The base of the capital represents the basket, the abacus the tile, and the volutes the bending leaves.

This column is also known as the Pillar of Beauty. Beauty is to adorn the inward man. The universe is the temple of the deity whom we serve, and beauty is the third pillar of his throne. Beauty shines through the whole of creation in symmetry and order.

A CORINTHIAN-STYLE PILLAR FROM ST. PETER'S BASILICA WITHIN THE VATICAN CITY, ITALY.

Robert Lomas's personal view

THE CORINTHIAN PILLAR OF BEAUTY IS PLACED IN THE SOUTH OF THE LODGE. IT IS THE SYMBOL OF AN UPRIGHT SOUL WHOSE ASCENDING SIDES HAVE BEEN FLUTED INTO BEAUTY BY THE CHISEL OF EDUCATION AND AT WHOSE SUMMIT INTELLIGENCE BREAKS FORTH INTO THE LEAFAGE AND TENDRILS OF WISDOM.

WHEN THE LODGE IS OPENED, THE JUNIOR WARDEN RAISES THE PILLAR OF BEAUTY AS A TOKEN OF THE LIGHT OF THE CENTER, NOW VISIBLE WITHIN THE OPEN LODGE. BUT WHEN THE LODGE IS CLOSED AND THAT SUPERIOR LIGHT IS REPLACED BY DARKNESS, THE PILLARS OF STRENGTH AND WISDOM PREVAIL AND NOW GOVERN THE OUTWARD ACTIONS OF THE BRETHREN.

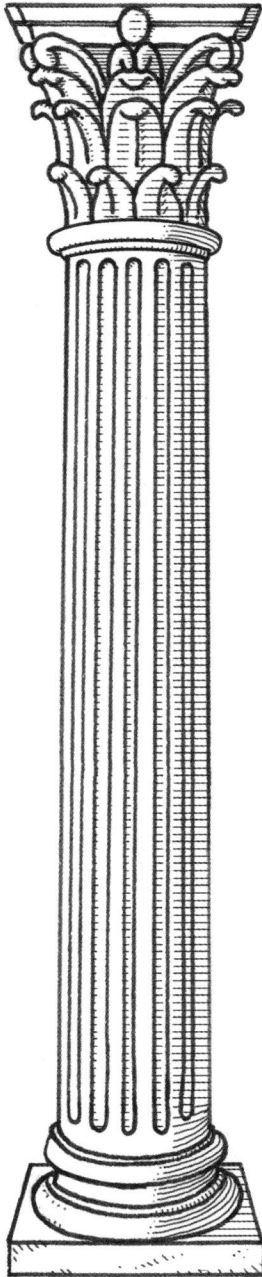

The Celestial Canopy

The heavens, God has stretched forth as a canopy, and the earth, he has planted as a footstool. He crowns his temple with stars, as with a diadem, and with his hand, he extends the power and glory. The sun and the moon are messengers of his will, and all his law is concordant.

THIS CELESTIAL CANOPY APPEARS IN AN EARLY NINETEENTH-CENTURY OIL PAINTING OF A TRACING BOARD.
From the collection of the Chancellor Robert R Livingston Masonic Library of Grand Lodge, New York, N.Y.

Robert Lomas's personal view

THE CELESTIAL CANOPY OF THE LODGE, PAINTED ON THE CEILING, SYMBOLIZES THE ETHEREAL NATURE OF A MASON. THE CHECKERED FLOOR AND THE CELESTIAL CANOPY ARE THE REVERSE OR OPPOSITE OF EACH OTHER. THE MASON'S ETHEREAL NATURE IS TENUOUS AND INVISIBLE, LIKE THE SUBTLE FRAGRANCE OF A FLOWER. ITS EXISTENCE IS NOT PHYSICALLY DEMONSTRABLE, BUT A MASONIC CANDIDATE ENTERS THE CRAFT WITH THE ACKNOWLEDGED DESIRE OF SEEKING TO CAST LIGHT ON THE NATURE OF HIS OWN BEING. THE ORDER ASSISTS HIM IN HIS SEARCH FOR THAT LIGHT THROUGH THE USE OF TEACHINGS AND SYMBOLS THAT HAVE BEEN DEVISED BY WISE AND COMPETENT INSTRUCTORS. THE MASON WHO YIELDS TO THE DISCIPLINE OF THE ORDER DOES MORE THAN IMPROVE HIS MORALS AND CHARACTER. HE ALSO BUILDS AN INNER ETHEREAL BODY TO MATCH THE BEAUTY OF THE CELESTIAL CANOPY.

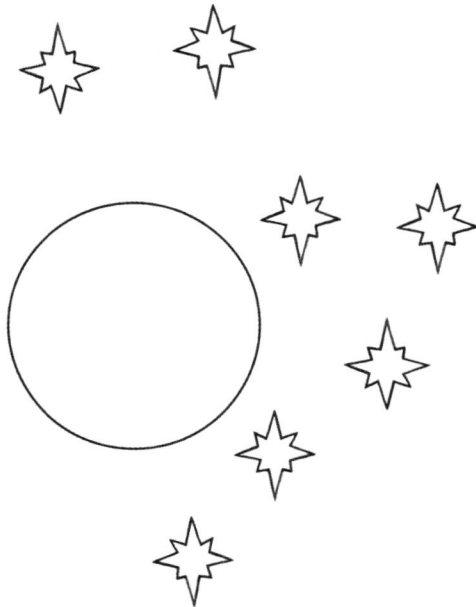

Jacob's Ladder

Rebecca, the beloved wife of Isaac, knowing by divine inspiration that a peculiar blessing was vested in the soul of her husband, desired to obtain it for her favorite son, Jacob. But there was a small problem: By birthright, the blessing belonged to Esau, her firstborn son. Jacob had no sooner fraudulently obtained his father's blessing than he was obliged to flee from the wrath of his brother, who in a moment of rage and disappointment threatened to kill him.

Jacob journeyed toward Padanaram, in the land of Mesopotamia. Weary and stranded in the desert, he lay down to rest, taking the earth for his bed, a stone for his pillow, and the canopy of heaven for a covering. In a vision, he saw a ladder, the top of which reached to the heavens, and the angels of the Lord were ascending and descending from it. It was then that God entered into a solemn covenant with Jacob: If Jacob would abide by God's laws and keep his commandments, then God would not only bring Jacob again to his father's house in peace and prosperity but also make him the leader of a great and mighty people.

Jacob's ladder had many staves or rounds, which point out as many moral virtues. However, the three principal virtues are faith, hope, and charity.

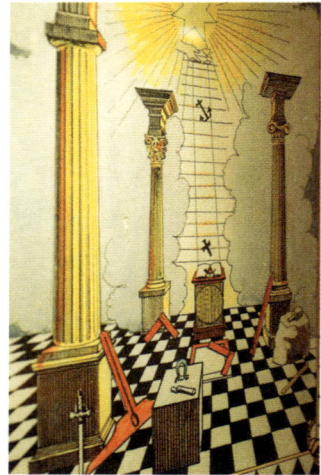

JACOB'S LATTER WITHIN A TRACING BOARD.

Robert Lomas's personal view

THE SYMBOL OF JACOB'S LADDER RESTS ON THE VOLUME OF THE SACRED LAW AND EXTENDS TO THE BRIGHT MORNING STAR, RISING IN THE EAST. IT REPRESENTS THE LOWER AND PHYSICAL PART OF A MASON, WHICH IS ANIMAL AND EARTHY AND STANDS ON THE EARTH. FROM THIS BASE, OUR SPIRIT REACHES TO THE CELESTIAL CANOPY. THESE SPIRITUAL AND CARNAL PARTS OF A MASON'S NATURE ARE IN PERPETUAL CONFLICT. THE MASTER MASON HAS LEARNED TO BRING ABOUT A PERFECT BALANCE BETWEEN THEM AND TO ESTABLISH HIMSELF IN STRENGTH, SO THAT HIS OWN SOUL STANDS FIRM AGAINST WEAKNESS AND TEMPTATION.

Faith

Faith is the foundation of justice, the bond of goodwill, and the chief support of civil society. We live and walk by faith. By it, we have a continual acknowledgment of a supreme being. By faith, we have access to the throne of grace and are justified, accepted, and finally received. A true and sincere faith is the evidence of things not seen but the substance of those hoped for. Faith will bring us to those blessed mansions, where we shall be eternally happy with God, the Great Architect of the Universe.

THE SYMBOL OF FAITH, AS IT APPEARS ON A HAND-PAINTED SILK APRON. From the collection of the Chancellor Robert R Livingston Masonic Library of Grand Lodge, New York, N.Y.

Robert Lomas's personal view

FAITH SYMBOLIZES THE POSSIBILITY OF ATTAINING MASONIC ENLIGHTENMENT. THE MASONIC PATH FROM WEST TO EAST IS NOT EASY TO TREAD. THE SPIRAL STEPS TO THE MIDDLE CHAMBER ARE STEEP AND CALL FOR FORTITUDE AND A STEADFAST SENSE OF PURPOSE. BUT FOR ALL THAT EFFORT, AS THE CLIMBER MOUNTS, IN FAITH OF REACHING THE LIGHT OF THE CENTER, BROAD VISTAS OPEN UP. WISDOM DESCENDS ON THE FAITHFUL MASON AS A SANCTIFYING AND INCREASING BRIGHTNESS. A MASON IS STRENGTHENED BY A POWER MIGHTIER THAN ANY INDIVIDUAL, AND AS THE HOODWINK FALLS AWAY THROUGH THE GATE, HE CAN SEE THE BEAUTIFUL LAND OF FAR DISTANCES. FAITH IN ATTAINING THIS VISTA SUSTAINS THE MASON ON HIS JOURNEY.

Hope

Hope is the anchor of the soul, both sure and steadfast. We must rely on almighty God to animate our endeavors and to teach us to fix our desires within the limits of his most blessed promises. So shall success attend us. If we believe something is impossible, then our despondence may make it so. However, he who perseveres in a just cause will ultimately overcome all difficulties.

THE SYMBOL OF HOPE, AS IT APPEARS ON A HAND-PAINTED SILK APRON. From the collection of the Chancellor Robert R Livingston Masonic Library of Grand Lodge, New York, N.Y.

Robert Lomas's personal view

MASONIC RITUAL SAYS THAT ST. JOHN, ONE OF THE PATRON SAINTS OF MASONRY, TEACHES, "HE WHO HATH THIS HOPE IN HIM PURIFIETH HIMSELF, EVEN AS THE MASTER WHOM HE IS SEEKING IS PURE."

THE ESSENCE OF THE MASONIC PHILOSOPHY IS THAT ALL MASONS ARE SEARCHING FOR SOMETHING IN THEIR OWN NATURE THAT THEY HAVE LOST. WITH PROPER INSTRUCTION AND BY THEIR OWN PATIENCE AND INDUSTRY, THEY HOPE TO FIND IT. THIS MISSING KNOWLEDGE IS SYMBOLIZED BY THE LOST WORD, AND THE HOPE OFFERED BY MASONRY IS THAT IT CAN BE FOUND BY THE APPLICATION OF THE MASONIC ART.

HOPE SYMBOLIZES OUR PERSISTENT DESIRE FOR THE REDISCOVERY OF THAT WITHIN OURSELVES THAT IS LOST.

Charity

Lovely in itself, charity is the brightest ornament that adorns our Masonic profession. It is the best test and surest proof of the sincerity of our religion. Benevolence, rendered by heaven-born charity, is an honor to the nation from which it springs and is nourished and cherished. Happy is the man who has sown in his breast the seeds of benevolence. He envies not his neighbor, he believes not a tale reported to his prejudice, he forgives the injuries of men, and he endeavors to blot them from his recollection. Then, brethren, let us remember that we are Free and Accepted Masons—ever ready to listen to him who craves our assistance—and from him who is in want,

THE SYMBOL OF CHARITY, AS IT APPEARS ON A HAND-PAINTED SILK APRON. From the collection of the Chancellor Robert R Livingston Masonic Library of Grand Lodge, New York, N.Y.

let us not withhold a liberal hand. So will a heartfelt satisfaction reward our labors, and the produce of love and charity will most assuredly follow.

Robert Lomas's personal view

AN ILLUMINED MASONIC CANDIDATE IS SAID TO ATTAIN WHAT IS KNOWN IN THE EAST AS THE STATE OF *SAMADHI*. IT ALSO KNOWN AS UNIVERSAL OR COSMIC CONSCIOUSNESS, BECAUSE WHEN IT IS EXPERIENCED, IT TRANSCENDS ALL SENSE OF PERSONAL INDIVIDUALIZATION, TIME, AND SPACE.

WHEN A MASON ENTERS THIS STATE OF MIND, THE BLISS AND PEACE SURPASS ALL TEMPORAL UNDERSTANDING. THE MASON HAS RISEN TO AN EXALTED STATE, WHERE THERE IS RESOLUTION IN BLISSFUL CONCORD WITH THE ETERNAL. ONCE THE MASON HAS EXPERIENCED THIS, HE IS IN CONSCIOUS SYMPATHY AND IDENTITY OF FEELING WITH ALL THAT LIVES AND FEELS. THIS TAKES THE FORM OF UNIVERSAL CHARITY AND LIMITLESS LOVE, WHICH ARE THE COROLLARIES OF PERCEIVING THE UNITY OF THE COSMOS. AS AN APPRENTICE, THE MASON WAS TOLD THAT THIS ATTAINMENT OF ILLUMINATION WAS THE SUMMIT OF THE MASONIC PROFESSION. ONCE REACHING IT, HE SEES THAT THERE IS A UNIVERSE WITHIN HIM AS WELL AS WITHOUT HIM. HE MICROCOSMICALLY SUMS UP AND CONTAINS ALL THAT IS MANIFESTED TO HIS TEMPORAL INTELLIGENCE AS THE VAST SPATIAL UNIVERSE AROUND HIM, WITH THIS INSIGHT HOW CAN HE FAIL TO PRACTICES CHARITY TO HIS FELLOW BEINGS?

The Mosaic Pavement

The mosaic pavement is the beautiful flooring of a Freemason's Lodge, which is variegated and checkered. This symbol points out the diversity of objects that decorate and adorn all of creation.

Our days are variegated and checkered by unpredictable events, both good and evil. This is why our lodge is furnished with mosaic work: to point out the uncertainty of all things here on Earth. Today, we may travel in prosperity, but tomorrow, we may totter on the

THE MOSAIC PAVEMENT IS A SYMBOL OF PHILOSOPHICAL TRUTH.

Robert Lomas's personal view

THE MASONIC RITUAL SAYS "THE SQUARE PAVEMENT IS FOR THE HIGH PRIEST TO WALK UPON," BUT IT IS NOT REFERRING MERELY TO THE JEWISH HIGH PRIEST OF CENTURIES AGO. IT IS A SYMBOL FOR EACH INDIVIDUAL MEMBER OF THE CRAFT. EVERY MASON SHOULD ASPIRE TO BECOME THE HIGH PRIEST OF HIS OWN PERSONAL TEMPLE AND TO MAKE OF IT A PLACE WHERE HE MAY MEET THE GREAT ARCHITECT OF THE UNIVERSE AND BECOME AWARE OF THE PLAN OF THE COSMOS.

EVERY LIVING BEING IN THIS DUALISTIC WORLD, WHETHER A MASON OR NOT, WALKS ON THE SQUARE PAVEMENT OF MINGLED GOOD AND EVIL. THE MOSAIC PAVEMENT IS A SYMBOL OF A PHILOSOPHICAL TRUTH. FOR THE MASON TO BECOME MASTER OF HIS FATE, HE MUST WALK ON THESE OPPOSITES IN THE SENSE OF TRANSCENDING AND DOMINATING THEM. HE MUST LEARN TO TRAMPLE ON HIS LOWER SENSUAL NATURE AND KEEP IT UNDER HIS SUBJECTION AND CONTROL. HE MUST BE ABLE TO RISE ABOVE THE MOTLEY OF GOOD AND EVIL AND TO BE INDIFFERENT TO THE UPS AND DOWNS OF FORTUNE THAT SWAY HIS THOUGHTS AND ACTIONS. THE MASON IS TRYING TO DEVELOP HIS INNATE SPIRITUAL POTENCIES, WHICH IS IMPOSSIBLE AS LONG AS HE IS OVERRULED BY MATERIAL TENDENCIES AND THE FLUCTUATING EMOTIONS OF PLEASURE AND PAIN THAT THEY INVOKE. BY RISING ABOVE THEM, THE MASON GAINS SERENITY AND MENTAL EQUILIBRIUM UNDER ALL CIRCUMSTANCES. IN THIS WAY, THE MASON WALKS ON THE CHECKERED GROUNDWORK OF EXISTENCE AND THE CONFLICTING TENDENCIES OF HIS MATERIAL NATURE.

uneven path of weakness, temptation, and adversity. Then, while such emblems are before us, we are morally instructed not to boast of anything, but to give heed to our ways and to walk uprightly and with humility before God. For while some of us are born to more elevated situations than others, when we are in the grave, we are all on the same level, with death destroying all distinctions. While our feet tread on this mosaic work, let our ideas return to the original from which we have been created. Let us, as good men and Masons, act as the dictates of reason prompt us: to practice charity, to maintain harmony, and to endeavor to live in unity and brotherly love.

The Blazing Star

The blazing star is the glory in the center and refers us to the sun, which enlightens the earth and, by its benign influence, dispenses its blessings to humankind.

THE BLAZING STAR SYMBOL TAKEN FROM A MODERN INTERPRETATION OF THE FIRST-DEGREE TRACING BOARD, CURRENTLY ON DISPLAY AT THE CHANCELLOR ROBERT R. LIVINGSTON MASONIC LIBRARY OF GRAND LODGE. Copyright Angel Millar. Reprinted with permission

Robert Lomas's personal view

THE BLAZING STAR IS ANOTHER NAME FOR THE SYMBOL OF THE SUN. THE SUN, IN TURN, IS A SYMBOL OF THE GREAT POTENTIAL INHERENT IN THE HIDDEN CENTER OF THE CANDIDATE'S SOUL. A MASON IS TAUGHT THAT THERE IS A MYSTERIOUS CENTER TO HIS BEING, WHICH IS AT FIRST ONLY DARKNESS VISIBLE. AS HE PROGRESSES INTO HIS OWN INTERIOR, HE REACHES THE BLAZING STAR OR GLORY AT HIS OWN CENTER. BY THIS AWE-INSPIRING LIGHT, HE SIMULTANEOUSLY KNOWS HIMSELF AND THE GREAT ARCHITECT AND REALIZES HIS UNITY WITH THE COSMIC PLAN AND THE POINTS OF FELLOWSHIP BETWEEN HIM AND THE PLAN. FROM THIS AWFUL AND SUBLIME EXPERIENCE, HIS INITIATED SOUL IS BROUGHT BACK TO ITS BODILY ENCASEMENT AND REUNITED TO THE COMPANIONS OF ITS FORMER TOILS. HE RESUMES HIS TEMPORAL LIFE WITH A CONSCIOUS REALIZATION OF HIS PLACE IN THE COSMOS. ONLY THEN IS HE ENTITLED TO THE NAME OF MASTER MASON. THE SECRETS OF FREEMASONRY AND OF INITIATION ARE CONCERNED WITH THIS PROCESS OF INTROVERSION OF THE SOUL TO ITS OWN CENTER AND THE VISION OF THE BLAZING STAR, WHICH SYMBOLIZES AWARENESS OF THE MYSTERIOUS NATURE OF THE CENTER.

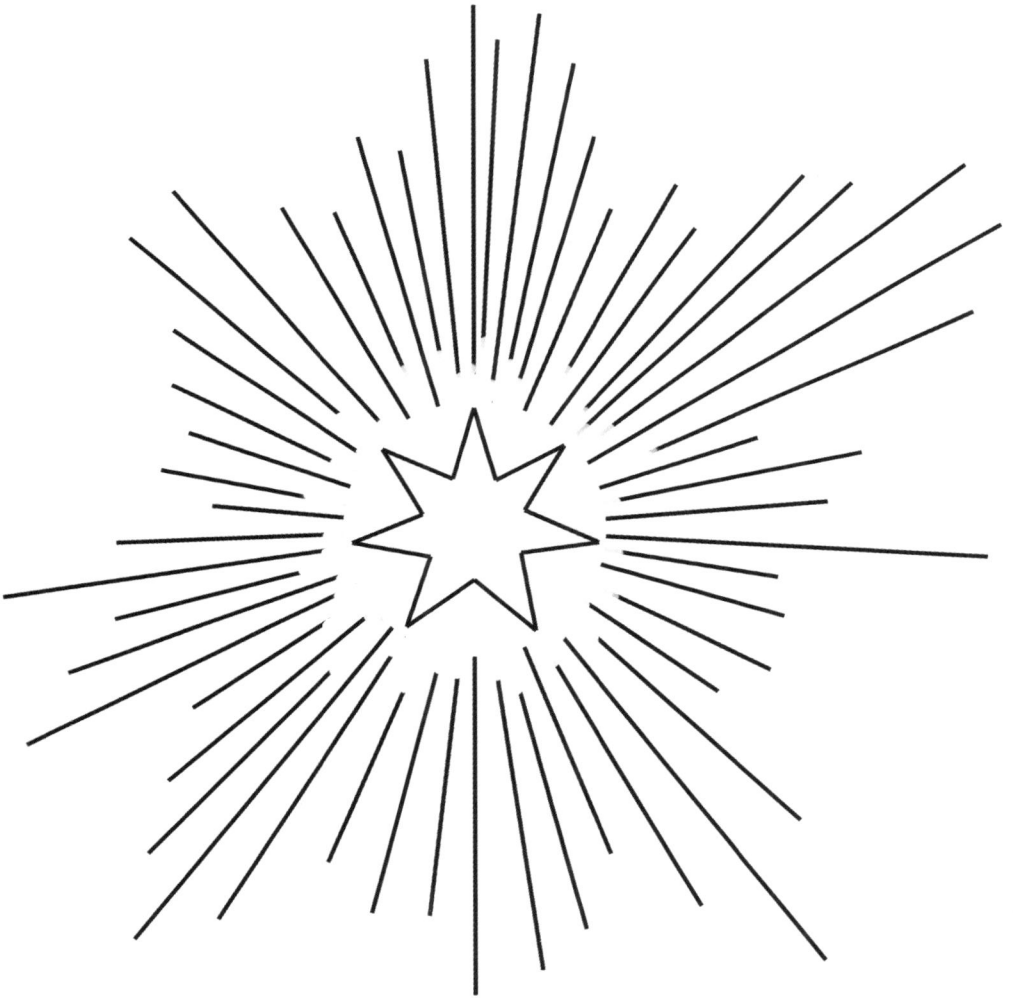

The Indented or Tessellated Border

The indented or tessellated border refers us to the planets, which, in their various revolutions, form a beautiful border or skirtwork around that grand luminary: the sun. In the same way, this border forms a skirtwork round a Freemason's Lodge.

TESSELLATED BOARDER SHOWN ON A THIRD-DEGREE TRACING BOARD. Courtesy of www.tracingboards.com

Robert Lomas's personal view

THE BRETHREN OF A MASONIC LODGE ARE PLACED IN DIFFERENT AND UNEQUAL DEGREES OF PER-CEPTION ON THE CHECKERED FLOOR OF LIFE, BUT THE TESSELLATED BORDER, WITH ITS TASSELS AT EACH CORNER, ENCLOSES EVERYONE ALIKE—WISE AND FOOLISH, LEARNED AND UNINFORMED. THE BORDER IS A SYMBOL OF THE UNIFYING NATURE OF LODGE MEMBERSHIP. THE SKIRTWORK SYMBOL-IZES A BORDER OF COMMON PROVIDENCE, AND FROM THE MUTUAL INTERPLAY OF THE LIGHT AND DARKNESS IN ALL MASONS COMES THE REALIZATION THAT WISDOM WILL AT LAST BE JUSTIFIED. MOREOVER, WE NEED NOT COMPLAIN OF THE PROCESSES, WHICH MAY TEMPORARILY INVOLVE SHARP AND PAINFUL CONTRASTS, ALTHOUGH THEY WILL WORK OUT TO A BENEFICIAL CONCLUSION. THE TESSELLATED BORDER SHOWS THAT THE CORPORATE SPIRIT OF THE LODGE ENFOLDS AND SUP-PORTS THE INDIVIDUAL BRETHREN.

The Tracing Board

The tracing board is used by the Master to lay lines and draw designs on, better enabling the brethren to carry on the intended structure with regularity and propriety. The Volume of the Sacred Law may justly be deemed the spiritual tracing board of the Great Architect of the Universe. In it are laid down such divine laws and moral plans that, were we conversant with it and adherent to it, would bring us to an ethereal mansion not made with hands but eternal in the heavens.

STRUCTURE DERIVES FROM THE TRACING BOARD.

Robert Lomas's personal view

IN ANCIENT TIMES, THE SYMBOLS OF THE DEGREE WERE DRAWN ON THE LODGE FLOOR BY THE RIGHT WORSHIPFUL MASTER USING CHALK AND CHARCOAL. DURING THE TRADITIONAL INSTALLATION CEREMONY, THE CANDIDATE WALKED THE STEPS OF THE DEGREE ABOVE THE SYMBOLS THAT ILLUMINATED THE KNOWLEDGE BEING IMPARTED. AT THE END OF THE CEREMONY, THE CANDIDATE MOPPED AWAY THE SYMBOLS TO HIDE THEM FROM THE EYES OF THE PROFANE. IN RECENT YEARS, THIS FRESHLY DRAWN SET OF SYMBOLS HAS BEEN LARGELY REPLACED BY ARTISTIC IMAGES OF THE SYMBOLS IN THE CONTEXT OF THE DEGREE. FROM STUDY OF THE TRACING BOARDS, THE MASON CAN DRAW ASIDE THE VEILS OF ALLEGORY THAT SHROUD THE TEACHINGS OF THE CRAFT.

THE CRAFT SOMETIMES CALLS ITSELF THE "SONS OF THE WIDOW." IN THIS NAME, THE SYMBOL OF FREEMASONRY AS A MYSTICAL AND BELOVED MOTHER IS INVOKED. WITHIN THE TRACING BOARD, THE CRAFT STANDS DRAPED WITH DARK AND FORBIDDING VEILS OF THE MOURNING WIDOW. AS WE LIFT THOSE VEILS, WE DISCOVER THE PRESENCE OF SOMETHING OF DEEPENING WONDER AND EVER-INCREASING BEAUTY—SOMETHING THAT WILL MAKE US AND OUR CRAFT GREATER THAN WE CURRENTLY ARE.

The Rough Ashlar

The Entered Apprentice works, marks, and indents on the rough ashlar. It is a stone, rough and unhewn as taken from the quarry, and by the industry and ingenuity of the workman, it is modeled, wrought into due form, and rendered fit for the intended structure. This symbol represents man in his infant or primitive state, rough and unpolished as that stone. Only through the kind care and attention of his parents or guardians, who give him a liberal and virtuous education, does his mind become cultivated, thereby rendering him a fit member of civilized society.

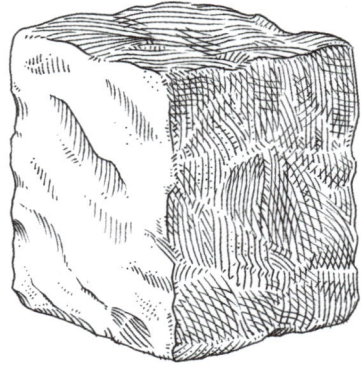

Robert Lomas's personal view

A MASON WHO DESIRES TO RISE TO THE HEIGHTS OF HIS OWN BEING MUST FIRST CRUSH HIS OWN LOWER NATURE AND INCLINATIONS. HE MUST PERFECT HIS CONDUCT THROUGH STRUGGLING AGAINST HIS OWN NATURAL PROPENSITIES. HIS BASE MATERIAL NATURE IS SYMBOLIZED BY THE ROUGH ASHLAR, AS IT IS DRAGGED FROM THE CLAY OF THE QUARRY. THE CANDIDATE IS GIVEN SPIRITUAL TOOLS TO WORK THE ROUGH ASHLAR OF HIS OWN NATURE INTO THE PERFECT CUBE OF AN ENLIGHTENED SOUL. AND THE CUBE CONTAINS A SECRET, SO THAT WHEN UNFOLDED, IT DENOTES AND TAKES THE FORM OF THE CROSS, MADE UP OF FOUR RIGHT ANGLES OR SQUARES.

The Perfect Ashlar

The perfect ashlar is for the experienced craftsman to try and adjust his jewels on. The perfect ashlar is a stone of a true die or square, fit only to be tried by the square and the compasses. This symbol represents man in the decline of his years, after a regular and well-spent life performing acts of piety and virtue. He can only be tried and approved by the square of God's word and the compass of his own self-convincing conscience.

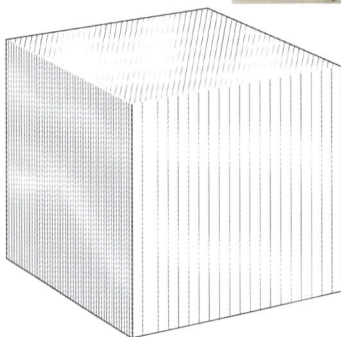

Robert Lomas's personal view

THE STATE OF SPIRITUAL DEVELOPMENT SIGNIFIED BY THE PERFECT ASHLAR IS THE WORK INVOLVED IN THE MASONIC SECOND DEGREE. TO ATTAIN THIS, THE MASON'S SOUL AND BODY MUST BE BROUGHT INTO A BALANCED RELATIONSHIP BEFORE PASSING THROUGH A CRUCIAL REGENERATIVE EXPERIENCE KNOWN AS THE CROSS OR TRANSITION FROM NATURAL TO SUPRANATURAL LIFE.

THE CROSS AS A PHILOSOPHICAL SYMBOL LONG PREDATES CHRISTIANITY. IN FREEMASONRY, IT IS SIGNIFICANT AS A SYMBOL OF THE FOUR PRIMORDIAL ELEMENTS (FIRE, WATER, AIR, AND EARTH) BROUGHT TOGETHER INTO A STATE OF BALANCED UNION. ALL NEWLY MADE MASONS HAVE TOO MUCH OR TOO LITTLE OF ONE OR ANOTHER ELEMENT IN THEIR COMPOSITION, AND THE NEED TO RESTORE THE INNER ELEMENTS OF THE BODY, MIND, SPIRIT, AND SOUL TO BALANCE AND HARMONY WITH OURSELVES IS THE LIFE PROBLEM WE ALL SHARE.

THE CROSS OF THE UNFOLDED PERFECT ASHLAR IS A CONSPICUOUS SYMBOL OF THE HUMAN SOUL. OUR EGO IS BOUND BY THE CROSS OF THE FOUR MATERIAL ELEMENTS, WHICH IT MUST SUBDUE INTO BALANCE AND HARMONY. THE MASONIC RITUAL SAYS," WE MUST MAKE ALL OUR PASSIONS AND PREJUDICES COINCIDE WITH THE STRICT LINE OF VIRTUE AND IN EVERY PURSUIT HAVE ETERNITY IN VIEW."

THE PERFECT ASHLAR SYMBOLIZES THE STATE OF BALANCE AND HARMONY THAT IS THE GOAL OF EVERY FELLOW OF THE CRAFT FREEMASON.

The Point within a Circle

In all regular, well-formed, well-constituted lodges, there is a point within a circle around which the brethren cannot err. This circle is bound between the North and the South by two grand parallel lines: one representing Moses and the other, King Solomon. On the upper part of this circle rests the Volume of the Sacred Law supporting Jacob's ladder, the top of which reaches to the heavens. In going around this circle, we must necessarily touch on both parallel lines and likewise on the sacred volume. While a Mason keeps himself thus circumscribed, he cannot err.

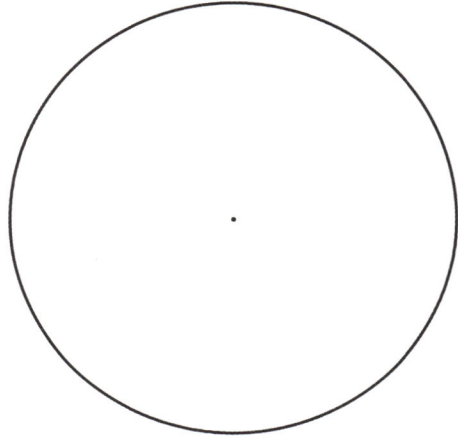

Robert Lomas's personal view

A DORMANT BUT VITAL PRINCIPLE EXISTS AS THE CENTRAL POINT OF THE CIRCLE OF A MASON'S INDIVIDUALITY. JUST AS THE OUTWARD UNIVERSE IS AN EXTERNALIZED PROJECTION OF THE GREAT ARCHITECT, SO IS THE OUTWARD INDIVIDUAL MASON THE EXTERNALIZATION OF AN INHERENT DIVINE SPARK, THROUGH WHICH PERSONAL SELF-WILL AND DESIRE HAVE BECOME DISLOCATED AND SHUT OFF THE MASON'S CONSCIOUSNESS. TO RECOVER CONTACT WITH THAT CENTRAL DIVINE PRINCIPLE IS THE PURPOSE OF FREEMASONRY. ONCE A MASON CEASES TO BE SIMPLY A RATIONALIZED ANIMAL AND BECOMES PRIVY TO MYSTERIES OF THE CENTER, HE RECOVERS THE LOST AND GENUINE SECRETS OF HIS OWN BEING. THE MASON WHO REACHES THAT POINT LIVES FROM THE CENTER, FOR IT IS THE END, THE OBJECT, AND THE GOAL OF HIS MASONIC EXISTENCE.

A MASON WHO HAS FOUND AND LIVES FROM THE DIVINE CENTER OF HIS BEING—THAT POINT FROM WHICH A MASTER MASON CANNOT ERR—POSSESSES WISDOM AND POWERS BEYOND THE IMAGINATION OF THE UNINITIATED WORLD.

Chalk, Charcoal, and Clay

Chalk is an ancient deposit, pure in its whiteness, and abundant. It is an emblem of Masonic secret wisdom, which is an ancient doctrine revealed and deposited from heavenly sources for the uplifting of man. It is free to whoever seeks it, and as such, it cannot fail to leave a mark on his mind.

Charcoal is an emblem of fervent heat. It symbolizes the need for the Masonic doctrine to be burned into the fabric of our being, mingled with our personal clay, and inscribed on the fleshy tablets of the heart. Like chalk and charcoal, the tracing board was personally imprinted on the earthy flooring of the lodge.

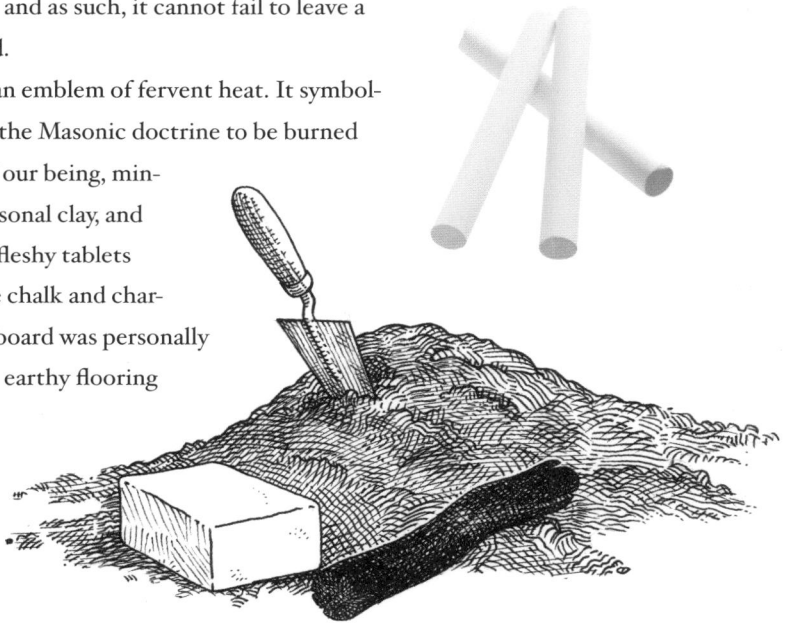

Robert Lomas's personal view

THESE MATERIALS—WHITE CHALK, BLACK CHARCOAL, AND MALLEABLE CLAY—SYMBOLIZE TRUTH, UNDERSTANDING, AND GROWTH. NOTHING IS MORE FREE THAN CHALK; ITS SLIGHTEST TOUCH LEAVES A TRACE. NOTHING IS MORE FERVENT THAN CHARCOAL; WHEN IT IS PROPERLY LIGHTED, NO METAL CAN RESIST ITS FORCE. NOTHING IS MORE ZEALOUS AND ADAPTABLE THAN CLAY; OUR MOTHER EARTH IS CONTINUALLY LABORING FOR OUR SUPPORT. FROM CLAY WE CAME, AND TO CLAY WE MUST ALL RETURN.

CHALK IS ABUNDANTLY FREE TO THE SERVICE OF MAN AND LEAVES ITS MARK ON WHATEVER IT TOUCHES. IT SYMBOLIZES THE SECRET MASONIC WISDOM, WHICH IS AN ANCIENT DOCTRINE REVEALED AND DEPOSITED FROM THE MYSTICAL CENTER FOR THE SPIRITUAL UPLIFTING OF ALL MASONS. ITS WHITENESS REPRESENTS THE PURITY OF MASONIC TEACHING, AND ITS NATURE SHOWS HOW EASILY THAT TEACHING ADHERES TO THOSE WHO SEEK IT OUT.

The Lewis

If you wished to give your son a Masonic name, you would call him Lewis, which denotes strength. This name is depicted in Masonic lodges by certain pieces of metal dovetailed into a stone, forming a cramp. And when combined with some of the mechanical powers, such as a system of pulleys, this device enables the operative mason to raise great weights to certain heights with little encumbrance and to fix them on their proper bases.

A Lewis, being the son of a Mason, has a duty to his aged parents to bear the heat and burden of the day, which they should be exempt from, by reason of their age. He is to assist them in time of need and thereby ensure that their final days are happy and comfortable. His privilege for so doing is to be made a Mason before any other person, however dignified.

THE LEWIS IS A SYMBOL OF STRENGTH.

Robert Lomas's personal view

THE NAME LEWIS IS TRADITIONALLY ASSOCIATED WITH THE CRAFT. IT IS THE NAME GIVEN TO THE SON OF A MASON. BUT THE SYMBOL OF THE LEWIS, AS ASSOCIATED WITH LIGHT, IS ALSO A DEVICE USED BY OPERATIVE MASONS TO LIFT AND PLACE WEIGHTS ON THEIR BASES. SYMBOLICALLY, THIS REFERS TO THE FACT THAT WHEN THE DIVINE LIGHT IS BROUGHT FORWARD FROM A MASON'S SUBMERGED DEPTHS AND DOVETAILED INTO HIS SOUL, HE BECOMES ABLE TO EASILY GRAPPLE WITH DIFFICULTIES, PROBLEMS, AND "WEIGHTS" OF ALL KINDS. THE NAME ALSO SYMBOLIZES A MASON'S MORAL JUDGMENT, WHICH TEACHES HIM TO JUDGE REAL VALUES AND, IN THE WORDS OF THE RITUAL, "FIX THEM ON THEIR PROPER BASES."

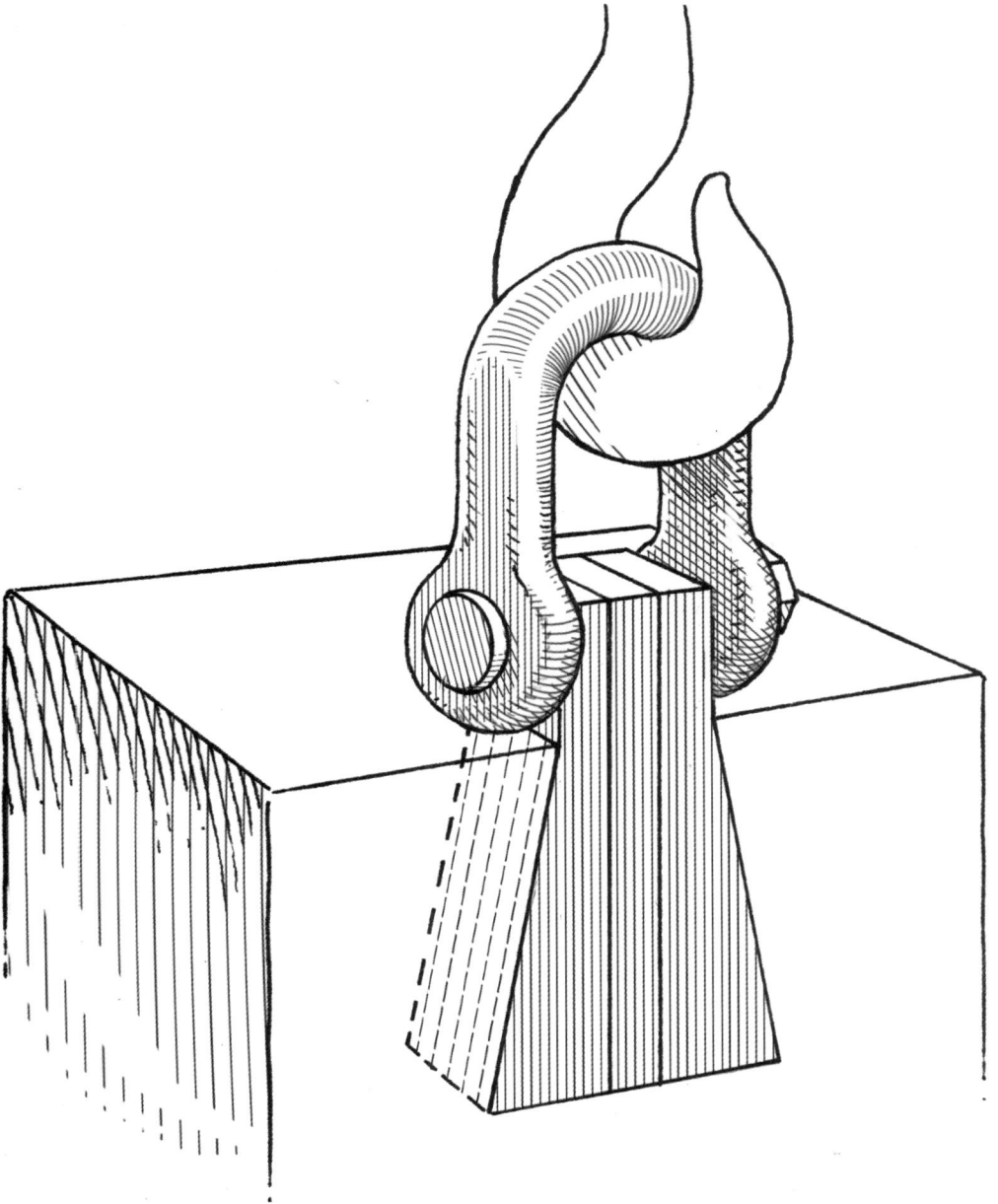

The Square and Compasses with Both Points Covered

Your progress in Masonry is marked by the position of the square and compasses. When you are made an Entered Apprentice, both points are hidden. This is the distinguishing badge of an Entered Apprentice.

THIS SQUARE AND COMPASSES WITH BOTH POINTS COVERED SYMBOL IS TAKEN FROM A MODERN INTERPRETATION OF THE FIRST-DEGREE TRACING BOARD, CURRENTLY ON DISPLAY AT THE CHANCELLOR ROBERT R LIVINGSTON MASONIC LIBRARY OF GRAND LODGE. Copyright Angel Millar. Reprinted with permission

Robert Lomas's personal view

IN FREEMASONRY, WE SPEAK OF THE GREAT ARCHITECT OF THE UNIVERSE AND COSMOS AS THE COSMIC TEMPLE BEING BUILT IN ACCORDANCE WITH THE DIVINE PLAN AND MEASURED OUT WITH THE HELP OF THE DIVINE COMPASSES AND SQUARE. THIS IDEA, WHICH IS THE BASIS OF MASONIC DOCTRINE AND PHILOSOPHY, IS THE FIRST SECRET REVEALED TO EVERY CANDIDATE. HE IS SHOWN THE SQUARE AND COMPASSES IMMEDIATELY AFTER HAVING HIS HOODWINK REMOVED. BECAUSE HE IS ONLY AN APPRENTICE, THE POINTS OF THE COMPASSES ARE HIDDEN BENEATH THE SQUARE; HE IS NOT YET PREPARED TO TAKE PART IN THE APPLICATION OF THE DIVINE PLAN. BUT AS A MASON, IT IS NOW HIS DUTY TO COOPERATE WITH THE GREAT ARCHITECT IN EXECUTING HIS PLAN AND ERECTING THE GREAT COSMIC TEMPLE. THE SQUARE THAT COVERS THE COMPASSES SYMBOLIZES THE SPIRITUAL TOOL HE WILL NEED TO MASTER TO SHAPE HIS SOUL INTO A PERFECT CUBE.

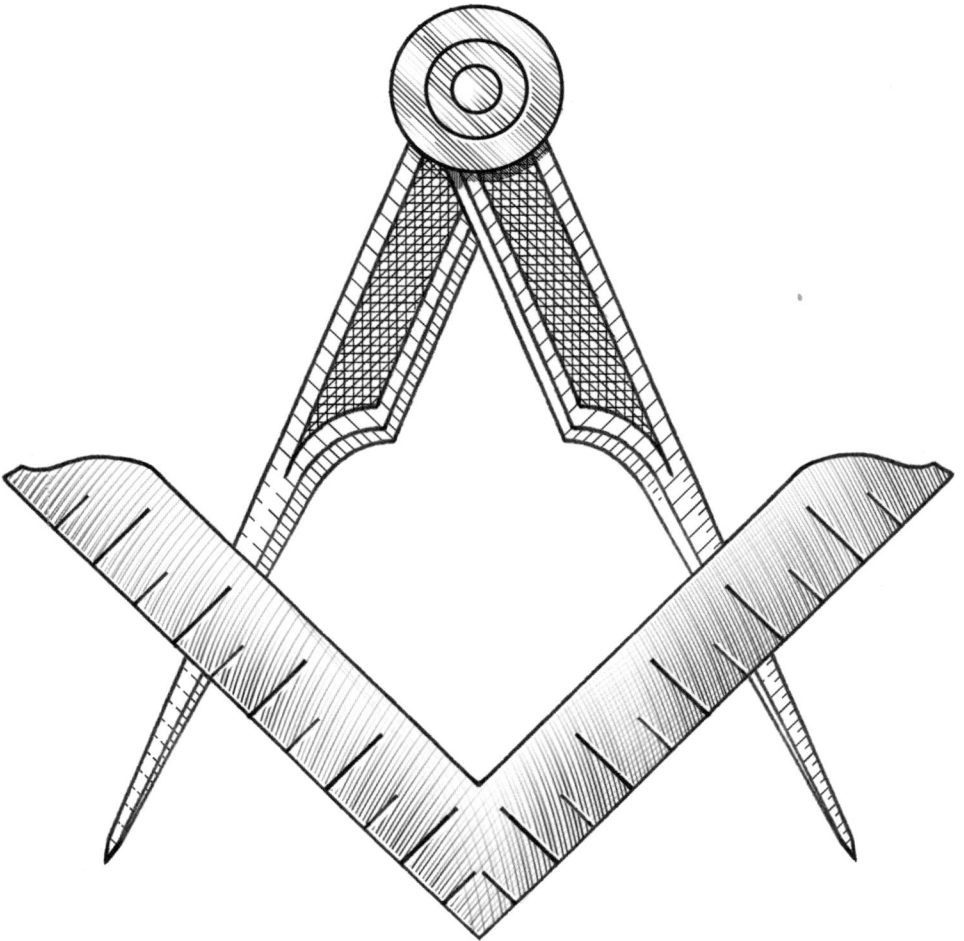

CHAPTER II

SYMBOLS OF THE
SECOND DEGREE

The Square and Compasses
with One Point Covered

When you were made an Entered Apprentice, both points of the compasses were hidden from your view, showing that you were newly admitted. Now that you are a Fellow of the Craft, one point is exposed, proving that you are midway in Freemasonry and thus superior to an Entered Apprentice but inferior to the status you will still likely attain.

Robert Lomas's personal view

AS A MASON PROGRESSES THROUGH HIS DEGREES, DARKNESS IS GRADUALLY BEING DISSOLVED BY LIGHT. IN THE DEGREE OF THE FELLOW OF THE CRAFT, ONE POINT OF THE GREAT ARCHITECT'S COMPASSES IS BROUGHT INTO SIGHT TO OVERLAY THE SQUARE OF HUMAN ACTIVITY IN SHAPING THE SOUL. HAVING BEEN INITIATED INTO THE MYSTIC AND COSMIC PRINCIPLES OF THE SQUARE AND COMPASSES, THE MASON SEES THAT THEY REST ON THE UNSHAKEABLE BASIS OF THE DIVINE PLAN. THE CHANGE IN THE VISIBILITY OF THE COMPASS POINTS REFLECTS THE FELLOW OF THE CRAFT'S MIDWAY POSITION IN THE CRAFT. HE CAN NOW DISCERN—IN BOTH THE COMPASSES AND IN HIMSELF—THE ONGOING CONFLICT OF DARKNESS AND LIGHT. AS THE POINTS OF THE COMPASSES EMERGE FROM DARKNESS, THEY SYMBOLIZE THAT, IN THE END, LIGHT ALWAYS CONQUERS. THIS EVOLVING SYMBOL IS PREPARING THE FELLOW OF THE CRAFT TO EXPECT TO MEET DIFFICULTIES AS HE ENDEAVORS TO FOCUS HIS UNDERSTANDING, AS SYMBOLIZED BY THE POINTS OF THE COMPASSES RISING FULLY INTO THE LIGHT.

A WOODEN SIGN FROM A TAVERN IN UPSTATE NEW YORK. From the collection of the Chancellor Robert R Livingston Masonic Library of Grand Lodge, New York, N.Y.

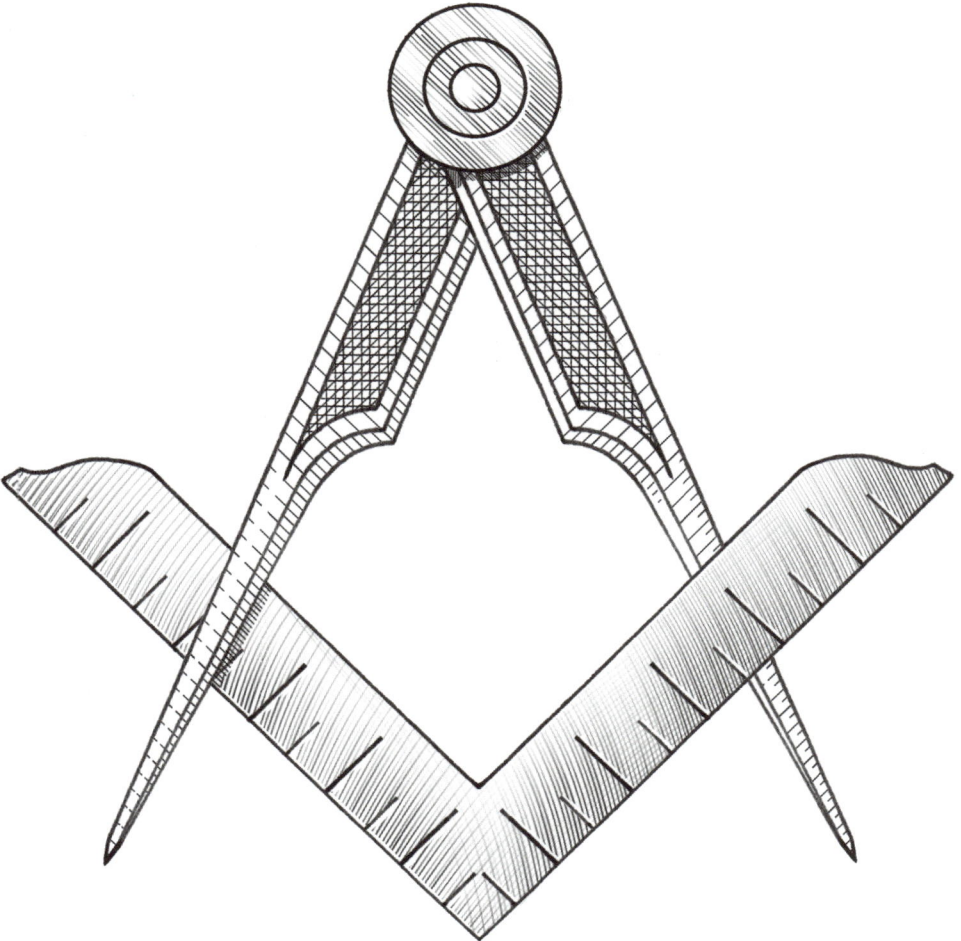

The Right-Hand Pillar

Jachin was the name of the right-hand pillar that stood at the entrance or porchway of King Solomon's temple. It was named after the great high priest who officiated at the temple's dedication, and it represents the power of the priest and the benevolent force of religion.

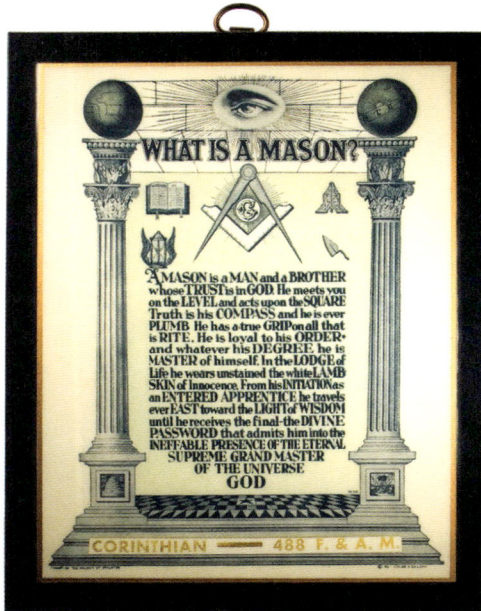

A SMALL WOODEN PLAQUE FROM THE COLLECTION OF THE CHANCELLOR ROBERT R LIVINGSTON MASONIC LIBRARY OF GRAND LODGE, NEW YORK, N.Y.

Robert Lomas's personal view

RECALL THAT THE LEFT-HAND PILLAR WAS NAMED FOR A KING AND RULER AND SYMBOLIZES THE FORCE OF SECULAR POWER IN SOCIETY. SIMILARLY, THE RIGHT-HAND PILLAR WAS NAMED FOR A HIGH PRIEST AND SYMBOLIZES THE POWER AND FORCE OF RELIGION IN THE LIFE OF SOCIETY. WISE ACTIVITY (BOAZ) MUST BE BALANCED WITH EQUALLY WISE PASSIVITY (JACHIN), IF A MASON IS TO BECOME ESTABLISHED IN STRENGTH AND TO STAND FIRM AND SPIRITUALLY CONSOLIDATED.

THIS IS NOT WORK TO BE HURRIED. THOSE THAT BUILD TEMPLES OF HUMANITY MUST WORK SLOWLY AND DO NOTHING IN EXCESS, CONSIDERING BUT THE FORCE OF TEMPORAL AND SPIRITUAL POWER.

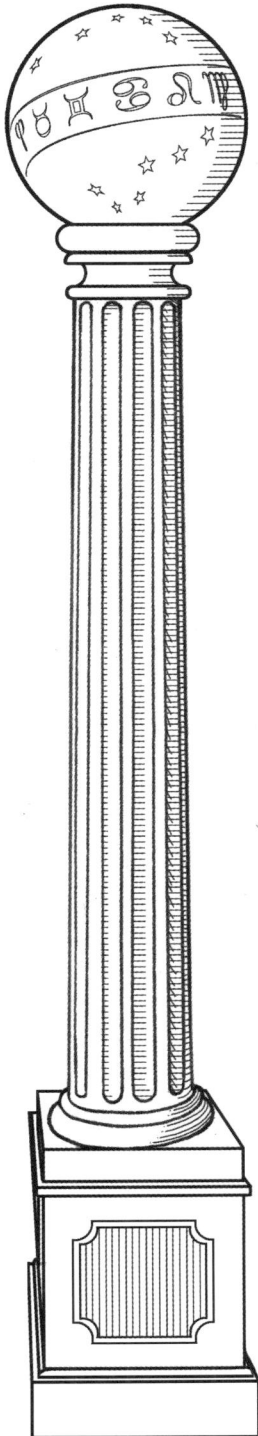

The Two Pillars at the Entrance to King Solomon's Temple

The pillar on the left of the porch of King Solomon's temple was called Boaz, and the pillar on the right, Jachin. The former denotes strength, and the latter, when conjoined, stability. The ritual says that each pillar was 17.5 cubits in height, 12 cubits in circumference, and 4 cubits in diameter.

The pillars were cast hollow the better to serve as archives for the Masons, who deposited the constitutional rolls within them. Each pillar's outer rim or shell was 4inches thick and made of molten brass. The shell was cast in the plain of Jordan in the clay ground between Succoth and Zeredathah, where King Solomon ordered those and all his holy vessels to be cast. The casting superintendent was Hiram Abif.

Robert Lomas's personal view

ALL MATTER IS COMPOSED OF POSITIVE AND NEGATIVE FORCES IN PERFECT BALANCE AND CONTAINS OBJECTS THAT WOULD DISINTEGRATE AND DISAPPEAR IF THEY DID NOT STAND FIRM IN PERFECT BALANCE. THE TWO PILLARS SYMBOLIZE THIS PERFECT INTEGRITY OF BODY AND SOUL, WHICH IS ESSENTIAL TO ACHIEVING SPIRITUAL PERFECTION.

IN ANCIENT PHILOSOPHY, ALL THINGS WERE CREATED FROM FIRE AND WATER—FIRE AS THE SPIRITUAL ELEMENT AND WATER AS THE MATERIAL ELEMENT. THE TWO PILLARS REPRESENT THESE UNIVERSAL PROPERTIES. IN THIS SYMBOLISM, THE PATH TO TRUE WISDOM IS AN ENTRANCE BETWEEN FIRE, ON THE RIGHT HAND, AND DEEP WATER, ON THE LEFT. THE PATH IS SO NARROW THAT THE MASON MUST TRAVEL IT ALONE. THIS NARROW PATH OF TRUE INITIATION IS SYMBOLIZED AS WE ENTER THE COSMIC TEMPLE BETWEEN THE SYMBOLIC PILLARS. FOR AS THE RITUAL SAYS "THE FORMER DENOTES STRENGTH THE LATTER TO ESTABLISH AND WHEN CONJOINED STABILITY, FOR GOD SAID 'IN STRENGTH WILL I ESTABLISH MY WORD IN THIS MINE HOUSE THAT IT WILL STAND FAST FOR EVER.'"

THIS EIGHTEENTH-CENTURY CERTIFICATE OF MEMBERSHIP IN THE "LOGE LE PARFAIT SILENCE" IN LYON, FRANCE IS SITUATED BETWEEN TWO PILLARS AND INCLUDES TEXT IN THREE LANGUAGES: FRENCH, ITALIAN, AND ENGLISH.

The Chapiters

The chapiters of each of these pillars were decorated with net-work, lily-work, and pomegranates. Each type of decoration had a symbolic meaning which is explained later. They also served to indicate the resting place of the secrets of Freemasonry.

THE CHAPITERS OFFER AN ADDITIONAL LAYER OF SYMBOLISM TO THE TWO PILLARS. Courtesy of www.tracingboards.com

Robert Lomas's personal view

THERE ARE ADDITIONAL LAYERS OF SYMBOLISM TO THE TWO PILLARS THAT STOOD AT THE ENTRANCE TO KING SOLOMON'S TEMPLE. THE CHAPITERS WERE FORMED HOLLOW WHEN THEY WERE CAST FROM MOLTEN BRASS ON THE PLAIN OF JORDAN, IN THE CLAY GROUND BETWEEN SUCCOTH AND ZEREDATHAH. THIS WORK OF CASTING WAS DIRECTED BY MASTER ARCHITECT HIRAM ABIF. HE CAST THE PILLARS HOLLOW SO THEY COULD SERVE AS A REPOSITORY OF THE ARCHIVES OF MASONRY, WHICH WERE DEPOSITED WITHIN THEM. TO MARK THE FACT THEY CONTAINED THE HIDDEN SECRETS OF MASONRY, THE CHAPITERS WERE DECORATED WITH SUITABLE SYMBOLS. EACH CHAPITER WAS 5 CUBITS HIGH.

The Net-Work

Net-work, which is made from connecting meshes, represents unity.

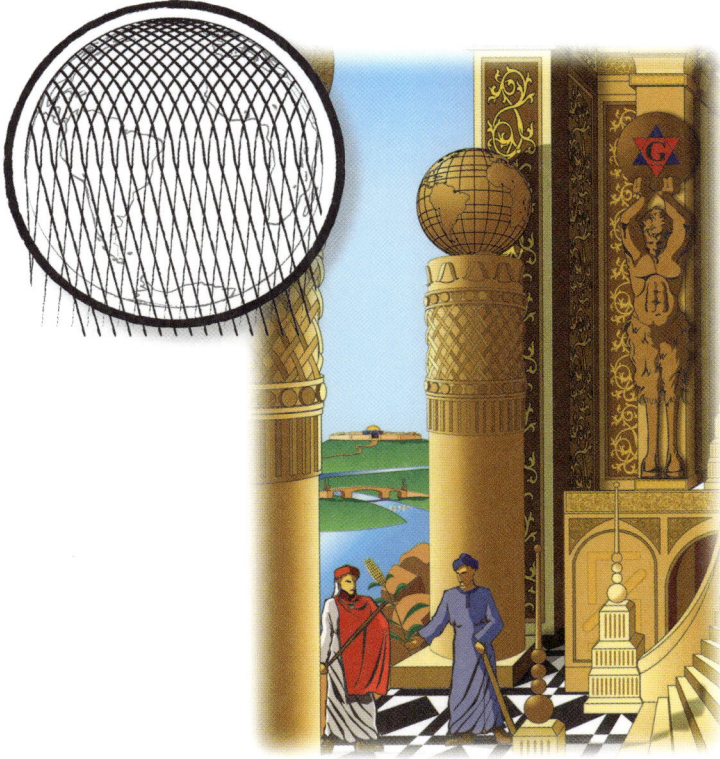

THE NET-WORK SYMBOLIZES THE UNIVERSAL UNITY AND
BROTHERHOOD OF MASONRY. Courtesy of www.tracingboards.com

Robert Lomas's personal view

THE RITUAL TELLS US THAT THE HEADS OF THE TWO PILLARS WERE ENRICHED WITH NET-WORK.

NET-WORK, BY THE UNITY AND INTERCONNECTED NATURE OF ITS MESHES, SYMBOLIZES THE

UNIVERSAL UNITY AND BROTHERHOOD OF MASONRY. THE NET-WORK WAS THE FINAL WORK DONE

BEFORE THE PILLARS WERE CONSIDERED FINISHED. IN THIS SYMBOLISM, THE BRETHREN ARE TOLD

THAT THE WORK ON THE TEMPLE OF HUMANITY WILL NOT BE COMPLETE UNTIL ALL PEOPLE CAN

HONOR ONE ANOTHER AS BRETHREN. THE HIDDEN RECORDS CONTAIN THE DIVINE PLAN OF HOW

THIS WAS TO BE ACHIEVED.

The Lily-Work

Lily-work, from its whiteness, represents peace.

THE LILY-WORK SIGNIFIES A LOVE MOST COMPLETE IN PERFECTION. Courtesy of www.tracingboards.com

Robert Lomas's personal view

THE LILY-WORK THAT ADORNS THE CHAPITERS IS A SYMBOL OF PURITY AND PEACE. ITS WHITENESS SPEAKS OF LIGHT AND TRUTH, AND THE LILIES REPRESENT PEACE. THE LILY IS A TRADITIONAL SYMBOL OF DIVINITY, PURITY, AND ABUNDANCE. IT SIGNIFIES A LOVE MOST COMPLETE IN PERFECTION, CHARITY, AND BENEDICTION. LILY-WORK SURROUNDS EACH OF THE TWO PILLARS, JUST AS THE BROTHERLY LOVE OF THE TESSELLATED BORDER SURROUNDS THE LODGE.

The Pomegranates

Pomegranates, from the exuberance of their seeds, represent plenty. There were two rows of pomegranates on each chapiter—one hundred in each row.

BECAUSE OF THE ABUNDANCE OF A POMEGRANATE'S SEEDS, IT SYMBOLIZES WEALTH. Courtesy of www.tracingboards.com

Robert Lomas's personal view

TO THE NATIONS OF ANTIQUITY, THE POMEGRANATE WAS A HIGHLY ESTEEMED SYMBOL. BECAUSE OF THE ABUNDANCE OF THE POMEGRANATE'S SEEDS, IT WAS KNOWN AS A SYMBOL OF WEALTH, ABUNDANCE, AND PLENTY. MASONS ARE TOLD THAT THE SKIRT OF AARON'S ROBE WAS DECORATED WITH GOLDEN BELLS AND POMEGRANATES, AND POMEGRANATES ALSO ADORNED THE GOLDEN CANDELABRA WITHIN THE TEMPLE. THERE WERE TWO ROWS—EACH CONTAINING ONE HUNDRED POMEGRANATES—ON EACH CHAPITER, SYMBOLIZING THE WEALTH AND RICHNESS OF KNOWLEDGE CONTAINED IN THE SECRET ARCHIVES OF FREEMASONRY.

The Globes

The pillars were further adorned with two spherical balls that contained maps of the celestial and terrestrial globes, pointing out that Masonry is a universal science.

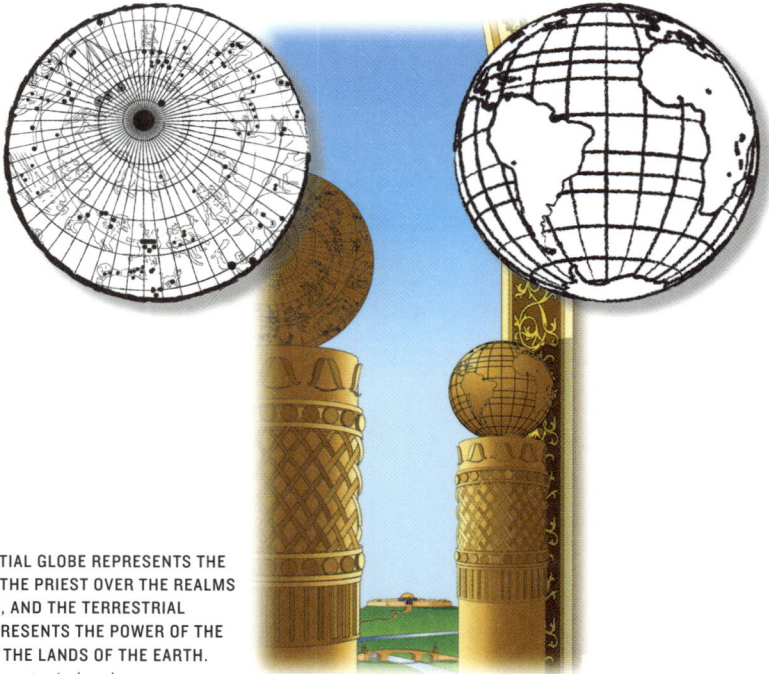

THE CELESTIAL GLOBE REPRESENTS THE POWER OF THE PRIEST OVER THE REALMS OF HEAVEN, AND THE TERRESTRIAL GLOBE REPRESENTS THE POWER OF THE KING OVER THE LANDS OF THE EARTH.
Courtesy of www.tracingboards.com

Robert Lomas's personal view

THE CHAPTERS OF THE TWO PILLARS WERE ALSO DECORATED WITH TWO SPHERICAL BALLS. THE PILLAR OF BOAZ HAD A TERRESTRIAL GLOBE, AND THE PILLAR OF JACHIN, A CELESTIAL GLOBE. THESE GLOBES, RESPECTIVELY, SYMBOLIZE THE POWER OF THE KING OVER THE LANDS OF THE EARTH AND THE POWER OF THE PRIEST OVER THE REALMS OF HEAVEN. THE CELESTIAL AND TERRESTRIAL GLOBES ARE ECHOED IN THE PILLARS OF THE SENIOR WARDEN AND JUNIOR WARDEN. WHEN THE LODGE IS OPENED, THE SENIOR WARDEN'S CELESTIAL GLOBE IS RAISED, AND THE JUNIOR WARDEN'S TERRESTRIAL GLOBE IS LOWERED TO SHOW THAT THE LODGE IS WORKING ON THE SPIRITUAL, RATHER THAN THE TEMPORAL, LEVEL.

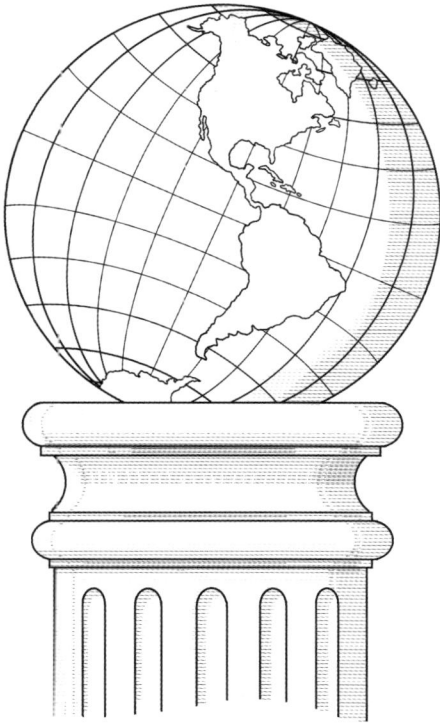

The Middle Chamber

Our ancient brethren went to receive their wages in the middle chamber of King Solomon's temple. They entered it through the porch or entrance on the south side, arriving at the foot of the winding staircase that led to the middle chamber.

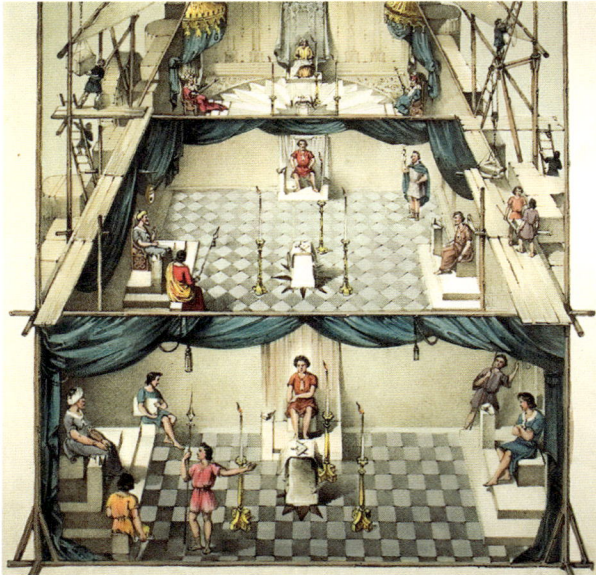

A RICHLY-COLORED LITHOGRAPH PRINT FROM A BOOK OF THE LODGE SHOWING THE MIDDLE CHAMBER, WHICH MASONS MUST PASS THROUGH BEFORE REACHING THE FIRE OF THE SPIRIT. From the collection of the Chancellor Robert R Livingston Masonic Library of Grand Lodge, New York, N.Y.

Robert Lomas's personal view

THE MIDDLE CHAMBER IS A SYMBOL OF THE HUMAN MIND. IT STANDS MIDWAY BETWEEN THINGS MATERIAL AND SPIRITUAL. IT IS REPRESENTED AS AN INTERMEDIATE HOLY PLACE THAT THE MASON MUST PASS THROUGH BEFORE REACHING THAT ULTIMATE HOLY OF HOLIES: THE FIRE OF THE SPIRIT. IT IS A MIDDLE CHAMBER, SO THE MASON IS LED TO FOLLOW A GRADUAL ASCENT FROM THE MATE-RIAL TO THE SPIRITUAL. THIS SYMBOLISM EXPLAINS WHY WE ASCEND TO PROGRESSIVELY HIGHER LEVELS BY SYMBOLICALLY OPENING UP FROM ONE DEGREE TO ANOTHER AND EXPOSING IN EACH LEVEL THE APPROPRIATE TRACING BOARD. BUT WE MUST NOT FORGET THAT EACH OPENING AND DEGREE IMPLIES AN UPLIFTING OF MIND AND HEART TO A HIGHER LEVEL OF CONTEMPLATION.

The Spiral Staircase

When the brethren approached the winding staircase, their ascent was opposed by the Junior Warden. He demanded of them the pass grip and the pass word. Only those who could give both correctly were allowed to proceed.

Those brethren who did pass went up a winding staircase consisting of three, five, seven, or more steps: three to rule a lodge, five to hold a lodge, and seven or more to make it perfect. The three steps represent the Right Worshipful Master and his two Wardens; the five steps represent the Right Worshipful Master, two Wardens, and two Fellows of the Craft; and the seven steps represent these positions plus two Entered Apprentices.

Three rule a lodge because at the building of King Solomon's temple, three Grand Masters held sway: Solomon, King of Israel; Hiram, King of Tyre; and Hiram Abif, master architect. Seven or more make it perfect because it took King Solomon seven years and more to build and dedicate the temple at Jerusalem to God's service. The seven steps also represent the seven liberal arts and sciences: grammar, rhetoric, logic, arithmetic, geometry, music, and astronomy.

When our ancient brethren reached the summit of the winding staircase, they arrived at the door of the middle chamber. They found it open but properly guarded by the ancient Senior Warden, who demanded of them the sign, token, and word of a Fellow of the Craft. After giving these convincing proofs, the brethren were allowed to pass. They then entered the middle chamber to receive their wages, which they did without scruple or diffidence. When they were in the chamber, their attention was drawn to certain Hebrew characters, which are now depicted in a Fellow of the Craft's Lodge by the letter G, which denotes the Grand Geometrician of the Universe.

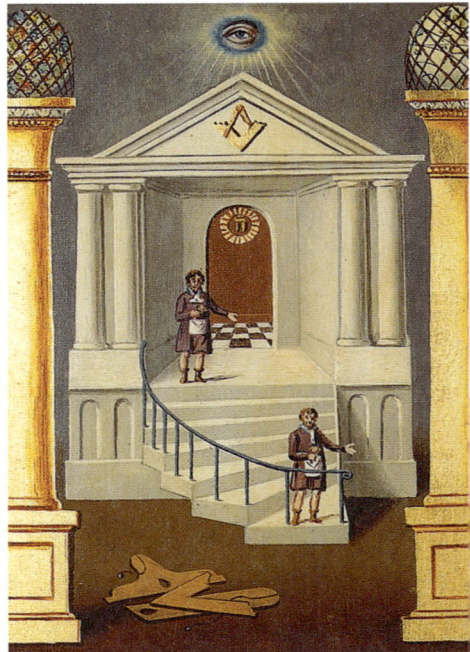

THE SPIRAL STAIRCASE, AS SEEN IN A RENDERING OF A SECOND-DEGREE TRACING BOARD.

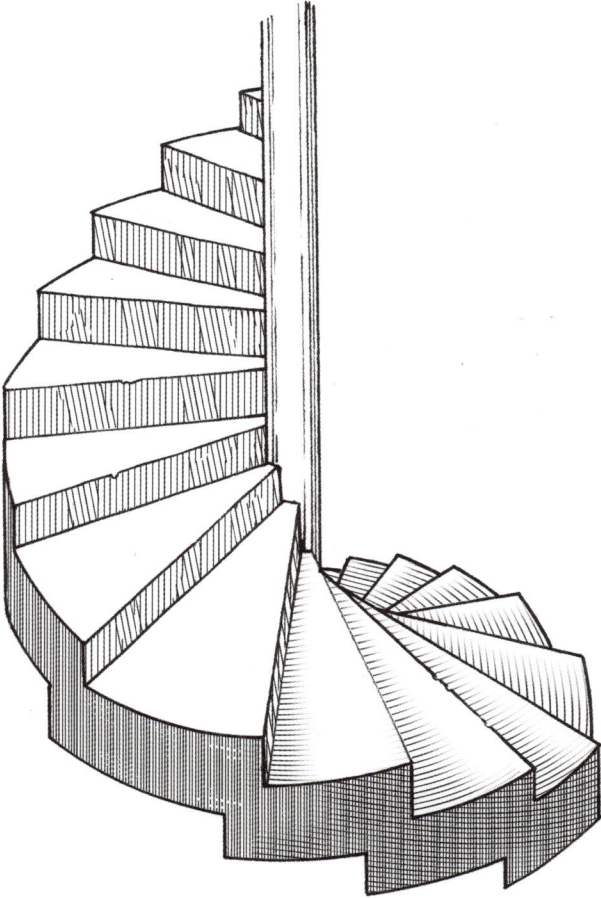

Robert Lomas's personal view

WHEN A CANDIDATE FOR FELLOW OF THE CRAFT FIRST ENTERS THE LODGE, HE TRACES A SQUARE PATH. IN DOING SO, HE VISITS THE FOUR SIDES AND SYMBOLIC METHODS OF GAINING KNOWLEDGE, EACH IN TURN. BUT THEN, HE IS DIRECTED TO MOUNT SPIRALLY BY A SERIES OF WINDING STEPS. THE LEVEL STEPS HAVE GIVEN WAY TO A SPIRAL ASCENT, SYMBOLIZING THAT THE CANDIDATE IS READY TO LEAVE THE LEVEL OF THE SENSE WORLD AND RISE TO THE LEVEL OF THE SUPRASENSUAL. AS HE ASCENDS THE WINDING STAIRCASE, THE CANDIDATE MENTALLY LEAVES BEHIND THE OUTER WORLD AND RISES INTO AN INNER SPIRITUAL WORLD. SYMBOLICALLY, AS HE CLIMBS THE SPIRAL STAIRWAY, HIS MIND ASCENDS TO THE SOURCE OF LIGHT. EXPLORING THESE NEW REGIONS AND LEARNING THEIR MANY SECRETS AND MYSTERIES IS HIS DUTY AS A FELLOW OF THE CRAFT.

The Wages

As noted earlier, our ancient brethren received their wages in the middle chamber of the temple. They received their wages without scruple or diffidence, well knowing that they were justly entitled to them. When the brethren were in the middle chamber, their attention was particularly arrested by certain Hebrew characters, which are now depicted in a Fellow of the Craft's Lodge by the letter G, which denotes the Grand Geometrician of the Universe, to whom we must all submit and whom we should strive most cheerfully to obey.

A LITHOGRAPH PRINT SHOWING ANCIENT BRETHREN RECEIVING THEIR WAGES. A MASON LEARNS THAT DIFFICULTY, ADVERSITY, AND PERSECUTION ARE HARDSHIPS (I.E., WAGES) HE MUST LEARN TO ACCEPT.

Robert Lomas's personal view

THE ROUGH ASHLAR CAN ONLY BE SQUARED AND PERFECTED BY CHIPPING AND POLISHING. THE MASON LEARNS THAT DIFFICULTY, ADVERSITY, AND PERSECUTION SERVE A USEFUL PURPOSE. THESE HARDSHIPS ARE HIS WAGES, AND HE MUST LEARN TO ACCEPT THEM, AS THE RITUAL SAYS, "WITHOUT SCRUPLE AND WITHOUT DIFFIDENCE, KNOWING THAT HE IS JUSTLY ENTITLED TO THEM, AND FROM THE CONFIDENCE HE HAS IN THE INTEGRITY OF HIS EMPLOYER."

WHEN A MASON SETS HIS FEET ON THE PATH TO THE LIGHT OF THE EAST, WHEN HE SEEKS PASSAGE BETWEEN THE PILLARS AND ENTERS DEEPER KNOWLEDGE, AND WHEN HE MOUNTS THE WINDING STAIRWAY TO THE HEIGHTS, HE MAKES A BREAK WITH HIS PAST AND PUTS HIS OLD METHODS OF LIVING BEHIND HIM. HE DETACHES HIMSELF FROM THE INTERESTS HE PREVIOUSLY PRIZED IN FAVOR OF SOMETHING BETTER. HE WILL FIND HIMSELF MOVED BETWEEN STATES OF LIGHT AND JOY AND PERIODS OF DARKNESS AND DISMAY. HE WILL DOUBT THE PATH ON WHICH HE HAS SET HIMSELF.

EXPERIENCES SUCH AS THIS CONSTITUTE HIS WAGES, AND HE MUST LEARN TO ACCEPT THEM WITHOUT COMPLAINING, AS THE RITUAL SAYS, "WITHOUT SCRUPLE OR DIFFIDENCE." THE FACT THAT WAGES ARE BEING PAID IS EVIDENCE OF SPIRITUAL PROGRESS. WHEN YOU REMAIN STAGNANT IN YOUR UNREGENERATE LIFE, YOU ARE SPIRITUALLY ASLEEP. BUT AS YOU AWAKE FROM YOUR TORPOR, YOU SET UP ADVERSE ENERGIES. THESE EXPERIENCES ARE SALUTARY LESSONS IN WISDOM AND CONDUCIVE TO THAT STABILITY OF SOUL THAT YOU WILL NEED IN ATTAINING HIGHER DEGREES.

An Ear of Corn Near a Pool of Water

An ear of corn near a pool of water denotes plenty. This symbol dates from the time that an army of Ephraimites crossed the River Jordan in a hostile manner against Jephtha, the renowned Gileaditish general. The Ephraimites had always been considered a clamorous and turbulent people. Jephtha tried to appease the Ephraimites but failed, so he gathered his army and fought them until they retreated. To render his victory decisive, Jephtha sent detachments of his army to secure the passages of the River Jordan, over which he knew the insurgents would flee. He gave strict orders to his guards, saying that if an Ephraimite fugitive came that way, he should immediately be slain, but if he evaded the truth or said nay, a test word was to be put to him to pronounce. If the fugitive could not pronounce the word properly, it would cost him his life.

King Solomon later had this test word adopted as a pass word in a Fellow of the Craft's Lodge. The pass word was used to prevent any unqualified person from ascending the winding staircase that led to the middle chamber of the temple.

IN THE SECOND-DEGREE CEREMONY, THE APPRENTICE IS GIVEN AN EAR OF CORN, WHICH IS A SYMBOL OF HIS GROWTH. Courtesy of www.tracingboards.com

Robert Lomas's personal view

IN THE SECOND-DEGREE CEREMONY, THE APPRENTICE MASON IS GIVEN AN EAR OF CORN AS HE
LEAVES THE LODGE, SO THAT HE MAY PREPARE PROPERLY TO PASS TO THE DEGREE OF FELLOW OF
THE CRAFT. THIS EAR OF CORN IS A SYMBOL OF THE APPRENTICE'S GROWTH. WHEN HE WAS FIRST
ADMITTED AS A DRY, UNNOURISHED SEED, HE WAS PLANTED IN THE GOOD, LEVEL EARTH OF THE
NORTHEAST CORNER OF THE LODGE. HE HAS BEEN NURTURED BY CAREFUL WATERING FROM THE
CALM, WISE POOL OF WISDOM THAT IS THE CORPORATE SOUL OF THE LODGE, AND HE HAS NOW
FLOWERED IN A HEAD OF SEED.

THE PASSWORD THAT DESCRIBES THE EAR OF CORN INCORPORATES THE SOUND OF A GENTLE
BREEZE, SYMBOLIZING THE BREATH OF DIVINE KNOWLEDGE THAT BLOWS FROM THE CENTER INTO
THE DEVELOPING MIND OF THE NEW FELLOW OF THE CRAFT. AS HIS HEAD OF SEED SWAYS LIGHTLY
IN THE BREEZE OF UNDERSTANDING, SO THE MASON GROWS IN AWARENESS OF THE CENTER.

The Five Noble Orders of Architecture

The five Masons needed to hold a lodge are represented by the five noble orders in architecture: the Tuscan, Doric, Ionic, Corinthian, and Composite.

Early humans, in full possession of wild and savage liberty, hid themselves in thickets of woods or in dens and caverns of the earth. In these poor recesses and gloomy solitudes, Masonry found them, and the Grand Geometrician of the Universe, pitying their forlorn situation, instructed them to build houses for their defense and comfort. The first efforts were small and the structures simple and rude—no more than a number of trees leaning together at the top, in the form of a cone, interwoven with twigs, and plastered with mud to exclude the air.

In this early period, we may suppose that each person desired to render his own house more convenient than that of his neighbor by improving on what had already been done. This led to considering the inconveniences of the round sort of habitation and to building others—more spacious and convenient—of the square form by placing tree trunks perpendicularly in the ground to form the sides and filling the interstices between them with branches that were closely woven and covered with clay. Horizontal beams were then placed on the upright trunks, which were strongly joined at the angles and thus kept the sides firm. The roof of the building was composed of joists, on which were laid several beds of reeds, leaves, and clay.

These ancient builders invented methods to make their huts more lasting and handsome, as well as convenient. They took off the bark and other unevenness from the trunks of the trees that formed the sides, raised them above the ground and humidity on stones, and covered them with flat stones or tiles to keep off the rain. They closed the spaces between the ends of the joists with clay or some other substance, and they covered the ends of the joists with boards, cut in the manner of triglyphs. The form of the roof was likewise altered. Because of its flatness, it was unfit to throw off the rain that fell in abundance during the winter seasons. So the builders raised it in the middle, giving it the form of a gable roof by placing rafters on the joists to support the clay, and they used other materials to create a covering.

From these simple forms, the orders of architecture began. Buildings of wood were set aside, and men began to erect solid and stately edifices of stone. Soon, these primitive huts grew into the first temples. Each of the different models had been improved to such a degree of perfection that it was, by way of eminence, denominated an order.

Of the five orders, three are of Greek origin and thus called Grecian orders. Distinguished by the names Doric, Ionic, and Corinthian, they exhibit three distinct characters of composition suggested by the diversity of form in the human frame. The other two orders are of Italian origin and called Roman orders; they are distinguished by the names Tuscan and Composite.

The Tuscan order is the simplest and most solid. It is placed first in the list of the five orders of architecture because of its plainness. The base of its column has few moldings. It has been compared to a sturdy laborer dressed in homely apparel.

THE FIVE NOBEL ORDERS OF ARCHITECTURE, TUSCAN, DORIC, IONIC, CORINTHIAN, AND COMPOSITE, ARE SHOWN LEFT TO RIGHT.

The Doric is the first of the Grecian orders and is placed second in the list of the five orders of architecture. Its column has no ornamentation except moldings on either base or capital. Its frieze is distinguished by triglyphs and metopes, and its cornice, by mutules. Being the most ancient of all the orders, the Doric retains more of the primitive hut style than any of the other orders. Its composition is both grand and noble. Because it was formed after the model of a muscular, full-grown man, delicate ornaments are repugnant to its characteristic solidity. The Doric order is principally used in warlike structures, where strength and noble simplicity are required.

TOSCANO   DORICO   IONICO   CORINTHO   COMPOSITO

Hauendo da trattare delli cinque Ordini di colonne, cioe Toscano, Dorico, Ionico, Corintho, et Composito, m'è parso che nel principio comunque, che si uedo le figure d'ogni specie di quello l'ha da trattare, ancor che non ui siano notate le sue misure particolari perche solo sono poste per dimostra una reoola oenerale liquale a una, per una particolarmente si dechiarera.

EACH OF THE FIVE NOBLE ORDERS REPRESENTS HOW A MASON CAN ENHANCE ALL ASPECTS OF HIS CHARACTER.

During this era, buildings were admirably calculated for strength and convenience but lacked something in grace and elegance. Continual observation of women supplied those characteristics, for the eye that is charmed with symmetry must be conscious of woman's elegance and beauty. This gave rise to the Ionic order. Its capital is adorned with volutes, and its cornice has dentils. The famous Temple of Diana at Ephesus (which took more than 200 years to build) was composed of this order. Both elegance and ingenuity were displayed in the invention of this column, modeled after a beautiful young woman.

A new capital was invented at Corinth by Calimachus, which gave rise to the Corinthian, which is deemed the richest of the orders. The capital of its column is adorned with two rows of leaves and eight volutes that sustain the abacus. This order is chiefly used in stately and superb structures.

The final order is the Composite, so named from being composed of parts of the other orders. Its capital is adorned with the two rows of leaves of the Corinthian and the volutes of the Ionic, and it has the quarter-round of the Tuscan and the Doric orders. The Composite's cornice has dentils or simple modillions. This order is used chiefly in structures where strength, elegance, and beauty are displayed.

Robert Lomas's personal view

THE FIVE NOBLE ORDERS OF ARCHITECTURE SHOW HOW A MASON CAN DEVELOP AND ENHANCE ALL ASPECTS OF HIS CHARACTER:

- THE TUSCAN PILLAR SHOWS THE VIRTUE OF THE PERSONAL EFFORT THAT MUST BE APPLIED TO DEVELOPING THE WISDOM OF THE SOUL; IT REPRESENTS PERSISTENCE.
- THE DORIC PILLAR REPRESENTS THE STRENGTH NEEDED TO BRING ABOUT CHANGE WITHIN YOUR SOUL AND THE VIRTUE OF WORKING FOR THE GOOD OF SOCIETY.
- THE IONIC PILLAR SHOWS THE NEED TO APPRECIATE AND CREATE BEAUTY WITHIN THE WORLD.
- THE CORINTHIAN PILLAR SHOWS HOW WISDOM, STRENGTH, AND BEAUTY MAY BE COMBINED TO PRODUCE A SOUL THAT IS STATELY AND IMPRESSIVE.
- THE COMPOSITE PILLAR SHOWS HOW ALL THE TEACHINGS OF THE CRAFT MUST BE BROUGHT TOGETHER TO FORM A STRUCTURE (I.E., A SOUL) THAT CAN DISPLAY STRENGTH, WISDOM, AND BEAUTY ACCORDING TO THE ASPECT FROM WHICH IT IS VIEWED.

SYMBOLS OF THE THIRD DEGREE

The Square and Compasses with Both Points Revealed

When you were made an Entered Apprentice, both points were hidden, and in the second degree, one was disclosed. Now you are a Master Mason, and the whole is exhibited, implying that you are now at liberty to work with both points to render complete the circle of your Masonic duties.

THE SQUARE AND COMPASSES OF THE MASTER MASON.

Robert Lomas's personal view

WHEN A CANDIDATE MASON PROGRESSES TO BECOME A MASTER MASON, THE POSITION OF THE SQUARE AND COMPASSES IS CHANGED TO REVEAL BOTH POINTS OF THE COMPASS AND THE SEPARATED SQUARE. NOW, THE MASTER MASON HAS FACED THE ULTIMATE TRIAL OF THE THIRD DEGREE: HE HAS SHOWN THAT HE UNDERSTANDS THAT HONOR, LOYALTY, AND SELF-SACRIFICE CAN BE MORE IMPORTANT THAN LIFE ITSELF. IN GAINING THIS KNOWLEDGE, HE HAS EXTENDED THE SCOPE OF HIS SOUL'S UNDERSTANDING. THE SQUARE SHOWS HOW HE HAS LABORED TO SHAPE HIS SOUL INTO A PERFECT CUBE, WHICH CAN BE TRIED AND PROVED ON ANY CORNER BY THE FREELY SEPARATED SQUARE. IN ADDITION, THE COMPASSES ARE NOW FREE TO HELP HIM FIND THE MYSTICAL CENTER— THAT POINT EQUIDISTANT FROM THE CIRCUMFERENCE AND MARKS THE SPOT FROM WHICH, ONCE FOUND, NO MASON CAN POSSIBLY ERR.

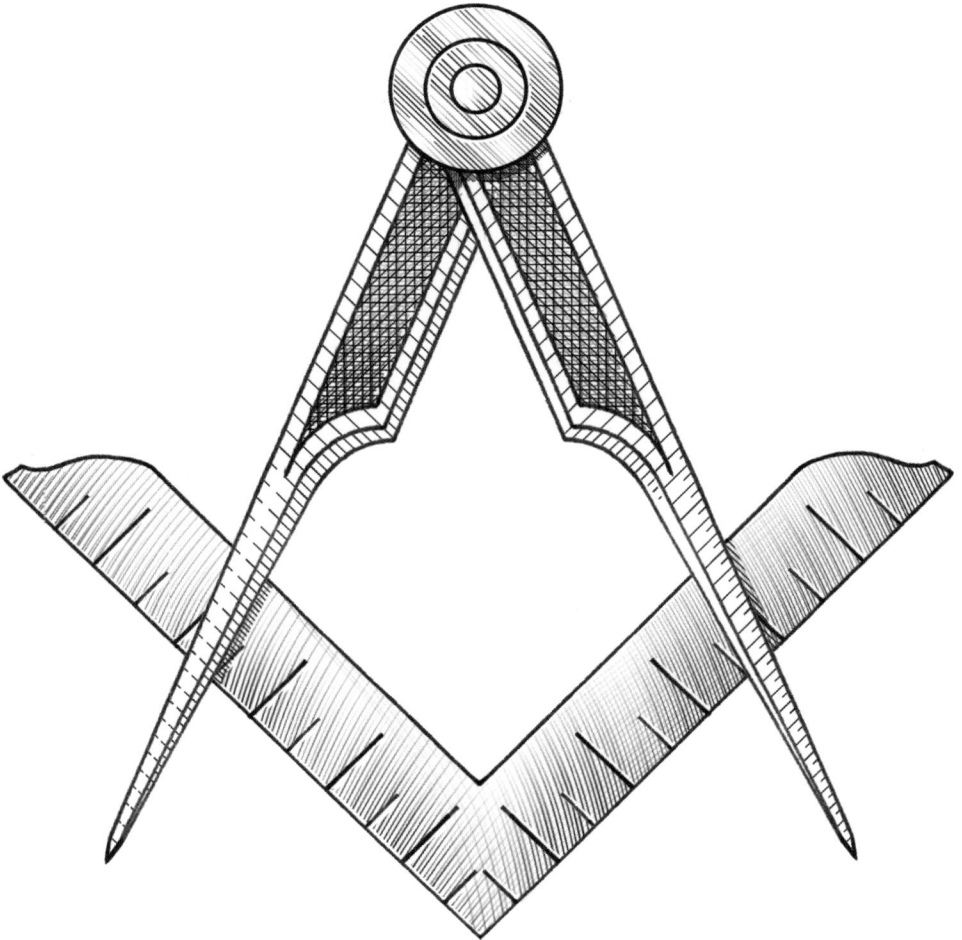

The Open Grave

The light of a Master Mason is darkness visible, serving only to express that gloom that rests on the prospect of futurity. It is this mysterious veil that the eye of human reason cannot penetrate unless assisted by the light that is from above. Yet even by this glimmering ray, you may perceive that you stand on the very brink of the grave into which you have just figuratively descended and that, when this transitory life has passed away, will again receive you into its cold bosom.

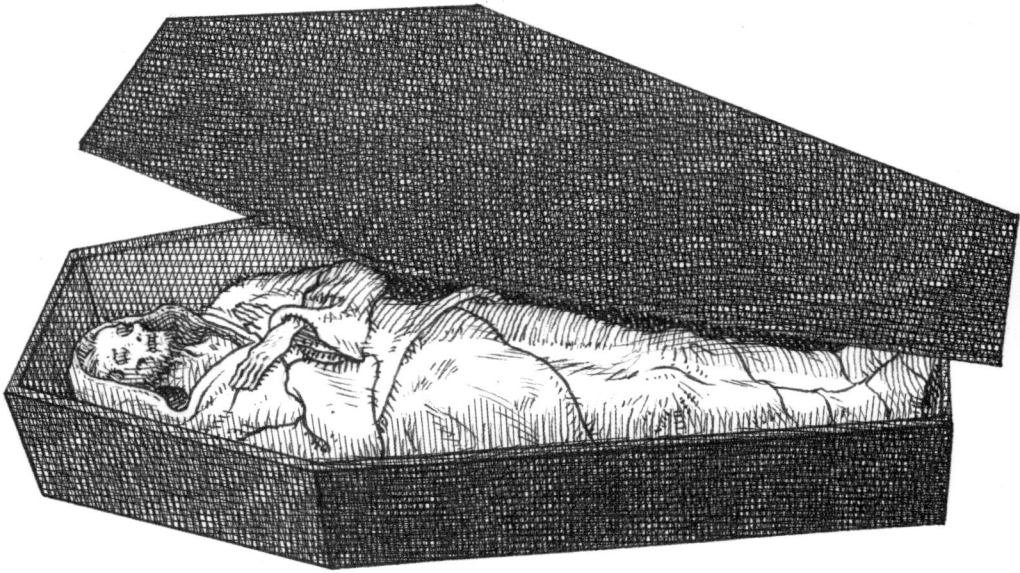

THE OPEN GRAVE IS A SYMBOL THAT HELPS REVEAL TO MASONS THE UNION BETWEEN THE INDIVIDUAL SOUL AND THE MYSTERY OF THE CENTER. Engraving by Sam Lacy from a drawing by J.A. Embeds Esq. after sketches by Joseph Gandy

Robert Lomas's personal view

AT THE CENTER OF EVERY MASON'S SOUL IS BURIED AN IMMORTAL PRINCIPLE—A VITAL SPARK THAT LINKS HIM TO THE DIVINE CENTER. IT IS NEVER EXTINGUISHED, NO MATTER HOW EVIL OR IMPERFECT HIS LIFE MAY BE.

THE LOST LIGHT FOR WHICH ALL MASONS SEARCH IS BURIED AT THE CENTER OF EACH INDIVIDUAL MASON. A MAN CAN REACH UP OR DOWN FROM THE CENTER OF HIS OWN BODY (I.E., 3 FEET BETWEEN NORTH AND SOUTH, I.E., HIGH AND LOW) AND CAN REACH OUT FROM THE CENTER OF HIS BODY (I.E., 3 FEET BETWEEN WEST AND EAST, I.E., THE LENGTH OF HIS ARMS). THESE ARE SYMBOLIC INDICATIONS BY WHICH THE RITUAL SUGGESTS THAT THE GRAVE OF HIRAM ABIF IS TO BE FOUND AT THE CENTER OF EVERY MASON WHO REPRESENTS HIM (I.E., IN HIS SOUL).

THIS SYMBOLISM GUIDES A MASON TO THE KNOWLEDGE THAT THE PURPOSE OF INITIATION IS TO REVEAL THE UNION BETWEEN THE INDIVIDUAL SOUL AND THE MYSTERY OF THE CENTER. THIS UNION IS REPRESENTED BY THE FAMILIAR CONJUNCTION OF THE SQUARE AND THE COMPASSES. THE SQUARE IS THE EMBLEM OF THE SOUL, AND THE COMPASSES ARE THE EMBLEM OF THE SPIRIT THAT DWELLS IN THAT SOUL. AS WE HAVE SEEN, THE MASON FIRST SEES THE POINTS OF THE COMPASSES CONCEALED BEHIND THE SQUARE, AND AS HE PROGRESSES, THOSE POINTS EMERGE FROM CONCEALMENT UNTIL BOTH RISE ABOVE THE SQUARE. THIS SYMBOLIZES A PROGRESSIVE SUBORDINATION OF THE SOUL AND THE CORRESPONDING RELEASE OF THE INNER SPIRIT INTO THE PERSONAL CONSCIOUSNESS OF THE MIND. IN THIS WAY, A MASON CAN WORK WITH BOTH POINTS OF THE COMPASSES TO BECOME AN EFFICIENT BUILDER OF HIS SPIRIT AND THUS RENDER COMPLETE THE CIRCLE OF HIS OWN BEING AS HE ATTAINS CONSCIOUS ALLIANCE WITH HIS TRUE SELF.

The Perfect Cube

We can change from a rough ashlar to a perfect cube and be carried from natural darkness into supernatural light. Just as the outer body can be opened for surgical investigation, so the lodge can be opened for us to understand the mechanism and purpose of our inner self. The spirit dwells in the mind, just as the mind suffuses the body. But only in the mind—once it has been rectified, purified, and worked from the rough ashlar to the perfect cube—can the center be brought to life and consciousness.

AN ALLEGORY FOR A MASON'S SOUL.

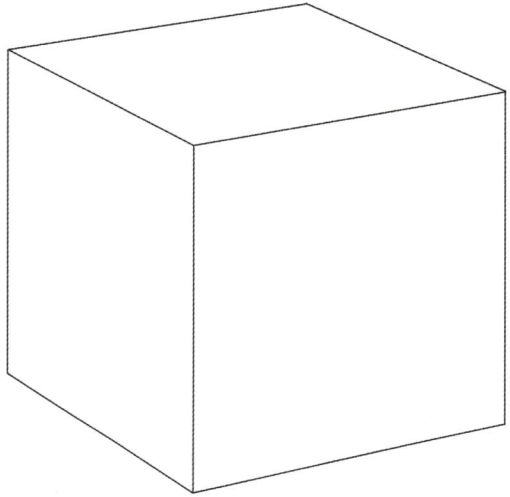

Robert Lomas's personal view

WHEN A MAN FIRST JOINS A LODGE, HIS SOUL IS THOUGHT OF AS A ROUGH STONE, FRESHLY HACKED FROM THE LIVING ROCK OF THE QUARRIES. IT HAS A COARSE AND CRUDE ASPECT, YET WITHIN IT, THERE IS A PERFECT CUBE OF POLISHED STONE. THE MASON IS GIVEN THE TOOLS TO WORK ON HIS SOUL AND ENCOURAGED TO MAKE DAILY PROGRESS IN SHAPING HIMSELF INTO A PERFECTED STATE. HE IS ENCOURAGED TO CONTROL HIS BASE URGES, SO THAT HIS SOUL MAY BECOME MORE REGULAR IN SHAPE. HE IS ALSO ENCOURAGED TO DEVELOP HIS MIND, SO THAT HE MIGHT ACQUIRE THE POLISH OF A LIBERAL EDUCATION. FINALLY, ABOVE ALL, HE IS ENCOURAGED TO BEHAVE HONESTLY AND FAIRLY, TO TREAT ALL SOCIETY IN A SQUARE AND HONEST WAY, UNTIL HE BECOMES A PERFECT SQUARE IN ALL HIS ASPECTS AND HIS SOUL ASSUMES THE SHAPE OF A PERFECT SQUARE AND ALL THREE DIMENSIONS.

The Porch

The porch stands before the entrance to the sanctum sanctorum.

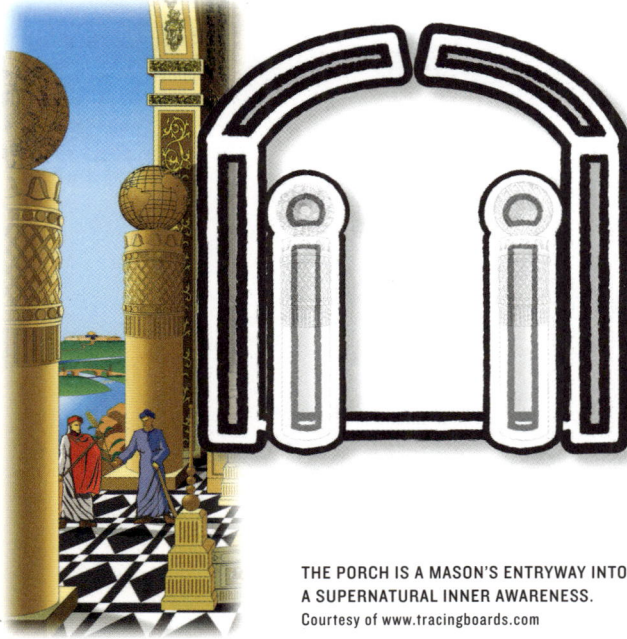

THE PORCH IS A MASON'S ENTRYWAY INTO
A SUPERNATURAL INNER AWARENESS.
Courtesy of www.tracingboards.com

Robert Lomas's personal view

THE PORCHWAY OF THE TEMPLE SYMBOLIZES AN OPENING INTO A SUPRANATURAL INNER AWARE-

NESS THAT CAN BE FOUND IN THE CENTRAL SANCTUARY. TO REACH IT, WE MUST LABOR AS WE

ASCEND THE WINDING STAIRWAY, GRADUALLY BUILDING OUR BODIES AND MINDS AS WE ADAPT TO A

SUBLIME DEGREE OF CONSCIOUSNESS. WE FEED ON THE ELEMENTS OF CONSECRATION THAT WERE

USED TO ESTABLISH THE LODGE THAT IS NOW A TEMPLE OF LIVING STONES.

OUR GROWING MINDS REQUIRE SUSTENANCE TO DEVELOP. SYMBOLICALLY, THE ELEMENTS

THAT CONSECRATE THE TEMPLE FEED OUR MINDS AS WE MAKE PROGRESS TOWARD THE INNER

SANCTUM. THE EAR OF CORN FASHIONS OUR MIND'S STRUCTURAL FORM. WINE VITALIZES AND

STIMULATES THE MIND AND STRENGTHENS ITS INTELLECT TO DEEPEN OUR INNER VISION. OIL IS

A LUBRICANT ENABLING THE DIFFERING PARTS OF OUR CONCISENESS TO RUN SMOOTHLY AND

WITHOUT FRICTION AS WE DEVELOP.

The Dormer

The dormer is the window that gives light to the sanctum sanctorum.

THE DORMER AS SEEN IN THE KNIGHTS TEMPLAR CHAPEL, FREEMASONS' HALL, MOLESWORTH STREET, IN DUBLIN, IRELAND.

Robert Lomas's personal view

THE DORMER IS THE WINDOW SET HIGH IN THE EASTERN ASPECT OF THE TEMPLE, WHERE THE RAYS OF THE RISING SUN SHINE ON THE DAWN OF THE VERNAL EQUINOX WHEN DAY AND NIGHT ARE IN PERFECT BALANCE. ONLY WHEN THE SUN RISES IN THE DUE EAST CAN ITS RAYS SHINE THROUGH THE DORMER AND ILLUMINATE THE SANCTUM SANCTORUM, OR INNER SACRED SPACE.

IN FREEMASONRY, WHENEVER THE RITUAL REFERS TO A TEMPLE, IT IS A SYMBOL OF THE SOUL OF A MASON. AT CERTAIN TIMES OF THE YEAR, IN THE SEASON OF BALANCE BETWEEN LIGHT AND DARK, A RAY OF SPIRITUAL TRUTH SHINES DIRECTLY FROM THE ETERNAL EAST. IF THE TEMPLE HAS BEEN BUILT WELL AND THE DORMER HAS BEEN CORRECTLY ALIGNED, THEN THE GOLDEN STREAKS OF THE DAWN'S LIGHT WILL SHINE AS A BEAM OF TRUTH TO ILLUMINATE THE STILL-DARK CENTER OF THE FREEMASON'S SOUL, SO THAT HE MAY KNOW THE GLORY OF TRUTH DEEP WITHIN HIMSELF.

The Square Pavement

The square pavement is for the high priest to walk on, meaning that every Mason—as the high priest of the temple of his own body—must walk upon the ever-changing occurrences of existence. He must stand superior to them, remaining stable, serene, and detached in the midst of events that elate or deject those whose affections are still focused on the transient and unreal. He must not try to pick out a timorous and pleasant way over the white squares only. Rather, with confidence and fortitude, he must tread the black ones too,

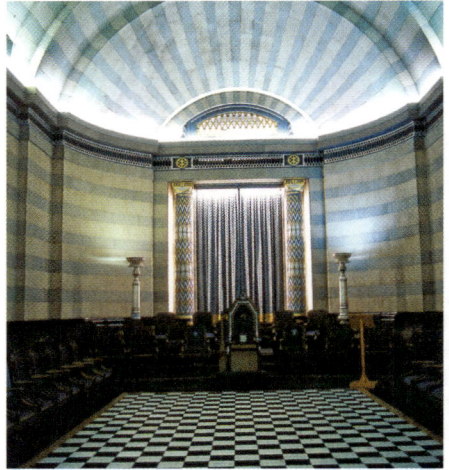

THE SQUARE PAVEMENT HELPS THE MASON DEVELOP HIS INNATE SPIRITUAL POTENCIES. Copyright and reproduced by permission of the Library and Museum of Freemasonry, London and Painton Cowen

Robert Lomas's personal view

THE CHECKERED FLOOR OF THE LODGE IS A MAJOR SYMBOL BUILT INTO THE LODGE FURNITURE. THE RITUAL TELLS US, "THE SQUARE PAVEMENT IS FOR THE HIGH PRIEST TO WALK UPON. "THIS STATEMENT REFERS NOT ONLY TO ANCIENT HIGH PRIESTS BUT TO ALL FREEMASONS. EVERY MASON MUST LEARN TO BECOME THE HIGH PRIEST OF HIS OWN PERSONAL TEMPLE AND TO MAKE OF IT A PLACE WHERE HE AND GREAT ARCHITECT MAY MEET.

EVERY MASON WALKS ON A SQUARE PAVEMENT OF MINGLED GOOD AND EVIL IN EVERY ACTION OF HIS LIFE. THE FLOORCLOTH IS A SYMBOL OF THIS ELEMENTARY PHILOSOPHICAL TRUTH. BUT THE MASON WHO ASPIRES TO BE MASTER OF HIS FATE MUST WALK ON THESE OPPOSITES AND SO TRANSCEND OR OVERCOME THEM. HE MUST TRAMPLE ON HIS LOWER SENSUAL NATURE AND KEEP IT IN SUBJECTION. HE MUST BECOME INDIFFERENT TO THE UPS AND DOWNS OF FORTUNE. THE MASON STRIVES TO DEVELOP HIS INNATE SPIRITUAL POTENCIES, WHICH IS NOT POSSIBLE WHEN HE IS OVERRULED BY FLUCTUATING EMOTIONS OF PLEASURE AND PAIN. BY ATTAINING SERENITY AND MENTAL EQUILIBRIUM UNDER ALL CIRCUMSTANCES, A MASON TRULY "WALKS UPON" THE CHECKERED GROUNDWORK OF EXISTENCE AND THE CONFLICTING TENDENCIES OF HIS MORE MATERIAL NATURE.

perceiving good and evil, pleasure and pain, birth and death, adversity and prosperity, and all the other opposites signified by the dual-colored squares. They are but alternating aspects of a single process and as of equal value to his own growth.

The Skirret

The skirret is a tool that acts on a center pin, from which a line is drawn to mark out ground for the foundation of an intended structure. It is used to prepare for laying the foundation and thus before the other tools of the Mason. Since we are not all operative masons but rather Free and Accepted, or speculative, Masons, we apply this tool to our morals. In this sense, the skirret points out the straight, undeviating line of conduct laid down for our pursuit in the Volume of the Sacred Law.

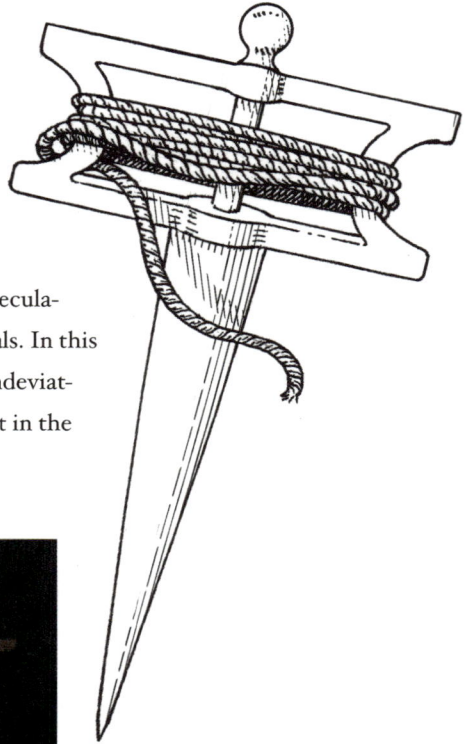

THIS SKIRRET, SHOWN HERE IN A MODERN INTERPRETATION OF A THIRD-DEGREE TRACING BOARD, SYMBOLIZES THE WAY TO FIND THE CENTER. Copyright Angel Millar. Reprinted with permission

Robert Lomas's personal view

THE SKIRRET SYMBOLIZES THE WAY TO FIND THE CENTER. WHEN PLACED AT THE CENTER OF A CIRCLE, EVERY POINT ON THE CIRCLE'S CIRCUMFERENCE IS EQUIDISTANT FROM IT. ONLY BY FINDING THE CENTER CAN THE MASON COME TO UNDERSTAND ITS MYSTERY. WHILE REFLECTING ON THE ROLE OF THE SKIRRET, HE REFLECTS ON HOW HE CAN FIND THE CENTER OF THE CIRCLE OF HIS BEING. AND IN DOING SO, AS THE RITUAL SAYS, HE "DELINEATES THE BUILDING" —THAT IS, HIS SOUL—SO THAT HE CAN PLACE THE CENTER PIN AND DRAW A TRUE LINE TO MARK OUT GROUND FOR THE BUILDING'S FOUNDATION.

The Pencil

With the pencil, the skillful artist delineates the building in a draft or plan that will instruct and guide the workmen. But again, because we are not all operative masons, we apply this tool to our morals. In this sense, using the pencil teaches us that our words and actions are observed and recorded by the Great Architect, to whom we must give an account of our conduct through life.

THE PENCIL, SHOWN HERE IN A MODERN INTERPRETATION OF A THIRD-DEGREE TRACING BOARD, NOT ONLY RECORDS A MASON'S PAST BUT ALSO DRAWS HIS PLANS FOR A BETTER FUTURE. Copyright Angel Millar. Reprinted with permission

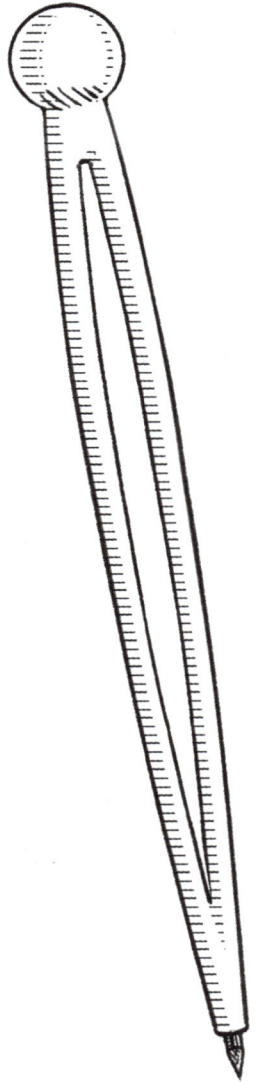

Robert Lomas's personal view

THE PENCIL SYMBOLIZES THE RECORDING OF OLD SCORES DUE BY THE MASON TO HIS FELLOW MEN, ALONG WITH OLD WRONGS THAT HAVE BEEN RIGHTED. THE WAGES OF OUR PAST BAD BEHAVIOR ARE RECORDED ON OUR SUBCONSCIOUS BY A PENCIL THAT OBSERVES AND RECORDS ALL OF OUR THOUGHTS, WORDS, AND ACTIONS. THE RITUAL SAYS THAT A PHILOSOPHICAL CANDIDATE RECEIVES THOSE WAGES WITHOUT "SCRUPLE OR DIFFIDENCE," KNOWING THAT HE IS JUSTLY ENTITLED TO THEM, AND HE IS GLAD TO PURGE HIMSELF OF OLD OFFENSES. WE ARE ALL INDEBTED TO SOMEONE FOR OUR PRESENT POSITION IN LIFE, AND WE MUST REPAY WHAT WE OWE TO HUMANITY. THE PENCIL NOT ONLY RECORDS OUR PAST, BUT IT ALSO DRAWS OUR PLANS FOR A BETTER FUTURE.

The Compasses

The compasses enable the skillful artist to determine the limits and proportions of a building with accuracy and precision. But because we are Free and Accepted, or speculative, Masons, not operative masons, we apply this tool to our morals. In this sense, the compasses remind us of the Great Architect's unerring and impartial justice. Having defined for our instruction the limits of good and evil, he will reward or punish us, as we have obeyed or disregarded his divine commands.

THE COMPASSES REPRESENT THE DIVINE PRINCIPLE ISSUED BY THE GREAT ARCHITECT.

Robert Lomas's personal view

THE COMPASSES, WHICH REST ON THE VOLUME OF THE SACRED LAW, REPRESENT THE DIVINE PRINCIPLE ISSUED BY THE GREAT ARCHITECT, WHICH IS TO BE MANIFESTED IN BOTH THE COSMOS AND IN THE INDIVIDUAL, ALLOWING BOTH TO FUNCTION AND BE UNDERSTOOD IN ACCORDANCE WITH THE LAWS THAT GOVERN THE UNIVERSE. THE COMPASSES SYMBOLIZE THE RANGE OF A DISCERNING MIND AND ITS ABILITY TO MEASURE A MASON'S SPIRIT. ALONG WITH THE SQUARE OF BODILY FORM, WHICH IS USED TO TRY AND PROVE THE SOUL, THE COMPASSES DELINEATE THE SHAPE OF A LIVING STONE FIT TO BE USED IN THE COSMIC TEMPLE.

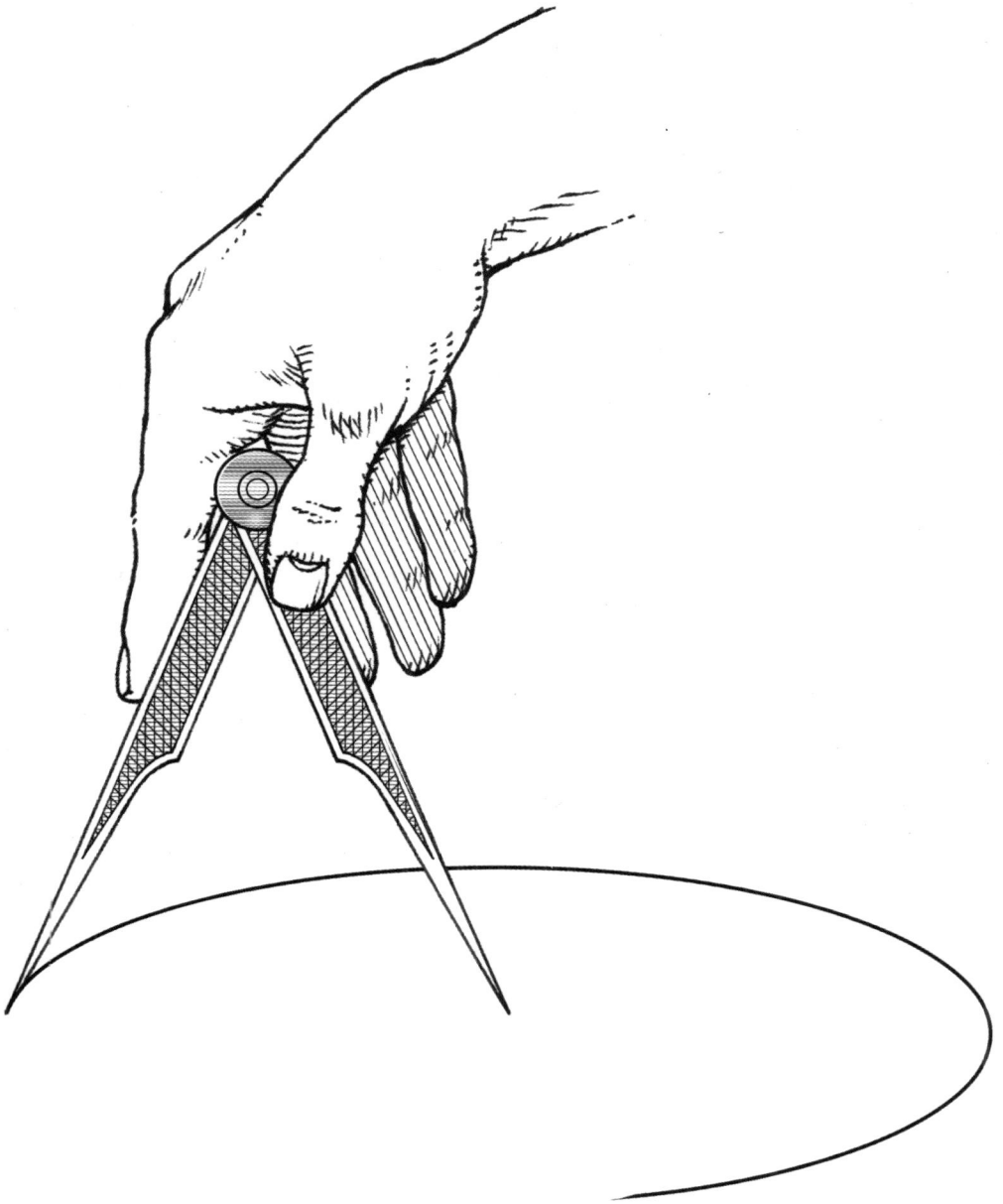

The Sprig of Acacia

The sprig of acacia marks the grave of a Master Mason. This tradition came about after the murder of Hiram Abif.

One day, twelve craftsmen who had joined in the original murder conspiracy came before King Solomon and offered a voluntary confession of all they knew. Out of concern for Hiram's safety, the king selected fifteen well-trusted Fellows of the Craft and ordered them to make a diligent search for the master architect to determine if he was still alive. The king also appointed a day for the Fellows to return to Jerusalem. After forming themselves into three lodges, they departed from the three entrances of the temple.

The Fellows of the Craft spent many days in fruitless search. Indeed, one lodge returned without having made any discovery of importance. But the second lodge was more fortunate. One evening, after having suffered the greatest deprivation and personal fatigue, one of the brethren, who was

THE SPRIG OF ACACIA HELPS THE MASON UNDERSTAND THE MYSTERY OF DEATH.

Robert Lomas's personal view

THE RITUAL AND THE TRACING BOARDS TELL US THAT A SPRIG OF ACACIA MARKED THE GRAVE OF THE MURDERED ARCHITECT. IT WAS LOOSELY PLANTED AND OFF-CENTER.

THE GRAVE SYMBOLIZES THE MASON'S SOUL, AND THE SPRIG OF ACACIA REPRESENTS THE DIVINE SEED PLANTED IN THAT SOIL. WHEN THE SPRIG OF ACACIA BLOOMS AT THE HEAD OF THE SOUL'S TOMB, THE MASON WILL UNDERSTAND THE MYSTERY OF THE DEATH OF HIRAM AND THE MYSTERY OF SPIRITUAL CONSCIOUSNESS—HOW PERCEPTION OF THE DIVINE CENTER OPENS UP HUMAN INTELLIGENCE TO THE UNIVERSAL AND OMNISCIENT MIND OF THE GREAT ARCHITECT. THE SPRIG OF ACACIA, WHICH STANDS FOR THE ETERNAL HUMAN SPIRIT, IS SYMBOLICALLY PLANTED AT THE HEAD OF THE GRAVE BECAUSE IT IS OUR SUPREME LIFE PRINCIPLE, FROM WHICH ALL OUR SUBORDINATE FACULTIES ISSUE.

resting, caught hold of a shrub that grew near. To his surprise, it came easily out of the ground. On closer examination, he found that the earth there had been recently disturbed. He therefore hailed his companions, and with their united endeavor, they reopened the grave. In it, they found the body of the Hiram, quite indecently interred.

The fellows covered the grave again, with all due respect and reverence. And to distinguish the spot, they stuck a sprig of acacia at the head of the grave. Then, they hastened to Jerusalem to impart the terrible news to King Solomon.

The Emblems of Mortality

The emblems of mortality will lead you to contemplate your inevitable destiny and to guide your reflections to that most interesting of all human studies: the knowledge of yourself. Be careful to perform your allotted task while it is yet day. Also continue to listen to the voice of nature, which bears witness that even in this perishable frame resides a vital and immortal principle. It inspires a holy confidence that the Lord of Life will enable us to trample the King of Terrors beneath our feet and lift our eyes to that bright morning star, whose rising brings peace and salvation to the faithful and obedient members of the human race.

WITH THIS SYMBOL, SHOWN ON THE APRON OF A GRAND SECRETARY, THE MASTER MASON ATTAINS KNOWLEDGE OF HIS TRUE SELF. From the collection of the Chancellor Robert R Livingston Masonic Library of Grand Lodge, New York, N.Y.

Robert Lomas's personal view

IN THE RITUAL OF THE THIRD DEGREE, AN IMPORTANT MOMENT OCCURS WHEN DARKNESS SUDDENLY GIVES WAY TO BEWILDERING LIGHT. BY THAT LIGHT, WHICH COMES FROM THE RISING OF THE BRIGHT MORNING STAR, THE NEWLY MADE MASTER MASON GAZES FOR THE FIRST TIME ON THE REMAINS OF HIS OWN PAST AND IS SHOWN THE EMBLEMS OF HIS OWN MORTALITY. THE MYSTICAL SPRIG OF ACACIA HAS BLOOMED AT THE HEAD OF HIS GRAVE, NOURISHED BY HIS PURIFIED MIND AND SOUL.

IN MASONIC CEREMONY, THIS IS WHEN THE MASON ATTAINS KNOWLEDGE OF HIS TRUE SELF. HIS EXPANSION OF CONSCIOUSNESS AND WISDOM HAS BECOME PART OF HIS NEW CHARACTER, AND HIS SPIRITUAL EVOLUTION HAS BEEN COMPLETED. HE NOW RETURNS, IN THE WORDS OF THE RITUAL, TO THE "COMPANIONS OF HIS FORMER TOIL" TO HELP THE REST OF HUMANITY REACH HIS LEVEL OF SPIRITUAL AWARENESS.

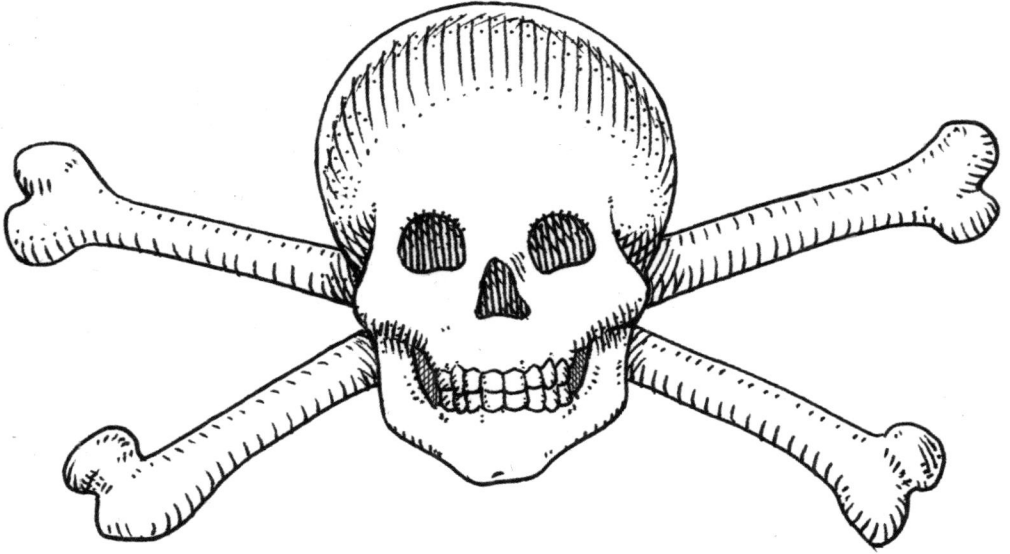

The Bright Morning Star

As the ritual has previously told us, we must be careful to perform our allotted task while it is yet day. Listen to the voice of nature, which bears witness that, even in this perishable frame, there resides a vital and immortal principle. It inspires a holy confidence that the Lord of Life will enable us to trample the King of Terrors beneath our feet and lift our eyes to that bright morning star, whose rising brings peace and tranquility to the faithful and obedient members of the human race.

THE BRIGHT MORNING STAR SYMBOLIZES THE ULTIMATE CORE OF OUR BEING.

Robert Lomas's personal view

THE STAR IN THE EAST OR FIVE-POINTED MORNING STAR SYMBOLIZES THE ULTIMATE CORE OF OUR BEING, BEYOND TIME AND SPACE. TO BECOME A REAL INITIATE, A MASON MUST EXPERIENCE THE PASSAGE THROUGH THE DIVINE DARK, THE UNSTABLE PSYCHIC REGION, TO FIND THE LIGHT OF THAT DISTANT BRIGHT MORNING STAR. ITS RAYS PROMISE THAT HE WILL ENDURE THE LAST AND GREATEST TRIAL TO THE END AND EMERGE TRIUMPHANT.

THE SYMBOLISM OF DEATH IS NOT THE PHYSICAL DEATH OF THE BODY BUT THE MYSTICAL DEATH OF THE EGO. ONLY WHEN THE CRAFT HAS TAUGHT THE MASON'S EGO HOW TO DIE DOES HIS SPIRIT OBTAIN FREEDOM. A MASTER MASON HAS DIED THAT DEATH AND EXPERIENCED THE TRANSFORMATION IT INVOLVES. HE HAS NO DREAD OF DEATH, FOR HE HAS ALREADY BEEN TO THE OTHER SIDE OF IT AND SEEN WHAT LIES BEYOND. HE KNOWS IT TO BE THE INEVITABLE COMPLE-MENT TO LIFE, AN INCIDENT OF EXISTENCE LIKE FALLING ASLEEP WHEN TIRED. HE HAS BALANCED HIS PILLARS AND BECOME, IN THE WORDS OF THE RITUAL, "ESTABLISHED IN STRENGTH." HE LIVES FROM THE CENTER, AND THE CENTER LIVES IN HIM. HE ENTERS HIS NEW LIFE WITH THE LIGHT OF HIS OWN MORNING STAR TO GUIDE HIM.

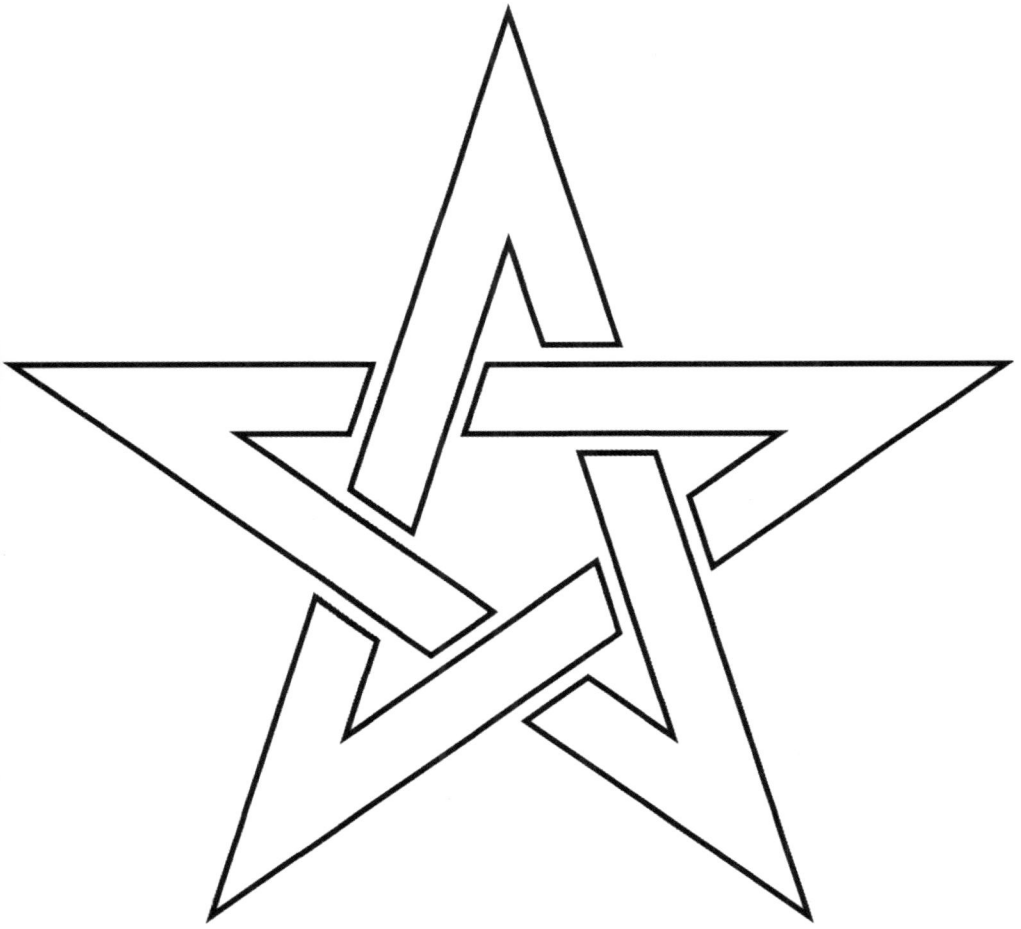

GENERAL SYMBOLS OF THE WIDER CRAFT

The Equilateral Triangle

Three mythical characters—two Hirams and one Solomon—combine to symbolize a threefold creativity. Wisdom—represented by Solomon, King of Israel—has the vision to create. Strength and resources—personified by Hiram, King of Tyre—projects the world of nature as the material out of which the creative idea is to take shape in the creature. Architectonic and geometrical power—personified by Hiram Abif—finally molds that idea into the beauty of objective form, the third aspect of creative energy. He represents the cosmic builder, the Great Architect by whom all things are made.

THE EQUILATERAL TRIANGLE SHOWN HERE IS PART OF A PENDANT THAT WAS GIVEN TO THE PAST HIGH PRIEST OF PHOENIX CHAPTER NO. 3 IN NEW YORK CITY. From the collection of the Chancellor Robert R Livingston Masonic Library of Grand Lodge, New York, N.Y.

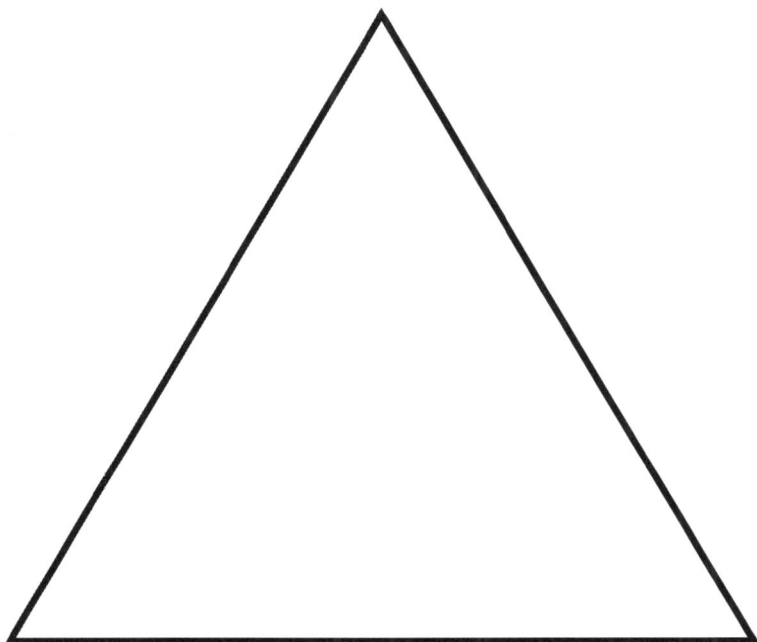

Robert Lomas's personal view

AN EQUILATERAL TRIANGLE, SOMETIMES SHOWN WITH A POINT AT ITS CENTER, IS A SYMBOL OF THE GREAT ARCHITECT. A GOLDEN VERSION OF THIS SYMBOL IS WORN BY COMPANIONS OF THE HOLY ROYAL ARCH.

THIS TRIANGLE HAS A TWOFOLD SIGNIFICANCE: FIRST, IT REPRESENTS THE SPIRITUAL, MENTAL, AND PHYSICAL PARTS OF THE MASON BROUGHT INTO PERFECT BALANCE AROUND THE LIFE PRINCIPLE OF THE CENTER. AND SECOND, IT REPRESENTS THE THREE PARTS OF THE GREAT ARCHITECT'S PLAN: THE VERY LARGE, EXEMPLIFIED BY RELATIVITY; THE VERY SMALL, EXEMPLIFIED BY QUANTUM MECHANICS; AND THE HUMAN SCALE, REPRESENTED BY NEWTONIAN MECHANICS. ALL THREE EXPLAIN PART OF THE MYSTERY OF THE CENTER, YET NONE ALONE IS ABLE TO EXPLAIN THE TOTALITY OF THE COSMIC LAW.

A MASON USES THE EQUILATERAL TRIANGLE TO SIGNIFY THAT HE IS STRIVING TO BRING HIS THREEFOLD NATURE—SENSES, REASON, AND SPIRITUAL INTELLECTUALITY—INTO BALANCE, SYMMETRY, AND UNITY. THIS SYMBOL ACKNOWLEDGES THAT THE VEIL OF FINITE EXISTENCE HAS BEEN DRAWN APART TO ALLOW HIM TO SEE THE LIGHT OF THE BRIGHT MORNING STAR RISING IN THE EAST OF HIS PERSONAL LODGE.

The Double Triangle (the Seal of Solomon)

The seal of Solomon comprises two interlaced equilateral triangles: one with its base to the sky and its point toward the earth, and the other with its base on the earth and its point to the sky. The triangles have similar symbolic meanings to the two pillars. The upward-facing triangle represents the king, with his power based on the earth and looking to heaven for guidance from the Great Architect. The other triangle, with its base in the heavens and its point reaching down to earth, represents the power of the priest, who draws his spiritual authority from the heavens and uses it to guide the actions of humans on the earth.

In a Royal Arch Chapter, seven lights are placed in the angles and center of this double triangle. Three represent wisdom, truth, and justice, and three represent truth, concordance, and peace. The seventh represents the mystical centre. Taken together, the whole represents the beauty and harmony that is visible in all the works of nature, where nothing is wanting or superfluous.

A VIEW OF THE ENTIRE PENDANT REFERENCED ON PAGE 240.
NOTE THE DATE 1818 IS ENGRAVED ON THE OUTER CIRCLE OF
THE PENDANT (LOWER LEFT). From the collection of the Chancellor
Robert R Livingston Masonic Library of Grand Lodge, New York, N.Y.

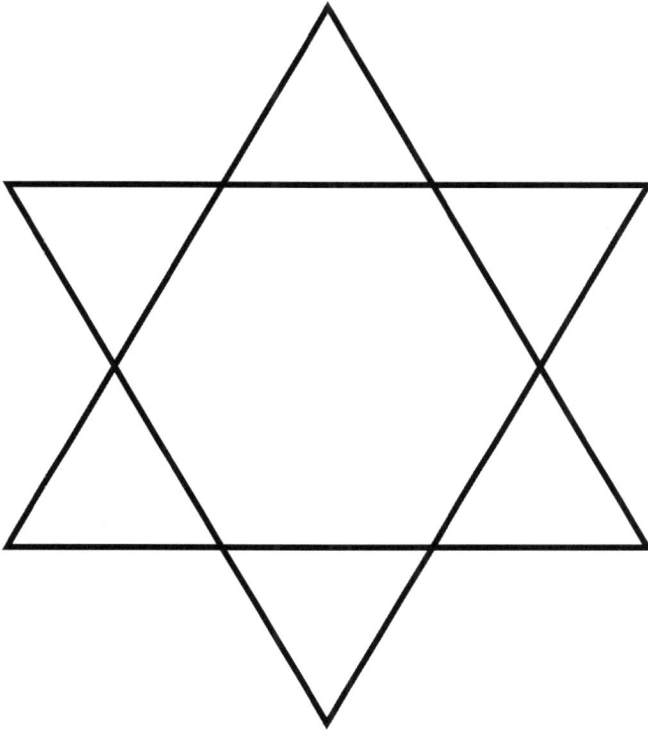

Robert Lomas's personal view

THE SEAL OF SOLOMON IS A SYMBOL THAT BUILDS ON THE UNION OF THE TWO PILLARS OF BOAZ AND JACHIN. THROUGH THIS SYMBOL, THE CANDIDATE IS TAUGHT TO SEE THAT TWO OPPOSITE BUT COMPLEMENTARY PRINCIPLES EXIST WITHIN HIM. BOTH BOAZ (SPIRIT) AND JACHIN (MATTER) ARE PRESENT. FOR SPIRIT TO BE EFFECTIVE, IT NEEDS A BODY IN WHICH TO EXPRESS ITSELF. FOR MATTER TO BECOME PERFECTED, IT MUST BE SUFFUSED BY SPIRIT. TO BE, AS THE RITUAL SAYS, "ESTABLISHED IN STRENGTH AND STAND FIRM FOR EVER" IMPLIES THE PERFECT BALANCE AND HARMONY OF THESE TWO OPPOSITES.

THIS SAME BASIC MASONIC TRUTH IS EXPRESSED IN THE UNITED SQUARE AND COMPASSES AND IN THE SYMBOL OF THE INTERLACED TRIANGLES KNOWN AS KING SOLOMON'S SEAL. THE INTERLACED TRIANGLES OF LIGHT SURROUNDING THE CENTRAL ALTAR IN THE DEGREE OF THE HOLY ROYAL ARCH OF JERUSALEM SYMBOLIZE THE UNION OF THE MASON'S PERCEPTIVE FACULTY WITH THE OBJECT OF HIS CONTEMPLATION: THE BLENDING OF THE HUMAN CONSCIOUSNESS WITH THE COSMIC LAW OF THE CENTER.

The Triple Tau

The Triple Tau is the symbol of a Royal Arch Mason. It signifies Hiram, King of Tyre, and Hiram Abif. It also signifies the temple of Jerusalem and is used in the Royal Arch by the wearer to reveal himself as a servant of the true God. The Triple Tau therefore reminds us of our constant duty to offer worship to the great Elohim—the most high, the everlasting, the almighty God.

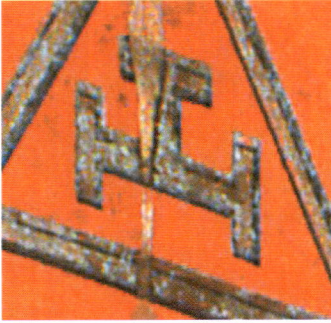

THE TRIPLE TAU SYMBOL AS SEEN ON THE LABEL OF A NINETEENTH-CENTURY BOTTLE OF LIQUEUR. Copyright and reproduced by permission of the Library and Museum of Freemasonry, London and Painton Cowen

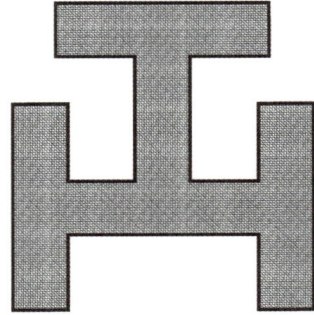

Robert Lomas's personal view

THE TAU CROSS, IN THE SHAPE OF THE LETTER T, IS A SYMBOL THAT DESCRIBES THE REGULAR STEPS A FREEMASON TAKES AS HE LEARNS THE SECRETS OF THE CENTER. THE RITUAL SAYS THAT WHEN THREE OF THESE SYMBOLS ARE COMBINED IN THE FORM OF A TRIPLE TAU, THEY SYMBOLIZE "A PLACE WHERE A PRECIOUS THING IS CONCEALED." THIS IS THE KNOWLEDGE OF THE CENTER, WHICH IS NOW HELD BY THE MASON WHO HAS TAKEN THE FIRST THREE REGULAR STEPS IN FREE-MASONRY AND HOLDS THE KNOWLEDGE OF EACH STEP.

THE SYMBOL HAS TWO RIGHT ANGLES AT THE EXTERIOR LINES AND TWO AT THE UNION OF THE CENTER. THERE ARE EIGHT RIGHT ANGLES IN ALL, CORRESPONDING TO TWO TRIANGLES, WHICH MAKES THE SYMBOL A CRYPTIC REPRESENTATION OF THE SEAL OF SOLOMON. THE ROYAL ARCH RITUAL SAYS THE SYMBOL CONTAINS A GIVEN NUMBER OF RIGHT ANGLES THAT "REPRESENT THE FIVE REGULAR PLATONIC BODIES."

WHEN WORN BY A MASTER MASON, THE TRIPLE TAU INDICATES THAT HE IS ABLE TO GOVERN THAT LODGE THAT IS WITHIN HIM. HE HAS PASSED THROUGH THE THREE DEGREES OF PURIFYING AND SELF-PERFECTING AND HAS SQUARED, LEVELED, AND HARMONIZED THE TRIPLE NATURE OF HIS BODY, SOUL, AND SPIRIT.

The Triangle within a Circle

The circle is an emblem of eternity, having neither a beginning nor an end. It is thus a fitting reminder of the purity, wisdom, and glory of the Omnipotent, which is without beginning or end. The triangle is a symbol of divine union and an emblem of the mysterious Triune, equally representing the attributes of the deity and his threefold essence. The triangle within the circle represents the great and awful name of God, the sacred, mysterious, and ineffable Tetragrammaton (the Hebrew name for the God of Israel).

THE TRIANGLE WITHIN A CIRCLE WITHIN A COLORED MASONIC WATERCOLOR FROM 1802. Copyright and reproduced by permission of the Library and Museum of Freemasonry, London

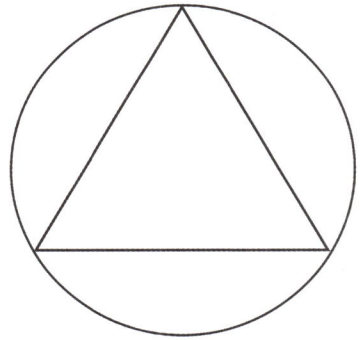

Robert Lomas's personal view

FREEMASONRY IS A SYSTEM OF RELIGIOUS PHILOSOPHY THAT PROVIDES US WITH A DOCTRINE OF THE UNIVERSE AND OF OUR PLACE IN IT. THE CRAFT AND ITS PHILOSOPHY HAS TWO PURPOSES:

1. THE FIRST PURPOSE IS TO SHOW THAT EVEN THOUGH HUMANS HAVE FALLEN AWAY FROM THE MYSTERIOUS CENTER TO THE CIRCUMFERENCE OF THE CIRCLE, WE MAY REGAIN THAT CENTER BY FINDING THE CENTER IN OURSELVES. THE GREAT ARCHITECT IS LIKE A CIRCLE WHOSE CENTER IS EVERYWHERE; THUS, IT FOLLOWS THAT A DIVINE CENTER IS, AS THE RITUAL SAYS, A "VITAL AND IMMORTAL PRINCIPLE," AND EXISTS WITHIN US.

2. THE SECOND PURPOSE IS TO TEACH THE WAY THAT CENTER MAY BE FOUND WITHIN US. THIS IS EMBODIED IN THE DISCIPLINE AND ORDEALS DELINEATED IN THE THREE DEGREES OF FREEMASONRY.

THE EQUILATERAL TRIANGLE IS SYMBOL OF THE GREAT ARCHITECT, AND THE CIRCLE IS A SYMBOL OF THE MASON. THE TRIANGLE WITHIN THE CIRCLE REMINDS EACH MASON THAT THE PATH TO THE CENTER IS WITHIN HIM.

The Keystone

At the building of King Solomon's temple, the valuable and curious keystone—containing many valuable coins and the ten letters in precious stonework that Hiram Abif took great pains to complete—was lost. It was supposed to have been taken away by some of the workmen. King Solomon offered a reward for the speedy return of the keystone or the making of another to take the place of the original.

An ingenious Entered Apprentice made a new keystone and fixed it in the vacancy in the arch. However, some of the Fellows of the Craft considered it a disgrace to the order to let someone of an inferior degree bear this honor. In the heat of jealousy, they took the new keystone and threw it into the Brook of Kedron, adjacent to the temple. A reward was also offered for the finding of this second stone. The Brother who had made it, together with two Entered Apprentices, looked for it, and when they found it, they received equally among them the last reward and with it the degree of Fellow of the Craft. The Brother who had made the keystone received the first reward for his ingenuity, and he and his two companions had the honor of fixing the stone in the arch a second time.

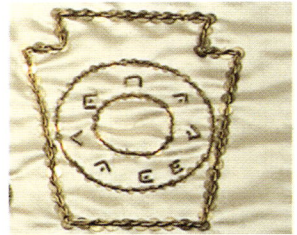

THE KEYSTONE AS SEEN ON A WHITE SILK APRON. From the collection of the Chancellor Robert R Livingston Masonic Library of Grand Lodge, New York, N.Y.

Robert Lomas's personal view

THE KEYSTONE IS THAT ESSENTIAL PART OF AN ARCH THAT JOINS THE TWO SIDES INTO A STRONG AND COHERENT WHOLE. WITHOUT THIS VITAL STONE, THE ARCH IS WEAK AND FLIMSY. IT IS NOT EVEN STRONG ENOUGH TO SUPPORT ITS OWN WEIGHT UNTIL THE KEYSTONE HAS BEEN PUT IN PLACE. THE KEYSTONE CAN BE OVERLOOKED, HOWEVER, AS IT IS NOT A REGULAR-SHAPED STONE. FOR MASONS, WHO ARE USED TO CREATING RECTANGULAR BLOCKS, THE KEYSTONE CAN APPEAR MISSHAPED AND MAY BE REJECTED BECAUSE IT IS NOT SQUARE AND DOES NOT FIT.

BUT THIS IS AN ILLUSION. THE KEYSTONE IS PERFECTLY SHAPED FOR ITS JOB WHEN PLACED IN THE CORRECT POSITION, AND IT CAN SUPPORT THE ENTIRE WEIGHT OF A BUILDING. LIKEWISE, A NEWLY MADE MASON MAY APPEAR ODD AND MALFORMED, ILLSUITED AND CLUMSY, BUT ONCE HE HAS FOUND HIS PLACE AND DEVELOPED HIS STRENGTHS, HE SERVES AS A VALUABLE SUPPORT FOR HIMSELF AND HIS BRETHREN.

The Vault

David intended to build a temple to God, but he bequeathed the enterprise to Solomon, his son. Solomon selected a place near Jerusalem. Finding the remains of Enoch's temple there and supposing them to be the ruins of a heathen temple, he selected Mount Morlah for the site of his temple to the true God. Under this temple, he built a secret vault, the approach to which was through eight other vaults, all underground, and to which a long and narrow passage led under the king's palace. In the ninth vault, Solomon held his private conferences with King Hiram of Tyre and Hiram Abif.

THE VAULT SYMBOLIZES THE DIVINE SPARK THAT IS DEEP WITHIN THE MASON'S SOUL AND ENABLES HIM TO RECOGNIZE THE LIGHT OF THE CENTER. Engraving by Sam Lacy from a drawing by J.A. Embeds Esq. after sketches by Joseph Gandy

Robert Lomas's personal view

THE RITUAL TELLS US THAT THE LOST WORD OF FREEMASONRY WAS FIRST GIVEN TO ENOCH AND HIDDEN IN A SECRET VAULT, WHICH WAS FOUND WHEN KING SOLOMON'S TEMPLE WAS BUILT ON THE SAME SPOT. THE WORD WAS HIDDEN AGAIN BY KING SOLOMON IN THE SECRET VAULT THAT REMAINED UNDER HIS TEMPLE. IT WAS FOUND AND RESTORED TO FREEMASONRY WHEN ZERUBBABEL REBUILT THE TEMPLE, AND IT CAN ONLY BE SPOKEN BY THREE ROYAL ARCH MASONS ACTING TOGETHER.

THE VAULT SYMBOLIZES THE DIVINE SPARK THAT IS DEEP WITHIN THE MASON'S SOUL AND ENABLES HIM TO RECOGNIZE THE LIGHT OF THE CENTER. SYMBOLICALLY, THE MASON STANDS IN THE PRESENCE OF THE STONE VAULT OR DENSE MATRIX, OUT OF WHICH HIS FINER BEING HAS EMERGED AND, OF HIS OWN HEAVENS, THE BRIGHT MORNING STAR HAS RISEN TO BATHE HIM IN THE LIGHT OF KNOWLEDGE. THIS LIGHT TRANSFORMS HIS CHARACTER FROM ONE OF CHAOS AND UNCONSCIOUSNESS INTO A PERFECT AND LUCID FORM, AS IT BECOMES A CO-CONSCIOUS VEHICLE WITH THE DIVINE PLAN.

The Uncompleted Temple

The death of Hiram, the chief architect, threw the workmen of the temple of King Solomon into great confusion. For a time, construction of the building was delayed because of the need for essential plans and an expert to direct the work. After the period of mourning had expired, King Solomon, upon consultation, appointed five superintendents—one for each of the five departments of architecture—and under their supervision, the building of the temple progressed. The work of completing the temple thus became the purpose of Freemasonry.

THE MASTER MASON WHO HAS NOT YET BEEN EXALTED TO THE ROYAL ARCH IS SYMBOLIZED AS AN UNFINISHED TEMPLE. From the British Library, London

Robert Lomas's personal view

FREEMASONRY DOES NOT DEAL WITH THE MATERIAL BUILDING OF ANY OUTWARD STRUCTURE BUT WITH THE DISORDERED TEMPLE OF THE HUMAN SOUL. THE RITUALS OF FREEMASONRY SYMBOLIZE SOMETHING DEEP AND PERSONAL: THE SHAPING OF THE MASON'S SOUL FROM THE ROUGH ASHLAR INTO THE PERFECT CUBE.

THE CRAFT DEGREES PROVIDE SOLEMN INSTRUCTION IN PREPARATION FOR THAT WORK. BUT THE WORK OF THE CRAFT IS NOT COMPLETE UNTIL THE MASTER MASON VENTURES INTO THE DARK VAULT OF HIS INNER BEING DURING THE RITUAL OF THE HOLY ROYAL ARCH. THE WORK REMAINS UNFINISHED WITHOUT ATTAINMENT OF THE ROYAL ARCH. THE MASTER MASON WHO HAS NOT YET BEEN EXALTED TO THE ROYAL ARCH IS THUS SYMBOLIZED AS AN UNFINISHED TEMPLE.

The Pillars, Circle, and Center

The circle is the symbol of infinity, whose center is everywhere and whose circumference is nowhere. You are infinity reduced and compressed to a point—but a point from which it is possible for you to consciously expand into an infinite being. Your personal, temporal self is but a separated, individualized point in the ocean of the universal spirit that encompasses you. By renouncing your personal self, you will transcend it and, losing the sense of separateness, grow into a conscious union with the one indivisible life that comprehends all.

The parallel lines that bound the circle declare that this indivisible life is everywhere, as characterized by two opposite aspects that are bound in perpetual equilibrium: spirit and matter; the formless and the formal; freedom and necessity; inflexible justice and boundless mercy. These parallels permeate the universe on all planes, characterizing every part of it and being present in every atom. But they are held together in eternal balance at one neutral, central point, where the opposites blend into unity.

That point in you is the center. To find it, you must follow a middle way, a straight and narrow path, turning neither to the right nor to the left and, in every pursuit, having the Eternal Unity in view.

THE PILLARS, CIRCLE, AND CENTER AS SEEN IN THE PRINT OF GEORGE WASHINGTON THAT APPEARS ON PAGE 95.
Library of Congress

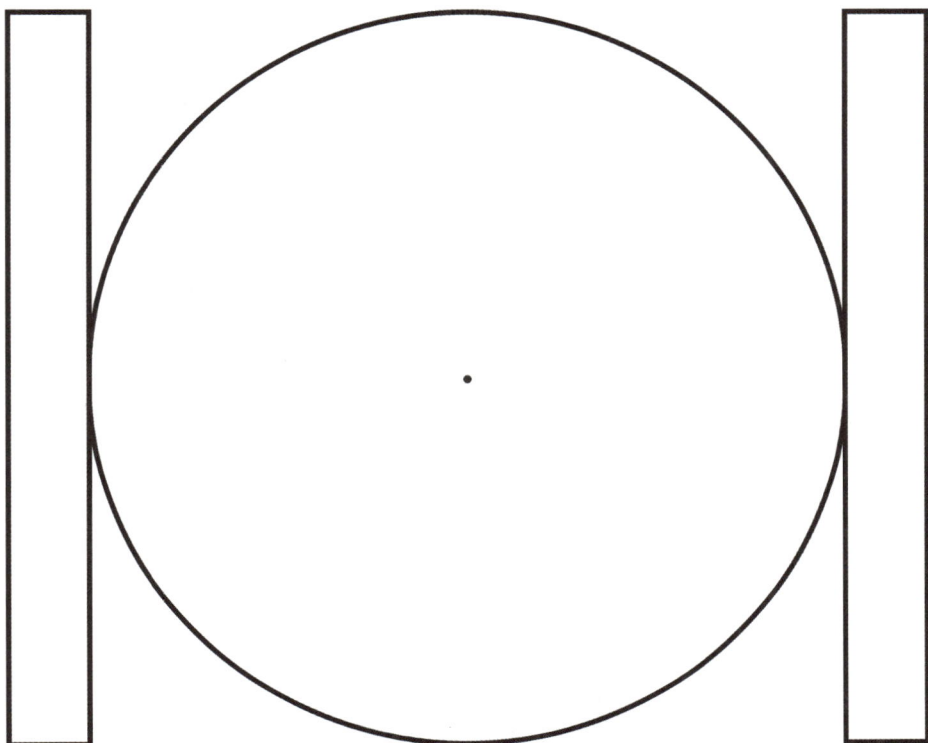

Robert Lomas's personal view

THE PILLARS, CIRCLE, AND CENTER SYMBOLIZE THE WHOLE PURPOSE OF THE CRAFT. WITH THIS

CENTER, WE HOPE TO REGAIN THE SECRETS OF OUR LOST NATURE. JUST AS THE LAWS OF THE

GREAT ARCHITECT ARE AT THE CENTER OF THE WHOLE UNIVERSE AND CONTROL IT, AND JUST AS

THE SUN IS THE CENTER AND LIFEGIVER OF OUR SOLAR SYSTEM—CONTROLLING AND FEEDING WITH

LIFE THE PLANETS CIRCLING ROUND IT—SO AT THE SECRET CENTER OF EACH INDIVIDUAL HUMAN

LIFE EXISTS A VITAL, IMMORTAL PRINCIPLE: THE SPIRIT AND THE SPIRITUAL WILL.

BY USING THIS FACULTY (ONCE WE HAVE FOUND IT), WE CAN NEVER ERR. THE RITUAL

SAYS THAT IT IS A POINT WITHIN THE CIRCLE OF OUR OWN NATURE, AND LIVING AS WE DO IN THIS

PHYSICAL WORLD, THE CIRCLE OF OUR EXISTENCE IS BOUNDED BY TWO GRAND PARALLEL LINES:

"ONE REPRESENTING MOSES; THE OTHER KING SOLOMON"—THAT IS TO SAY, LAW AND WISDOM,

THE DIVINE LAWS REGULATING THE UNIVERSE ON THE ONE HAND AND THE DIVINE WISDOM ON THE

OTHER. THE MASON WHO KEEPS HIMSELF THUS CIRCUMSCRIBED CANNOT ERR.

PART THREE

A PRACTICAL
INTRODUCTION
TO THE
TRACING BOARDS

AFTER EACH CEREMONY HAS TAUGHT THE candidate about the individual symbols and provided training to sensitize him to their importance, the symbols are combined into a composite image called a tracing board. The tracing board is used for two purposes:

1. It shows how the symbols can be combined to provide greater insight into the issues being considered.
2. It provides a focus for Masonic reflection, in which the candidate is drawn to consider what message the combination of symbols can impart.

The method of teaching is to reveal the tracing board and then provide a ritual explanation of its Masonic meaning.

There are six boards that lead toward a full understanding of the final mystic symbol, known as the center—the point from which no Mason can err.

THE TRACING BOARDS

THE FIRST-DEGREE TRACING BOARD

The first-degree tracing board shows the newly made Mason a vision of the philosophical scope of his Craft. The checkered floor of the lodge, encompassing both darkness and light, stretches out to meet the distant sky, which in turn is split into day and night. The sun, in the northeast corner, is shown governing the day and illuminating the rough ashlar, which is shaded by the pillar of beauty. The moon, in the northwest corner, is shown to govern the night, and its rays of knowledge illuminate the perfect ashlar, which stands before the pillar of strength, supported by a Lewis.

On the floor lie the working tools of the officers of a lodge—the square, the level, and the plumb rule—illuminated by the sun at its meridian. In the center of the lodge stands the altar, supporting the three great landmarks of the square, the compasses, and the Volume of the Sacred Law. The altar supports the base of Jacob's ladder, which reaches toward the rising of the bright morning star in the east, and on the ladder are the seven angelic officers of the Grand Lodge above, including faith, hope, and charity. On the face of the altar is the symbol of the center, the point from which no Master Mason can err. The altar is illuminated by the bright morning star, and its shadow falls on the tracing board, showing the divine plan,

Courtesy of www.tracingboards.com

still in darkness, and working tools of the Installed Master, whose job is to bring it into the light.

The working tools of all the degrees are distributed about these main symbolic landmarks.

THE SECOND-DEGREE TRACING BOARD

The second-degree tracing board shows the candidate arriving at the foot of the spiral staircase that winds up to the inner chamber, where he will receive his wages. He has left the distant city and crossed the stream of flowing water and the fields full of ears of corn to stand at the porchway, or entrance, to King Solomon's temple. There, he is challenged by the Junior Warden, who stands before the temple entrance,

between the terrestrial and celestial pillars of Boaz and Jachin. These pillars denote strength and, when conjoined, establish stability.

Black, equilateral lozenges adorn the beautiful white pavement of the porchway. The checkered pavement of the upper hallway leads to the dark and mysterious center of the temple, which conceals a sacred symbol of the Great Architect of the Universe. The entrance to the middle chamber is guarded by the Senior Warden. His duty is to challenge each Fellow of the Craft, demanding the pass grip and pass word of his degree and so proving him worthy to receive his wages.

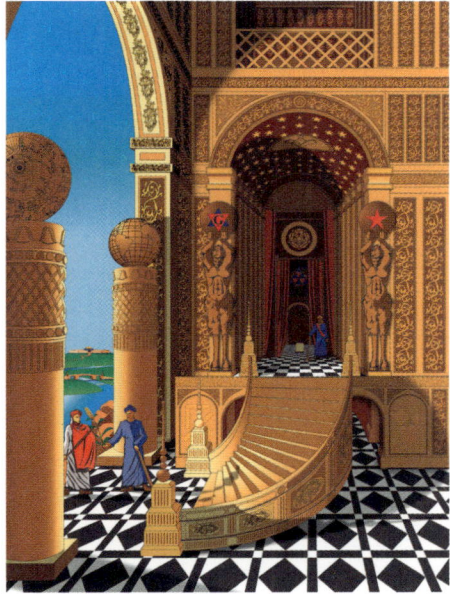

Courtesy of www.tracingboards.com

THE MARK TRACING BOARD

The Mark tracing board was set in the interior of King Solomon's temple just before the Masons finished the building work. It shows a view through the uncompleted arch, toward the quarry by the Brook of Kedron. In the distance stand the hills and the eternal city, and a blazing star shines in the heavens above them. The Junior

Warden stands by the entrance of the quarry to supervise the work.

The porchway is framed by the threefold symbol of the Triple Tau and enhanced by the two pillars of Boaz and Jachin. Against one of the pillars, the double-headed axe of the Senior Warden stands ready to test the integrity of all Mark Masons. The floor of the porchway shows the checkered pavement leading down—first to the lozenge pavement and finally to the black-and-white labyrinth, at the center of which stands the cubical altar.

BRO GEORGE WASHINGTON DEPICTED STANDING AMIDST IMAGES DRAWN FROM THE TRACING BOARDS.

In the foreground are the perfect ashlar, the keystone, and the perfect double cube. Blue lozenges are set in the red border of the board, symbolizing the infinite extent of the lodge. At the corners stand the mysterious symbols that Hiram Abif carved onto the four faces of the keystone.

THE THIRD-DEGREE TRACING BOARD

The third-degree tracing board shows the shallow grave in which the mortal remains of the Grand Master, Hiram Abif, were found by the lodge of Fellows of the Craft who searched for him. They reverently covered him with white cloth, as a badge of innocence, and marked his grave with a sprig of acacia at the head. Around the grave were placed the tools of the Master Mason, which remind us to carry out our allotted tasks while it is yet day and to listen to the voice of nature. Within our perishable frame resides a vital and

Courtesy of www.tracingboards.com

immortal principle. It inspires a holy confidence that the Lord of Life will enable us to trample the King of Terrors beneath our feet and lift our eyes to that bright morning star, whose rising brings peace and tranquility to the faithful and obedient members of the human race.

A square, the badge of the Master Mason, is placed on his chest, and the plan, the skirret, the compasses, the pencil, the level, and the plumb rule are arranged on his shroud. At his feet are the emblems of mortality, which lead a Mason to contemplate his inevitable destiny and guide his reflections toward that most interesting and useful of all human studies: the knowledge of oneself.

THE ROYAL ARCH TRACING BOARD

The tracing board of the Holy Royal Arch shows the discovery of the secret vault beneath the ruins of King Solomon's Temple by the three sojourners employed by the Sanhedrin of Jerusalem to rebuild the temple. They are lifting the keystone from the archway to give access to the secret chamber, containing the sacred altar and the lost word of Masonry.

The shaft of light from the sun falls into the dark vault, which contains the lost word carved onto face of the pedestal. The pedestal is set in an equilateral triangle, which is the ancient Enochian symbol of the Great Architect.

The checkered pavement represents the uncertainty of life and the instability of things terrestrial, and the pedestal of pure white marble—in the form of a true double cube—is the perfect emblem of innocence and purity. It is placed within a circle, which is an emblem of eternity, having neither beginning nor end. The circle reminds us of the purity, wisdom, and glory of the Omnipotent, which is without beginning or end.

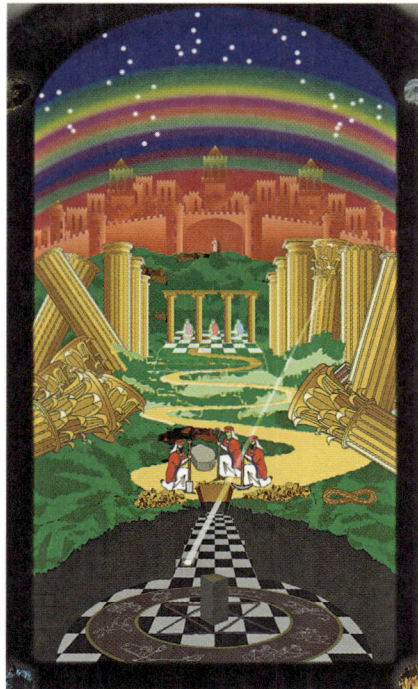

Courtesy of www.tracingboards.com

In the background, at the end of the spiral path, are the three principals of the Sanhedrin: Zerubbabel, Haggia, and Joshua. They stand between the pillars of stability and the pillars of knowledge. Behind them is the eternal city and above it, the rainbow and the Holy Royal Arch of the heavens.

THE TRACING BOARD OF THE CENTER

The tracing board of the center shows the development of a Masonic Candidate to a Master Mason. Each of the four steps—from Candidate to Entered Apprentice to Fellow of the Craft and finally to Master Mason—are placed within the circle, which encloses the mystical center. The shadows of the figures represent the positions of the sun when the various steps are taken: The Candidate with his sun in the northeast corner, the Entered Apprentice with his sun in the southeast corner, the Fellow of the Craft with the sun rising at the vernal equinox, and the Master Mason with the sun at high noon, when a man casts no shadow.

The lodge is set up with its symbols tracing the spiral path to the center on the black-and-white pavement. The two lines of symbols represent the descent to the dark square of death and the ascent to the light of the bright morning star.

This board sums up the complete spiritual journey from Masonic Candidate to Master Mason. Freemasonry is based on three grand principles: brotherly love, relief, and truth. In our social gatherings, we practice brotherly love, and through our charitable giving, we practice relief. And lastly, we must not neglect the inquiring and intellectual Masonic quest for truth, which should be the driving force behind our urge to make visible the light of the center.

Courtesy of www.tracingboards.com

THE CENTER

The Masonic ritual prescribes a formal idialogue between the Worshipful Master and his Wardens which goes as follows.

> *Worshipful Master:* Brother Junior Warden, while contemplating the
> duties of your office, what have you observed?
>
> *Junior Warden:* A profound symbol, Brother Master.
>
> *Worshipful Master:* Brother Senior Warden, where is this profound
> symbol to be found?
>
> *Senior Warden:* In the center of the lodge, Brother Master.
>
> *Worshipful Master:* Brother Junior Warden, how may the Brethren rec-
> ognize this symbol?
>
> *Junior Warden:* By the letter G, shining from the center of a blazing
> star, Brother Master.
>
> *Worshipful Master:* Brother Senior Warden, to what does this symbol
> refer?
>
> *Senior Warden:* To the Grand Geometrician of the Cosmos, to which
> you, I, and all must show respect, Brother Master.

So brethren, let us remember, wherever we are, whatever we do, the all-seeing eye of the Grand Geometrician of the Cosmos sees all of us and all actions throughout the universe. May we persevere as faithful Brethren of the Craft and apply geometry with fervency and zeal to reach that point from which no Master Mason can ever err.

ENDNOTES

PREFACE

1. Thomas W. Jackson. Review of The Secret Science of Masonic Initiation by Robert Lomas *The Northern Light*. August 2009, p. 23.

CHAPTER 1

1. R. Dawkins. *The Ancestor's Tale*. London: Wiedenfield and Nicholson, 2005. p. 25.

2. R. Cann, et al. "L Polymorphic sites and mechanisms of evolution in human mitochondrial DNA." *Genetics*, 106 (1984), 479–499.

3. B. Sykes. *The Seven Daughters of Eve*. London: Bantam, 2001. p. 336.

4. J. Shreeve. *The Neanderthal Enigma*. New York: William Morrow, 1995.

5. M. Henderson. "Scratches that trace the ascent of man." *Times*, Jan. 11, 2002. p. 5.

6. D. Lewis-Williams. *The Mind in the Cave*. London: Thames and Hudson, 1998. p. 29.

7. C. G. Jung. *Man and his Symbols*. London: Aldus, 1964.

8. Ibid.

9. Phaedo 75b.

10. C. G. Jung. *Man and His Symbols*. London: Aldus, 1964.

11. Ibid.

12. M. Gimbutas. *The Language of the Goddess*. London: Thames and Hudson, 2001.

13. Ibid.

14. B. Edwards. *Drawing on the Right Side of the Brain*. London: Fontana/Collins, 1987.

15. Ibid.

16. B. Edwards. *Drawing on the Artist Within*. London: Collins, 1987.

17. Ibid.

18. Ibid.

19. Ibid.

20. Ibid.

21. S. Mithen. *The Prehistory of the Mind*. London: Phoenix, 1996.

CHAPTER 2

1. C. G. Jung. *Man and His Symbols*. London: Aldus, 1964.

2. G. M. Edelman. *Wider Than the Sky: A Revolutionary View of Consciousness*. London: Penguin, 2004.

3. D. Lewis-Williams. *The Mind in the Cave*. London: Thames and Hudson, 2004.

4. Ibid.

5. Ibid.

6. M. Gimbutas. *The Language of the Goddess*. London: Thames and Hudson, 2001.

7. Ibid.

8. Ibid.

9. C. Renfrew and P. Bahn. *Archaeology, Theories, Methods and Practice*. London: Thames & Hudson, 1998.

10. C. Renfrew. *Bronze Age Migrations in the Aegean*. London: Birchall, 1973.

11. M. Gimbutas. *The Living Goddess*. Los Angeles: University of California Press, 1999.

12. Ibid.

13. J. Mellaart. *Çatalhöyük*. London: Thames & Hudson, 1967.

14. *Çatalhöyük 1997 Archive Report*. http://www.catalhoyuk.com/archive_reports/1997/ar97_03.html.

15. M. Gimbutas. *The Living Goddess*. Los Angeles: University of California Press, 1999.

16. Ibid.

17. R. Lomas and C. Knight. *Uriel's Machine*. Beverly, MA: Fair Winds Press, 1999.

18. M. Gimbutas. *The Living Goddess*. Los Angeles: University of California Press, 1999.

19. Ibid.

20. Ibid.

21. Ibid.

22. R. Lomas and C. Knight. *Uriel's Machine*. Beverly, MA: Fair Winds Press, 1999.

23. R. Lomas. *Turning the Hiram Key*. Beverly, MA: Fair Winds Press, 2005.

24. R. Lomas and C. Knight. *Uriel's Machine*. Beverly, MA: Fair Winds Press, 1999.

CHAPTER 3

1. D. Schmandt-Besserat. *How Writing Came About*. Houston: University of Texas Press, 1996.

2. Ibid.

3. J. Jacobs. *The Economy of Cities*. London: Pelican, 1968.

4. D. Schmandt-Besserat. *How Writing Came About*. Houston: University of Texas Press, 1996.

5. Ibid.

6. W. J. Hackwell. *Signs, Letters and Words*. New York: Charles Scribner's Sons, 1989.

7. D. Schmandt-Besserat. *How Writing Came About*. Houston: University of Texas Press, 1996.

8. M. Gimbutas. *The Language of the Goddess*. London: Thames and Hudson, 2001.

9. R. Lomas. *Turning the Templar Key*. Beverly, MA: Fair Winds Press, 2009.

10. M. Gimbutas. *The Language of the Goddess*. London: Thames and Hudson, 2001.

11. D. Schmandt-Besserat. *How Writing Came About*. Houston: University of Texas Press, 1996.

12. W. J. Hackwell. *Signs, Letters and Words*. New York: Charles Scribner's Sons, 1989.

CHAPTER 4

1. I. McGilchrist. *The Master and His Emissary*. New Haven, CT: Yale University Press, 2009.

2. R. W. Sperry.

3. I. McGilchrist. *The Master and His Emissary*. New Haven, CT: Yale University Press, 2009.

4. R. Arnheim. *Visual Thinking*. Berkeley: University of California Press, 1969.

5. G. Logan. *Knowth and the Passage Tombs of Ireland*. London: Thames & Hudson, 1986.

CHAPTER 5

1. R. Lomas. *Turning the Templar Key*. Beverly, MA: Fair Winds Press, 2007.

2. Ibid.

3. R. Gourlay, *Daily Telegraph*, July 2000.

4. R. Lomas. *Turning the Hiram Key*. Beverly, MA: Fair Winds Press, 2005.

5. Ibid.

6. R. Lomas. *Turning the Templar Key*. Beverly, MA: Fair Winds Press, 2007.

CHAPTER 6

1. R. Lomas. *The Invisible College*. London: Transworld, 2009.

2. Ibid.

3. J. Wallis. *A Defense of the Royal Society*. London, 1678.

4. "John Wallis." School of Mathematics and Statistics, University of St. Andrews, Scotland. http://www-history.mcs.st-andrews.ac.uk/Biographies/Wallis.html.

5. M. Jammer. *Einstein and Religion: Physics and Theology*. Princeton, NJ: Princeton University Press, 2004.

6. "Oxford Mathematics and Mathematicians." Mathematical Institute, University of Oxford. http://www.maths.ox.ac.uk/about/history.

7. R. Recorde. *The Whetstone of Witte*. http://www.archive.org/details/TheWhetstoneOfWitte.

8. "The General Scholium to Isaac Newton's *Principia mathematica*." Newton Project Canada. http://www.isaacnewton.ca/gen_scholium/scholium.htm.

9. "John Wallis." School of Mathematics and Statistics, University of St. Andrews, Scotland. http://202.38.126.65/navigate/math/history/Mathematicians/Wallis.html.

10. "Isaac Newton's Life." Isaac Newton Institute for Mathematical Sciences. http://www.newton.ac.uk/newtlife.html.

11. D. R. Wilkins. "Sir Isaac Newton." School of Mathematics, Trinity College. http://www.maths.tcd.ie/pub/HistMath/People/Newton/RouseBall/RB_Newton.html.

12. Ibid.

13. "Newton's *Philosophiae Naturalis Principia Mathematica*." Stanford Encyclopedia of Philosophy. http://plato.stanford.edu/entries/newton-principia.

14. W. W. Rouse Ball. *A Short Account of the History of Mathematics*. New York: Dover Press, 1908.

15. I. Newton. *Mathematical Principles of Natural Philosophy*. Berkeley: University of California Press, 1934 (1725). p. 370.

16. R. Penrose. *The Road to Reality*. New York: Knopf, 2005.

17. DeGroot, 2004.

18. Zimmerman, 1996.

19. DeGroot, 2004.

CHAPTER 7

1. This apron was presented to the Grand Lodge of Pennsylvania by the Washington Benevolent Society on July 3, 1829. Today, it can be seen in the Grand Lodge Museum at the Masonic Temple in Philadelphia.

2. W. J. Hackwell. *Signs, Letters, Words: Archaeology Discovers Writing*. New York: Charles Scribner's Sons, 1987.

3. R. Lomas. *The Invisible College*. London: Transworld, 2009.

4. Close to the Embankment underground station.

5. "How to Use the Euro Name and Symbol." European Commission Economic and Financial Affairs. http://ec.europa.eu/economy_finance/euro/cash/symbol/index_en.htm.

CHAPTER 8

1. The Masons who signed this statement included the following: Josiah Bartlett, of King Solomon's Lodge, Massachusetts; William Ellery, of St. Andrew's Lodge, Boston; Benjamin Franklin of St. John's Lodge, Philadelphia; Elbridge Gerry, of Philanthropic Lodge, Massachusetts; Lyman Hall, of Solomon's Lodge, Georgia; John Hancock, of St. Andrew's Lodge, Boston; Joseph Hewes, of Hanover Lodge, North Carolina; William Hooper, of Hanover Lodge, North Carolina; Philip Livingston, of Holland Lodge, New York; Thomas McKean, of Perseverance Lodge, Pennsylvania; Thomas Nelson Jr., of Yorktown Lodge, Virginia; Robert Treat Paine, of the Grand Lodge of Massachusetts; John Penn, of Unanimity Lodge, North Carolina; Roger Sherman, lodge unknown (but his Masonic apron is in the collection at Yale University); Richard Stockton, of St. John's Lodge, New Jersey; Matthew Thornton, of the British Military Lodge of the Regiment of Foot; George Walton, of Solomon's Lodge, Georgia; William Whipple, of St. John's Lodge, New Jersey.

2. S. B. Morris. "Masonic Papers: American Freemasons and the Spirit of Freedom." Pietre-Stones Review of Freemasonry. http://www.freemasons-freemasonry.com/brentmorris1.html.

3. "James Madison." American President: An Online Reference Resource. Miller Center of Public Affairs, University of Virginia. http://millercenter.org/academic/americanpresident/madison/essays/biography/1.

4. "The Framers of the Constitution." U.S. Constitution Online. http://www.usconstitution.net/constframe.html.

5. S. B. Morris. "Masonic Papers: American Freemasons and the Spirit of Freedom." Pietre-Stones Review of Freemasonry. http://www.freemasons-freemasonry.com/brentmorris1.html.

CHAPTER 9

1. J. F. Kennedy. "Special Message to the Congress on Urgent National Needs." May 25, 1961. John F. Kennedy Presidential Library and Museum. http://www.jfklibrary.org/Historical+Resources/Archives/Reference+Desk/Speeches/JFK/Urgent+National+Needs+Page+4.htm.

2. "Freemasons in Space." Grand Lodge of British Columbia and Yukon. http://www.freemasonry.bcy.ca/biography/spacemason.

3. "James E. Webb." National Aeronautics and Space Administration. http://history.nasa.gov/Biographies/webb.html.

4. T. Wolfe. "One Giant Leap to Nowhere." *New York Times*. July 18, 2009. http://www.nytimes.com/2009/07/19/opinion/19wolfe.html?pagewanted=3&_r=1.

5. December 1969 issue, p. 13, of the *New Age Magazine*, the official magazine of the Supreme Council 33° A.&A. Scottish Rite of Freemasonry of the Southern Jurisdiction, Washington, DC.

6. "The Story of Tranquility Lodge 2000." Tranquility Lodge History. Tranquility Lodge 2000. http://www.tl2k.org/history.htm.

7. Ibid.

ACKNOWLEDGMENTS

I would like to thank the folks at Fair Winds Press. John Gettings for proposing the idea of this book to me, sourcing the images and managing the production; Will Kiestler for his hard work in developing the concept and sharing his challenging ideas; and Matt Marinovich for editing the text.

I also thank my agents Bill Hamiliton and Charlies Brotherstone of A M Heath Ltd for all their hard work in making sure the project came to fruition.

My brother Masons of the Lodge of Living Stones, have helped me study and understand the symbols and been a sounding board for many of my ideas and I thank them for the regular intellectual stimulation of our lodge meetings and discussions.

And finally I would like to thank my family for their continuing support of my writing efforts.

ABOUT THE AUTHOR

Dr. Robert Lomas has written several cult classics about the history of Freemasonry, including *The Invisible College*, *Freemasonry and the Birth of Modern Science*, *The Man who Invented the Twentieth Century*, *Turning the Hiram Key*, *Turning the Solomon Key*, and *Turning the Templar Key*. His work with co-author Christopher Knight in *The Hiram Key* was used by novelist Dan Brown to create characters and symbols in his bestsellers *The Da Vinci Code* and *The Lost Symbol*. And some Freemasons believe Lomas is the inspiration for the protagonist, Dr. Robert Langdon.

Lomas holds a degree in electrical engineering and a Ph.D. for his research into solid state physics and crystalline structures. He has established himself as one of the world's leading authorities on the history of science, and lectures on information systems at Bradford University's world-ranking school of management. He is a popular speaker on the Masonic lecture circuit, a regular speaker at the Orkney Science Festival, and is much in demand for live Webcast lectures to Masonic groups around the world.

INDEX